A CANADIAN HISTORY OF
FIRE ENGINES

A CANADIAN HISTORY OF
FIRE ENGINES

Donal Baird

Vanwell Publishing Limited
St. Catharines, Ontario

Copyright© 2001 by Donal Baird. All rights reserved. No part of this publication may be reproduced or transmitted in any form or by any means, electronic or mechanical, including photocopying, recording, or any information storage and retrieval system, without either prior permission in writing from the publisher or a license permitting restricted copying.

Vanwell Publishing acknowledges the financial support of the Government of Canada through the book Publishing Industry Development Program for our publishing activities.

Design: Linda Moroz-Irvine

Vanwell Publishing Limited,
1 Northrup Crescent
P.O. Box 2131
St. Catharines, Ontario L2R 7S2

Printed in Canada

Canadian Cataloguing in Publication Data

Baird, Donal M.
    A Canadian history of fire engines

Includes bibliographical references and index.
ISBN 1-55125-054-3

1. Fire engines – Canada – History.   I. Title.

TH9371.B34 2000   628.9'259'0971   C00-932058-X

Table of Contents

Introduction: A War and its Weapons vii

I   Goosenecks to Squirreltails: The Hand Engines 11

II   The Coffee Pots: Steam-Powered Pumping 39

III   Horse Power, Trucks and Wagons 71

IV   Hand Cranks and Hard Tires: First Automobiles 103

V   Time of the T-Heads: A Successful Formula 137

VI   The Modern Era: Advancing Technology 171

VII   Postwar to 2000: An Expanding Mission 199

Appendix 231

Bibliographical Notes 235

Bibliography 238

Index 239

Dedicated to those who, over two centuries, have had the courage and foresight to look for and try out better tools for firefighting.

Introduction   A WAR AND ITS WEAPONS

Much of the romantic appeal of the municipal fire service has been in its firefighting vehicles— "apparatus," to give the hoary, mystical term firefighters use. All modes of transportation have their fascination; all the more so when they are used for emergency service and are as distinctive as fire engines. For the firefighters themselves, the glamour and capabilities of their fire apparatus have always had significant impact on their *esprit de corps*. Even now, when the nature of their emergency responses has widened greatly, firefighting still dominates their thinking and the design of their vehicles.

The earliest technology in firefighting equipment crossed the Atlantic ocean from Germany, Holland and Britain during the eighteenth century. The heart of this technology was, and still is, the pump that supplies the water needed to extinguish fires. Americans and Canadians soon developed their own style of fire apparatus to suit their unique problems and, for the most part, North America has differed from the rest of the world ever since. Only recently, in a shrinking globe, has there been the beginning of acceptance of one another's equipment worldwide.

The fire record of North America has been dismal compared to most of Europe. We have been a careless and wasteful frontier society, experiencing more and larger fires than anybody else. This situation led to calls for more and bigger firefighting weapons, and a dependence on fighting fires rather than preventing them. As a result, Canada and the United States tend to be unique in the world in their fire protection methods and in their view of how the fire service should be organized.

The early French then English settlers of Canada hurriedly established their pioneer towns in a wilderness and were very vulnerable to fire. Their primitively heated homes were built of wood and, with limited resources and weak transportation links, they could not replace lost property easily. On top of this, it was not until the late 1700s that there was a fire insurance market to cover losses and the beginnings of a community firefighting capability.

It was only after more than a century of existence and some severe losses that the first cities, like Montréal and Québec, tried seriously to control the threat of fire. As in the more advanced American seaboard cities, this began with rudimentary fire prevention regulations, the provision of buckets, ladders and hooks, and the appointment of fire wardens to keep order on the fire scene.

Under these regulations, householders were required to maintain a pair of fire buckets for common use. When there was a fire, everyone was expected to come running with buckets, axes and saws. The best grade of fire bucket was made of leather, sewn or riveted, with a leather-wrapped rope handle. Wooden buckets were also used, but they were heavier. Owners had their names on their buckets in order to claim them from the pile after the fire had been put out.

The results of these methods were ineffectual. Measures were limited to a bucket brigade directing intermittent splashes of water from the nearest well or pond, tearing away burning shingles and trim boards to prevent the involvement of neighbouring houses; and rescuing what furniture or commercial stocks could be carried out. This situation existed not only in the primitive colonies. Europe, too, had little in the way of effective firefighting organization at that time.

Not until the latter part of the eighteenth century did the idea of organized firefighting crews take form in Montréal and Québec. Steps were taken with the old tools under the French colonial regime, but it remained for the British fire insurance companies, the British army garrisons and the early volunteer fire companies in the developing cities of the American colonies to create a model of what could be done with a pumping engine.

The United Empire Loyalists came from the United States with an established expectation of organized fire protection measures such as they had become accustomed to back home. There, the first volunteer fire companies had been started by citizens at large as mutual assistance associations, providing insurance for and salvage of one another's goods. They progressed further to serious combat with fires when workable fire engines became available from England. The most famous of the instigators of self-protection was Benjamin Franklin. Because of the Loyalist element in Canada and the work of the British garrison engines, Halifax and Saint John organized fire engine companies soon after these towns had been established.

The earliest volunteer units, referred to as fire clubs or protection companies, supplied themselves with baskets or canvas bags to carry away valuables, bed keys to dismantle bed frames, and other useful tools for rescuing property. Firefighting became paramount only when the fire engine came upon the scene. Ever since, a critical element in the success of the fire control function has been the technology of firefighting vehicles that could be rushed through the streets to a fire location. The aim has been to the stop loss of life and property, and the traditional emphasis was placed predominantly on extinguishing rather than preventing fires.

The bucket, hook and axe brand of firefighting had severe limitations, but tearing down small buildings and pulling away burning shingles sometimes stopped a fire from spreading from one building to another. Some hook-and-ladder companies persisted in this technique throughout the hand fire engine era. In St. Catharines, Ontario, for example, the ladder company seemed more enterprising than their fellow volunteers of the engine companies, even in the 1860s, doing some good work with their big hook while the engines malfunctioned or the hose leaked and lost all of its water pressure. Later on, the use of explosives to demolish structures in the path of a large fire was a kindred effort at fire control. This method was also ineffectual, as demolished buildings still burned well.

It remained for the availability and acceptance of the practical, pumping fire engine—capable of directing a continuous stream of water on a fire from a distance—to make some degree of organization desirable and to prove it worthwhile.

Thus began a 300-year history of improvements in both the organization of fire control, and the technology of the equipment, especially in the vehicles and their functions. Although the men, organization and apparatus enabled the fire service to contend with the increasingly large and more varied risks of fire, their enemy would continue to threaten the economic welfare, the creature comforts and the very existence of the community, not to mention the citizens' lives. There would always be bigger, taller buildings and more dangerous hazards appearing on the scene to cause greater loss of life and property, followed by a scramble to catch up.

Firefighting is labour intensive, and is needed on very short notice for brief periods. In our era, when the majority of the population is guarded by career firefighters, the effort to reduce labour through mechanization is a leading concern. There has however been limited success in reducing the labour involved in firefighting.

The best solution to both this problem and the issue of satisfactory fire control are now seen to be the incorporation of fire safety measures into buildings and the education of citizens in fire safety awareness. These are endorsed by the fire service people, but there is little likelihood that firefighters and their colourful apparatus will ever be put out of business. On the contrary, fire services have expanded their activity into a proliferation of other emergency responses to events that threaten lives and property in this increasingly complex world. Fire departments now respond to traffic accidents, hazardous goods incidents, and medical emergencies. Of course, this expansion of their roles entails modifications to their vehicles and to the equipment they carry.

This book has been written largely as a companion volume to my earlier *The Story of Firefighting in Canada,* and deals with the history of fires and firefighting organizations in Canada.

An early fifteenth century tub-type fire engine on skids, in fairly common use in Germany then. It was apparently the pioneer in 250 years of hand fire engines around the world. (From Ewbank's Hydraulics and Mechanics)

An early single-cylinder skid fire engine with carrying handles in Japan, possibly inspired by visiting Royal Navy engines. It was simple in construction and would be handy in the narrow alleys of Japanese towns. (Tokyo Fire Dept Museum)

An early Montréal three-wheeled hand engine, said to be a gift of the Phoenix Insurance Office in 1804. It supplied a line of leather hose, although the riveted form shown was probably added somewhat later. (Chateau de Ramezay)

Origins of the Fire Pump

A colourful and important form of community service was brought to North America's first cities and towns with the evolution of a practical, mobile firefighting pump. For almost one hundred years, beginning late in the eighteenth century, volunteer fire companies armed with muscle-powered fire engines defended their pioneer towns. These young communities were struggling to become bases of commerce and civilization in a raw, new country.

The volunteers kept the combustible wooden towns alive in the face of a constant threat of destruction by all-consuming conflagrations. This neighbour-helping-neighbour initiative was one of the first essential municipal services and was made possible by the primitive technology that gave the volunteer fireman the tools of his trade. As may be expected for the period, this technology originated in Europe and was improved and adapted in the United States for North American uses.

Humans possibly learned that water could extinguish a fire even before they knew how to light one themselves, and when they developed water-carrying utensils, the first bucket brigades were formed. For many centuries, pottery, skin, wood and leather buckets would remain the principal weapon for controlling unfriendly fires. It probably took people much longer to realize that water could be more effectively used if thrown in

Chapter I

Goosenecks to Squirreltails: The Hand Engines

a fine, aimed stream. This would also be safer for the firefighter, who could stand farther away.

The Egyptians designed a sophisticated device for this purpose. It was a basic two-cylinder force pump and was fitted with an air chamber to dampen pulsation and give continuity to the stream between pump strokes. This invention is recorded as having been proposed several centuries B.C. by Ctesibius of Alexandria and is described in the Commentaries of Heron's *Spiritalia*. Whether the technology of the day was able to make the pump work adequately is unknown.

A long search ensued to devise mechanical means to throw bigger and better streams of water at fires. With bronze available, the Romans progressed from squeezing wineskin bags to the syringe, or squirt, making use of this device with their *Vigiles*, the first recorded firemen. The squirt was a bronze cylinder about two feet long, with handles on each side and a plunger inside. Operated by two or three men on the street, it could throw a brief jet of water with some accuracy onto a roof or into a window—a decided advantage over a hand-thrown bucketful. The Romans spread this device through Europe and it was still in use in the sixteenth century. The squirt appeared, or possibly reappeared, in England at the end of the 1500s, long after the Romans had left.

The Romans must have progressed to a two-cylinder force pump of sorts, because they had them during their occupation of Britain. However this device, eventually to become the universal fire-

Royal Navy ships often fought fires in ports where they were stationed. The little shipboard engines had no wheels and must have looked like this when taken ashore. (Drawing by Audrey Matheson)

fighting machine, was lost as the Dark Ages closed in. At any rate, the Egyptian pump surfaced again in Germany during the seventeenth century and was subsequently employed throughout the western world for firefighting until supplanted by steam-driven pumps.

In the Middle Ages, European cities were at the mercy of fire, protected as they were only by squirts, bucket brigades and hooks for pulling down buildings—all in the hands of casual firefighting forces. By the 1600s however, efforts were being made to progress beyond these weak weapons. German inventors had produced a giant squirt operated by a crank and screw-driven piston, but it was apparently not really practicable. A single-cylinder force pump set inside a half-puncheon, mounted on sled runners, was a step in the right direction. It had a universal swivelling nozzle mounted on top, the embryonic stage of the gooseneck to follow.

An inventor named John Hautsch in the German city of Nuremberg furthered progress with a pump set into a rectangular box on wheels. The pump was much like that of the Egyptian Ctesibius; namely, two cylinders operated alternately by a rocking arm. The top of the box was perforated with holes so that the water was strained of debris when poured in. The two cylinders smoothed the intermittent squirting action, making for a more steady stream. It is possible that Hautsch had devised an air chamber as well. His fire engine appeared in 1656, an appropriate development for a noted metalworking city.

The Great Fire of London in 1666 and the subsequent rise of the fire insurance companies had stimulated similar efforts in Britain. There had been squirts and some primitive pumps available

Discovered under a pile of salt in a fishing shed at Trinity, Newfoundland, this 1811 Hopwood bedposter engine has no foot treadles and no means of steering. (Newfoundland Historic Resources Collection)

during the fire. The single-cylinder pump designs had metal cylinders and pistons or leather bellows construction. Unfortunately, London Common Council, in trying to upgrade fire defences afterward, merely acquired more of the squirts and ineffectual single-cylinder pumps they had relied on for some twenty years. This decision was made in spite of the advantages of the double pump, demonstrated by the London Waterworks as early as 1582.

Portable firefighting pumps became fairly well developed in Holland in the latter part of the seventeenth century, numbers of them being exported to Britain and other countries. One was ordered for Québec (and possibly one for Louisbourg) in the French Colonial era, although it never arrived. The Dutch led the way in fire engine development until the production of competitive engines in Britain after 1700. The geniuses behind the Dutch engines were John and Nicholas van der Heide, superintendents of fire engines for the City of Amsterdam.

The Dutch must have found their pumps effective since Amsterdam had more than sixty van der Heide engines in service in 1695. The nearest six responded to any fire alarm. It is not known whether they had an air chamber or pulsation damping device that early, but the Amsterdam operation must have made the world sit up and take notice of fire engines as an effective means to deliver water onto fires.

Richard Newsham's Engine

It remained, however, for Richard Newsham of London to build a fire engine in 1721 sufficiently improved to receive the nod

Drawing of a bedposter engine in the Newsham style with gooseneck nozzle. It is designed to be filled with buckets from wells and ponds—before the introduction of hose. (Drawing by Audrey Matheson)

of historians looking for the inventor of the first successful fire engine. Newsham did not add anything basic to what had been done in Germany and Holland. He simply refined what already had been accomplished. A contemporary, Fowkes of Wapping, built very similar engines. But all fire engines from now on would copy the Newsham model in some way.

Newsham's engine consisted of a rectangular, watertight wooden box—the larger ones on wheels—inside of which the two-cylinder, single-acting pump was mounted. The two pump pistons were worked up and down alternately by a rocking arm see-sawed under muscle power. A long nozzle on a swivelling base, referred to as a "gooseneck," was located on top of the pump to direct the discharge onto the fire.

PRIZE FIRE ENGINE MANUFACTORY.

CRAIG STREET, MONTREAL.

Exhibition of Industry of all Nations, LONDON, 1851. **PRIZE MEDAL.** See Jury Reports, Page 179.

L'Exposition Universelle, a Paris, 1855. **1re MÉDAILLE,** Rapports du Jury Mixte International, P. 225.

First Prize and Diploma, Provincial Exhibition, Montreal, September, 1853.

THE Subscriber is now prepared to execute orders for FIRE ENGINES of every grade found to be useful and suitable for private Companies, Manufactories, Railways, Villages, Towns and Cities, and will warrant the Machines furnished to give entire satisfaction or no sale.

Having successfully met the World's competition at London and Paris, he considers it merely necessary to say that his Engines cannot be surpassed for all the qualities which render an Engine valuable, viz :—strength, convenience, ease of operation, simplicity of design, and, therefore, non-liability to derangement.

GEORGE PERRY,
Craig Street

Montreal, October, 1857.

A commercial directory in Montréal carried this advertisement for fire engines built by the Perry firm in 1857. This was late in the hand engine era, the steamer being just over the horizon. (Baird Historical Collection, BHC)

There were a number of significant improvements in the design of Newsham's machine. Most important was the return of the air chamber in the discharge pipe to dampen the pulsation of the piston strokes and make the stream from the nozzle continuous. There was also a smooth linkage using chains between the actuating arms, or "brakes," and the pump. To supplement the efforts of the pumpermen bending their backs over the brakes on either side of the machine, handrails on top allowed several men to stand on top of the engine's body and operate foot treadles, throwing their weight from one foot to the other. The rails produced a distinctive appearance and the type became known as a "bedposter."

At one end of the Newsham engine, inside a box called a "condensing case," stood the tall air chamber mounted on top of the pump. Up through the top of the chamber came the discharge pipe with the gooseneck nozzle on it. Hose was not yet in use, and the engine had to be stationed directly before the building on fire so that the stream of water could reach the flames.

Aside from the working parts of iron, copper, brass and leather, the machine was made of wood with iron braces and solid, iron-bound wooden wheels. There was no provision for steering around a corner—the front wheels were fixed, so that the whole end of the fire engine had to be lifted to negotiate a turn. Speed of response to fires over the rough streets was obviously very limited.

From Newsham through Adam Nuttall in 1850, a number of prominent hand fire engine makers—including Nathaniel Hadley, Charles Simpkin and Moses Merryweather—comprised the ancestors of Merryweather and Sons, a firm that built fire engines for a full century, through the eras of steam and gasoline power. Merryweather also absorbed Shand, Mason and Company, descended from the Phillipe, Hopwood and Tilley firms of hand engine builders. Fire engines bearing all of these names appear to have seen service in Canada in early times, many sent out by British fire insurance companies.

British warships in the early nineteenth century carried one or more portable fire pumps, usually carried with handles, like a sedan chair. They were simple, with gooseneck nozzles, and worked like the land fire engines. British army garrisons had engines as well; they were often the first in the garrison towns in Canada and they demonstrated to the townsfolk what was possible in firefighting.

The English builders eventually developed hand-powered fire engines with larger bodies, drawn by horses and on which the paid insurance company firemen could ride. They also utilized horse-drawn wagons arranged for carrying portable engines on board.

American and Canadian builders, on the other hand, endeavoured to keep their engines light. North American firemen all worked on a volunteer basis and, in the big cities, long resisted any change to horse-drawn engines, being content to haul them through the streets themselves at a brisk trot. A position on the hauling rope was a place of honour, not to be surrendered to a mere horse. When another fire company was spotted enroute to a fire there would be a furious race to get there first. Cash awards for being first to put water on a fire were usually given. Equally important in the eyes of the volunteers, however, was the prestige of being first.

First Engines in Canada

Establishing the existence and nature of the first fire engines from the records presents difficulties, because even the hand-held squirt was described as a fire engine. The first identifiable fire engines in North America often have been taken to be two Newsham machines imported for the City of New York in 1731, but it can be shown that Boston had pre-Newsham engines somewhat earlier.

Some locally-built early hand engines were entirely unsuccessful and hardly worth considering in tracing the history of the device. The faulty pair of local engines first used in Saint John, New

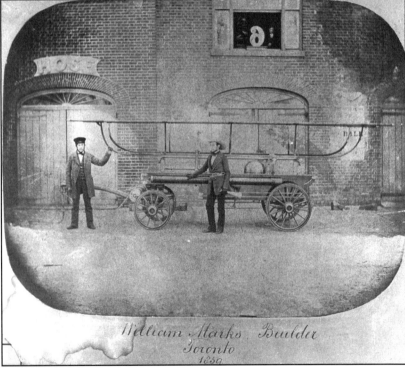

Brunswick in 1786 seem to be in this category. A bedposter that arrived in the town of Shelburne, Nova Scotia, on board a British man-of-war in 1786 was long considered the first fire engine in Canada. The best claim however rests with the two engines acquired for each of Montréal and Québec City in 1765, unless the British had engines in their garrisons earlier. Québec City merchants had ordered a Dutch-style engine much earlier, in 1691, but for some reason it failed to arrive.

The Montréal and Québec engines were surely English, as they had been sponsored by the governor. Much later, the small towns of Cote St. Paul and Berthier were described as having second-hand engines dating from 1774 and 1776. The former was built by the pioneer manufacturer Phillipe. These may have been the original Montréal and Québec machines. Halifax and Saint John obtained fire engines in 1783 and 1787, respectively. They were English bedposter engines, made of oak, and measured eight feet long and four-and-a-half feet wide. Like the Shelburne engine, they looked like Newsham's, having the same chain linkage between the rocker arm and pump; however they might have been Fowkes's.

After 1800, the Alliance Insurance Company donated larger British engines to Montréal and Toronto, machines bearing the company name having been in service there previously. The Montréal engine was a London-built Tilley. It was considered rather heavy, at about a ton, for the roughly sixty gallons per minute it would pump.

Halifax received one of its early fire engines from the fire insurance company bearing the city's name in 1827; it was probably a

---

Top: An unusual tricycle fire engine from Québec City. It was probably that built by Lemoine in 1849 and appears to have only one cylinder. It looks awkward and not very efficient for its weight. (Service Incendie Québec)

Bottom: William Marks of Toronto built engines for that city around 1860. Judging from this 1859 model, they appear to have been very similar to the Button piano engines. Other engines for Toronto were imported by the fire insurance companies. (Toronto Fire Dept)

A fine example of a later Perry engine with a copper tub and an unusual squirrel-tail suction hose, the proud possession of the Cayuga, Ontario Fire Department. (BHC)

Hopwood machine. In some cases, insurance companies merely made contributions toward the purchase of engines or supported an individual fire company's general funds.

The first hand fire engines in North America, then, were British imports. After about 1840, Canadian- and American-built engines were the rule. As municipal governments took on the responsibility for fire protection, the preference on the part of the British insurance companies for the English engines was no longer a factor. The background of some of the English engines in Canada is hazy—some in the smaller towns were evidently insurance engines castoff from larger centres which had moved to improved, second-generation machines. A few of the earlier engines were privately owned, maintained by merchants in Montréal, St. John's and Saint John.

The American Style

While colonial America initially bought English engines because they were the best and they were "in the family," not long after the War of Independence the craft of building fire engines was being

mastered in New York and Philadelphia. One of the first prominent builders was Richard Mason in Philadelphia, credited with introducing the fore-and-aft style engine, with the pumping brakes at the ends instead of the sides. John Agnew's firm was descended from Mason's, and produced the large and beautiful Philadelphia Double-Deckers. None of these distinctive fire engines seem to have come into Canada except on a brief visit.

New York builders tended to follow the English pattern for a time, using the sidestroke arrangement. In the Boston area, two manufacturers chose the fore- and aft-configuration and this became popular throughout New England. Crossing the border, it became common in Canada as well.

The first of these two builders was Ephriam Thayer in 1790, who, followed by his son Stephen, built a great many of his relatively compact, spartan engines for American fire companies. William

Top: An 1852 James Smith piano engine, *Prince of Wales*, served No. 8 Company in the Sand Point section of Saint John. After a sojourn in the Nova Scotia Firefighters' Museum, it is now in the Old No. 2 Engine House Museum in Saint John, a station that was built for hand engines. (BHC)

Bottom: A beautifully maintained Button squirrel-tail engine of the Dunnville, Ontario Fire Department. It has folding brakes and two eduction (discharge) pipes leading to the front end for attaching hose. (BHC)

This Smith hand tub shown at Black Creek Pioneer Museum is said to have been given to Toronto in 1837 by the British American Insurance Company, though some records disagree. It has a long eduction pipe instead of a gooseneck nozzle. (Black Creek Pioneer Museum)

Hunneman, once an apprentice to Paul Revere, the silversmith, learned about fire engines under Thayer. He started his own fire engine business in Roxbury, Massachussetts, in 1792. In its ensuing almost one hundred years, the Hunneman Company produced many hundreds of engines, some finding their way to remote parts of the world. They were probably the largest of all hand fire engine producers. Winnipeg and Victoria started out with Hunneman engines, both delivered by water.

Hunneman's engines differed from the English and their American copies, having their pumping brakes at the ends like Mason's and Thayer's. Hunneman also had the pump mounted in the centre of the body instead of at one end. With the fore-and-aft layout, fixed brake arms long enough to accommodate the number of firemen needed to operate any but the smallest pumps would project far out to the sides. This would be impractical when racing through the streets, so it was necessary to devise brakes that folded to the sides when not in use.

About the time the Thayer and Hunneman engines appeared, American engines were being fitted with steering front wheels. On these, and on the Button companies' engines, there was an arched iron frame on the front of the body, under which the wheels could turn a full ninety degrees. This was called the crane-neck type.

Perry's Gold Medal Machine

A number of Hunneman engines went into service in Montréal, the Maritime Provinces and Ontario in the early 1800s, but it was not long before his market was taken over by a Canadian manufacturer. About 1840, a Montréal tradesman named George Perry—who is said to have worked in the Hunneman factory for a time—and his several brothers commenced building fire engines on the Hunneman pattern.

Fire engines were built mostly of wood. The Perry brothers were cabinetmakers by trade and volunteer firemen by avocation. The Perrys had become tired of hearing how an engine built in Montréal by one Antoine LePage was the most powerful in the city. This impelled them to outperform the rival engine by building a better one.

One Perry brother, Alfred, was a famous hero among the firemen of Montréal and, as a prominent example of the competitive spirit among them, eagerly promoted plans for a more powerful machine. He was in a good position to evaluate the engines' effectiveness since his fire company, the Union, was supplied with a Perry engine. In any case, the Perry product did not differ very much from the basic Hunneman design and the two are not always quickly differentiated.

The Perry fire engine business seems to have been on a small scale until the name gained international fame, beginning with the first world's fair, held at the Crystal Palace in London in 1851. When a large collection of agricultural products, manufactured goods and curios was put together and shipped to London for a Canadian display, the Perry brothers responded with their usual unbridled competitive spirit. As volunteer firemen and fire engine builders they saw their chance to show their prowess, and quite likely gain recognition in the same league as the British and Americans.

The Perrys obtained the backing of the Canadian exhibition commissioners, and Alfred went along to Prince Albert's Great Exhibition to look after the engine. He succeeded in promoting official pumping contests and won a Great Medal, the only one awarded to Canada at the exhibition. In the tests prescribed by the jury, a contemporary account said, "No other engine threw a column of water so high as this, or discharged so great a body of water per man." To Perry's regret, no American fire engines showed up in London.

In Paris four years later Alfred Perry repeated his performance, this time against twenty-two fire engines from England and all

A folding brake, squirrel-tail engine rigged for horse draught. It appears to have been brought out of reserve for a parade, no longer having its crew of volunteer haulers. (Harold Doherty)

Inset: A Fredericton, New Brunswick version of the fore-and-aft engine, one of several built by bicycle-maker George Taylor in 1863. It had suction intake on one side, discharge on the other. (Harold Doherty)

This nicely preserved Smith piano engine, typical of many that served in the Maritime provinces, belonged to the Alma Section of the Union Engine Company of Halifax. It is now in the N.S. Firefighters' Museum, Yarmouth. (BHC)

across Europe. A Lemoine engine from Québec City was also there, but still none from the United States. In addition to winning another gold medal, the renowned Montréal fireman took his engine out of the exhibition hall to help fight a major fire in an army warehouse. The Perry fire engine impressed a large international crowd with its ability to draft water from the River Seine, while the Paris engines had to be filled by bucket brigades.

The *London Illustrated News* reported, "The Canadian engine was put in charge of Mr. Perry, an officer of the Canadian Fire Department, and drawing its water direct from the Seine with its own suction, kept several other engines supplied with a constant stream. At one time, Mr. Perry put on his jet and the stream was so strong and effective as to attract the attention of Marshal Magnan and his staff."

"Enjine! Enjine! Make way for the Enjine!" was the cry. Both stopping the fire and getting to the scene ahead of rival fire companies were equally in their minds. (Drawing by Audrey Matheson)

With the resultant international fame and seemingly little serious competition at home, the Perry fire engine began to sell widely in Eastern Canada. The west was still unsettled, but in the growing outpost city of Victoria, a Perry engine was purchased. The Perry was a small, plain, but relatively powerful engine compared to the big English ones and the later designs of American engines, such as the "piano" types developed by Button and Smith and popular in some Canadian cities. These other engines were not generally of a greater capacity, notwithstanding their more impressive appearance.

Working against George Perry, in whose name the business operated, were several factors that explain why he did not go on to greater things, such as manufacturing steam fire engines and other apparatus of the post hand engine era. Only the fame gained in England and France finally established his product as serious competition for the major American manufacturers. The Canadian market was small and far-flung. The Maritimes certainly had close ties and established trading patterns with New England. The Prairies were not yet settled and the West Coast cities traded with San Francisco. They all usually bought American engines.

The Perrys were also late in the game, for the major centres were beginning to look at the experimental steam fire engines before the first decade of the Perry engine had been completed.

The Perry company is believed to have stopped building fire engines in 1870 or soon thereafter. Montréal purchased two small Perry engines in 1869 for use in the outskirts of the city, on the side of Mount Royal. This was unusual for a fully paid fire department, but a special circumstance owing to a poor water supply. The age of hand-powered fire engine building was about to end, because the requirements of small villages could now be met from the supply of castoffs from the cities.

The Pianos

Among the major hand engine builders of the United States, James Smith of New York City and L. Button and Company of Watertown, NY supplied a considerable number of fire engines to Canadian fire departments. Smith built several styles of engine in the first half of the nineteenth century, the heyday of hand engine production. He first manufactured models similar to the English bedposter, that is, side-stroke with the pump, condensing case and gooseneck nozzle at one end.

When Button and Company introduced the piano engine in 1838—so-called because its enclosed rectangular box resembled pianos of the day—Smith and others followed suit. The piano, with increasing pumping capacities, had long side

---

Top: It was Natal Day for the Village of Truro, Nova Scotia, in 1887 when this hose reel with leather hose was "dressed" for the occasion. Even this rudimentary vehicle was a matter of interest in a small village. (BHC)

Bottom: A hose reel racing team of the Halifax Union Engine Company ready for action on the track. The race to put a hoseline in action was a hard-fought competition in the latter nineteenth century and is still practised today in competitive musters. (Halifax Fire Dept)

brakes to accommodate more men, and the brakes frequently folded upward to reduce the width of the machine when travelling. The pumps were more often located toward the centre of the body, with only the air chamber showing above the covered deck. The often elaborate condensing case was eliminated.

By this time, the gooseneck nozzle mounted on top of the engine was no longer needed. Threaded discharge connections were now provided at the side for the attachment of hose lines. Suction hose had also become standard equipment and was carried in two or more lengths mounted on the sides of the body. Button, Cowing and Jeffers each introduced a permanently attached suction hose, connected at one end of the engine and bent up over the top, out of the way when not in use. This inspired the name squirrel-tail for these engines. The style became common particularly in Ontario and parts of the west, where numerous Button engines were used. For the older cities originally equipped with gooseneck engines, the piano was a second generation weapon, replacing the older, less effective machines between 1840 and 1850.

Some gooseneck engines were adapted to the riveted leather leading and suction hose after these became available in North America between 1818 and 1822. Many engines continued to be built with discharge outlets taken off the top of the air chamber. A long discharge pipe curving down from this high point to the far end of the engine allowed the connection of hose at an accessible point, although many converted engines had the hose coupled directly on the gooseneck.

American volunteer fire companies, in the bigger cities particularly, were highly competitive, not only in practical performance but in the beauty and parade qualities of their apparatus. As a result American hand fire engines were often elaborately carved and decorated with pictorial art at great expense to the company members. This art reached a peak in the illumination of the condensing cases of the gooseneck and Philadelphia engines by prominent artists. Piano engines might be finished in polished and inlaid woods like rosewood and mahogany, according to the vanity and purse of the fire company.

By contrast, Canadian fire companies only occasionally went beyond a little gilt trim. The Perry engine that went to London in 1851 was decorated to meet anticipated American competition. Its side panels had painted scenes of Montréal. Queen Victoria admired it as "a very good and novel kind of engine," but it was derided by the British press as small and not very robust-looking.

Other Canadian Engines

As might be expected for those times, a number of hand fire engines were built for fire departments by local foundries or blacksmiths. These seem to have been mostly single efforts, proving that fire engine building was not quite as easy as it appeared. The criteria for success were light weight and minimum pumping effort in relation to the stream of water delivered and—most important—reliability.

Only the Perrys of Montréal became manufacturers of hand fire engines of any significance in Canada. They fought aspiring competition locally on the part of two builders, Lemoine in Québec City and LePage in Montréal. Public competitions were somewhat indecisive, but the Perry engine was evidently lighter and less cumbersome. The smaller, more manoeuverable Perry machine also outshone the big English engines when it came to getting through the snowdrifts of Canadian winters. Alfred Perry described the Alliance engine as going at a snail's pace with twenty men hauling; it was difficult to turn and required thirty or forty men to haul it in heavy snow.

There is no information on the LePage engine, except that there was one in service with a Montréal fire company. Nor is there any indication of other sales successes. The Lemoine engine is similarly recorded in service with only one Québec fire company. It was

Top: A Fredericton hose company in parade dress. Their mascot picked a shady spot under the four-wheeler. The reel was probably locally built. (Harold Doherty)

Bottom: An interesting lineup of firefighting strength—a ladder cart, two-wheel reel, folding brake hand engine, four-wheeled reel and an Amoskeag steamer in the doorway of one of the Yarmouth fire company stations. (Paul Cleveland)

unique in its tricycle design, with only one pump cylinder, possibly double-acting, and fore-and-aft pumping brakes.

Most of the five or more small hand engines in the Fredericton, New Brunswick, Fire Department appear to have been locally built by a self-taught engineer named George Taylor, who was in charge of the waterworks and built the first bicycle in town. Saint John also had several fire engines built by local concerns such as the Phoenix Foundry. A large piano engine built by David Bradley in 1858 for the adjoining city of Portland, eventually became a competition engine in Lynn, Massachussets, in the latter part of the century. It had a solid mahogany body eleven feet long, eight-inch-diameter pump pistons, and it was able to beat all of the Saint John engines in competition. It did not fare so well against the later ten-inch engines in the New England competitive musters. The Hamilton, Ontario, Fire Department still parades the little "Victoria," a local product of the Fisher Company, in a small version of the Hunneman type.

Several of Toronto's piano fire engines were squirrel-tails, built by William Marks of Temperance Street around 1860. They were replacements for earlier gooseneck types and resembled the Button engines very closely.

Fire Hose: A Dramatic Development

In 1772 sewn leather discharge or leading hose had been invented in Holland by the van der Heides, John and Nicholas, superintendents of fire apparatus for Amsterdam.

The historian Ewbank quotes an early source as saying, "The Dutch and others used a long flexible tube of leather, sailcloth or the like, which they carry or conduct in the hand from one room to the other as the occasion arises, so that the engine may be applied where the fire is only withinside." This quaintly described the next great technological advance after the perfection of the fire pump itself. The Dutch hose was made in fifty-foot lengths with brass screw couplings.

This step permitted the removal of the gooseneck nozzle from the top of the engine in favour of a portable nozzle held by hand at the end of a hose line. It is obvious from the design of some of the English engines in Canada around 1800 that they were built for the use of leading hose. Perhaps they used sewn canvas hose. The first Québec City engines came with forty feet of hose, the length then used in Britain. Some small engines, such as the Montréal Phoenix of 1804, had no gooseneck nozzle, operating only with hose. The first Toronto engine also was equipped with hose when delivered in 1808. The Americans, however, appear to have waited for the advent of the more reliable leather, rivetted-seam variety in 1818.

Merryweather manufactured leather hose after its introduction from Holland late in the eighteenth century and it was sewn with twine. Single copper riveting was adopted by this firm in 1830, followed later by the standard double row of rivets for the higher pressures of steam-powered pumping about 1870.

Philadelphia is credited with the first appearance of the riveted seam for leather hose in 1818, increasing its reliability, and this was eagerly adopted by Canadian and American firemen. The impression is clear that any predecessor hose of any kind was not in wide use in either country, even when it came with the engines. There is no doubt that sewn leather hose would be perishable compared to the engines themselves and might soon be discarded.

Now the fight against fire would no longer be primarily a rearguard, defensive operation, fought from the outside. Previously, the firemen had to accept that the interior of the building on fire would be gutted. Now, as Ewbank says, bold firefighters could go into the smoky interior to do battle at close quarters before the flames took over the structure. This was increasingly important as buildings became larger and more valuable.

An important result was the transition of the firefighter from a mere thrower of water to a courageous, enterprising specialist in a hazardous occupation. The fire engines were more protected, on the other hand, than the gooseneck engines sometimes damaged as a result of having to be close to the fire, much like the later water towers.

It was not too great a step further for the van der Heides to create a hose for the other end of their pumps so that water could be drawn in from a distant source. Heretofore it could come only from the tub reservoir—part of the engine's body. Their solution, particularly for Amsterdam with its numerous canals, involved a portable canvas bag, like a funnel, on a stand. Filling this with buckets at the canal bank caused water to flow under a slight head through a hose-like tube to the tub of the pump. A long bucket brigade was thus often avoided. With improving hose, the Dutch inventors built new engines equipped with a direct hose inlet to the pump.

The North Americans did not adopt the van der Heides' gravity-flow hose line. They waited for the appearance of a short, non-collapsing section of hose that would withstand a vacuum. Now the need for labour-intensive operations with buckets was eliminated altogether. Fire engines could lift water directly from wells, cisterns and natural bodies of water. They could draft from carters' puncheons on wagons or work in relay to supply a stream of water from a considerable distance, as Alfred Perry did at the fire in Paris. The men who pumped the brakes were not too pleased at having to work far from the fire—they were accustomed to having a ringside seat.

The first hard suction hose appeared in the United States in 1822 on an engine in the City of Providence, Rhode Island. It was a Philadelphia-built machine and the idea spread quickly, with many old engines converted to take suction from either the tub or hose at the turn of a valve. It was this ability to supply a stream from draft to a remote point that made the Perry engine so dramatically effective in Paris in 1855. According to Perry, the Paris Fire Regiment had no engines with this capability.

As piped waterworks systems began to appear in towns toward the middle of the nineteenth century, they were usually so weak that the hand fire engines still had to supply the hose streams. They did this by removing a plug from the hydrant, filling a pit surrounding it and taking suction there. The term "fireplug" remains in use to this day. Even when a waterworks became strong enough to deliver better hose streams directly from hydrants than the fire engines could, some volunteer fire companies insisted on connecting their pumps just the same.

Riveted leather hose was heavy and required constant care, with applications of beef tallow and neatsfoot oil to keep it soft and pliable. Nevertheless, it proved more reliable than twine-sewn canvas at one-quarter of the weight. Leather hose continued to be used in major Canadian fire departments until the 1870s when *gutta percha* rubber, and then circular woven, cotton-covered rubber hose replaced it.

Leather hose was normally oak-tanned, overweight cowhide, fastened into a one-and-one-half or two-inch-diameter tube with a double row of copper wire rivets. Complete with threaded brass couplings and iron rings at intervals for handles, it weighed some eighty pounds per fifty-foot length. Such hose withstood pressures of two hundred pounds, but if not cared for diligently it would become mouldy, too stiff to handle and crack.

At first fire engines might carry one or two lengths of leading hose, but when they were moved from near the fire to the water source, several hundred feet were assigned to each company. This called for the development of the hose jumper or leader cart, a reel mounted on two wheels. It was towed behind the engine at first, then as the amount of hose increased, the reel was pulled separately. The New York-style gooseneck engines often carried a reel of hose on top, but this practice was uncommon in Canada. The two-wheel reel eventually grew into a four-wheeler with larger hose capacity for ambitious fire companies with larger-capacity pumps. Insufficient hose to reach a fire from the nearest water source was a frequent frustration.

Around the 1860s the volunteers of St. Catharines, Ontario, frequently complained about insufficient hose, leaks and the poor condition of this part of their equipment. It is possible to read between the lines that the problem was due to both lack of funds to purchase more hose and indifferent maintenance.

Early Water Supplies: The Carters

As the universal fire extinguishing medium, water is for the most part plentiful and cheap. It is also indispensable for other uses vital to the community. There has been strong incentive for communities to make it available whether from wells, cisterns or water mains. For firefighting, water is needed in a hurry and in large quantities.

In the beginning, a well in the town square might serve all citizens for all purposes. A bucket brigade could dip from the nearest well, pond, brook or harbour, fresh water or salt. When fire engines came into use, the buckets filled them from the same sources. As the engines' capacity increased, cisterns or wooden tanks sunk into the ground were installed at key points to provide sufficient volumes. With hose, sources within reasonable hose length of potential fires were needed, or it would be back to the buckets for the firemen.

At the same time, the supply of domestic water to householders was taken on by private enterprise as carters with horse and wagon made door-to-door sales. Particularly in towns where there might be a poor well supply but a handy harbour or river,

A representation of a volunteer company's spider carriage at cleaning and maintenance time. Such elaborate carriages were expensive and quite possibly were paid for out of the fire company's own funds. (Drawing by Audrey Matheson)

carters sold water by the pail from a hogshead mounted on a two-wheeled cart, or a sled in winter. Dogs might pull smaller carts in Montréal and Ottawa. City fathers made use of this resource by paying for each load carters delivered to a fire, with a premium for the first loads to arrive.

In Montréal the carters hauled water from the adjacent St. Lawrence River. In their eagerness to be first on the fire scene they often arrived with only half a barrelful left, the rest having splashed out on the way. Even after the first water mains with fireplugs were installed, the carters might have water on hand for the pumps before the firemen could get the plug connection made, thus prolonging their usefulness.

Conditions were much the same in Toronto, or York as it was called at the beginning of the hand engine era. Even after the installation of the first hydrants on the commercially-owned waterworks, the pressure was too weak and the hydrants too few, so the carters served usefully for a few years longer. Their wood-stave puncheons held sixty to eighty gallons of water. The offer of rewards for promptness began in 1825, the normal reward for a load delivered to a fire being initially a York shilling.

This system of water supply was legislated in 1834, when all carters were required to have a water puncheon and to respond to fires on pain of a twenty-shilling fine for nonappearance, although the premiums for arriving first on the scene still applied. To improve their chances of earning them, the carters, who might be hauling other loads all day, placed full water puncheons on their carts for the night so as to be ready for a quick start.

The loads brought to fires were counted by giving the carter a receipt in the form of a tin or lead tally about the size of a fifty-cent piece. With a premium on speed and much spillage on the bumpy streets en route, the 1834 regulations called for refusal of the premium if the puncheon was less than three-quarters full. The carters soon devised a canvas flap to contain the splashing and often became involved in wild races with one another.

The Toronto carters did not have a very good reputation and were sometimes suspected of arson to promote revenue. Since they were able to respond quickly when they had a loaded puncheon and did not go on foot like the firemen, they frequently reached the fire first. This situation gave them the chance on occasion to bargain on a price for helping the fire victims salvage their goods from the burning building.

Manning the Brakes

Because the hand fire engine required several shifts of twelve to twenty or more men to work the pumping brakes, to say nothing of hauling it smartly along on the way to fires, the volunteer fire company was a large group, some forty to eighty men. The whole fire department was a loose organization of individual companies, each a tightly knit social and service club of significance in the community.

Some companies became rowdy and their rivalries occasionally interfered with effective firefighting. Competition on the sports field helped some to dampen their high spirits. This included pumping contests and hose-reel races. Some companies maintained special reels for racing use only.

Hand fire engines varied considerably in size, but they were essentially the same in operating principle, at least as far as Canada was concerned. Two opposing beams, or brakes, on opposite sides or ends of the machine were rocked up and down at sixty to a hundred times a minute by two rows of firemen. The connecting arm between them alternately depressed the two single-acting pistons, each with its inlet and outlet valves. A few rotary pumps operated by cranks were used in the United States, but there is no evidence of them in Canada.

The wooden body was normally divided into three compartments. There was a small toolbox section and the main tub, a reservoir frequently lined with copper for waterproofing, divided in two parts. A bulkhead with many small holes drilled in it cut off a smaller section called the feeder box, into which water was dumped. Filtered for debris through the holes, the water reached the main tub with the pump and its suction inlet. In the later engines with suction hose, a valve controlled whether tub or hose suction was used.

Pumping capacity was in the area of sixty to a hundred gallons per minute for typical earlier engines, a pressure sufficient to project a forceful stream onto a roof or into an upstairs window. Nozzles were around five- to seven-eighths of an inch in diameter. Some later engines were capable of discharging several hundred gallons per minute and might require forty or more men on the brakes at

A detail of a Cowing engine with its elaborate brasswork. The volunteers raised the funds to pay for these extras in order to outshine competing fire companies. Canadian engines were only occasionally as elaborately decorated as their American counterparts. (BHC)

The unusual cart-mounted hosereel of Alma Section, Union Engine Company, Halifax. The department had a single engine company divided into a number of sections, each equivalent to one company elsewhere. (Now at Nova Scotia Firefighters' Museum, Yarmouth)

A fine example of the more elaborate and aptly named spider hose carriage with spring-mounted bells, hauling rope, running lamp and parade decorations, preparing for a parade in Baltimore. The American veteran firemen's associations still put great effort into their parade machines. (BHC)

The pump cylinders were single-acting, open at the top, of brass or iron, and had leather packing. Piston diameters ran from five to ten inches and the stroke from eight to eighteen inches. The largest engines, designated as first class, had pistons of nine or ten inches in diameter.

The urge to win pumping contests as well as to fight fires better led to the purchase of bigger and better fire engines, the volunteers often paying the cost from their own pockets. Pumping prowess was generally decided on the basis of the greatest horizontal or vertical distance water could be thrown through a specified size of nozzle. Continuous effort did not count for much, a momentary splash being enough to make the wet mark that would be measured.

It was on the basis of such a splash that the Perry engines won at London and Paris. Montréal's Union Engine Company was equipped in 1850 with a Perry engine built expressly to challenge the LePage engine of the rival Montréal Engine Company. A contest to see which machine could wet a tower of Notre Dame Church at the highest point broke down in a squabble, both having thrown water higher than a hundred and forty feet.

once. Under competition conditions, hand engines operating for only brief periods were able to throw small streams of water in excess of two hundred feet horizontally or a hundred and eighty feet vertically. On occasion they were known to beat early steam fire engines in this respect. Naturally any contest was one of both machines and pumping crews.

It was decided then to settle the matter on the basis of the classic hand engine-era test of "washing." A test of volume pumped, this challenge involved partly filling the tubs of both engines, then having them pump water into each other's tub. The one pumping fastest would overflow the other's tub, thus washing it.

This contest broke up in disorder when the LePage team claimed the Perry supporters pulled the Montréal's hose out of their engine as it was about to overflow. To be washed was a particular disgrace. When pumping in a relay at a fire, top performance was assured by the opportunity for the first crew in the line to wash the second and the need for the second crew to avoid being washed.

A shift of firemen could pump for about ten minutes before needing relief, if they were not working the brakes too quickly. Relieving pumpers stepped in while the pumping continued. This was tricky and resulted in as many broken knuckles as did inter-company fistfights.

Reels and Carts

As fire departments and their equipment developed beyond 1800, the citizens saw more than just engines dashing through the streets. The hose-reel, sometimes manned by an independent hose company, took on particular importance when hydrant systems capable of feeding a hose without benefit of a pump were installed. Hand engines began to be laid up.

By 1850, the hook-and-ladder cart and its crew had joined the scene in all the major centres. Previously many cities required ladders and hooks to be maintained around the town where they could be brought out quickly. The "hook" in hook and ladder was a demolition hook, one of the first fire defence tools. Mounted on the end of a pole so that it could be raised up to engage eavestroughs, trim boards or roofing, the heavy iron hook had a chain attached for pulling these combustible parts away from buildings. Sometimes flimsy early buildings were pulled down completely to stop the spread of fires. Ladders of the hand apparatus era were made with heavy, solid beams of wood. There were no extension ladders.

Other hand-drawn vehicles included the occasional cart for carrying buckets or tarpaulins and salvage bags for protecting building contents. All hand-drawn vehicles were fitted with a tongue for steering and a long loop of rope for hauling. A reel for rolling up the hauling rope was provided under the front end. The heavy engines had no brakes and had a restraining rope at the rear for control going down hills.

After the later development of the soda-acid chemical engine and its great success on horse-drawn fire apparatus, two-wheeled, hand-drawn chemical carts became popular in villages and industrial plants. This device was in some cases a successor to the hand pumping engine in places too small to maintain steam fire engines.

There were times, especially in heavy snow conditions, when passing horses were summarily commandeered to help haul an engine to a fire. On muddy streets the firemen might take to the sidewalks with their apparatus, scattering pedestrians. This got them into considerable trouble in Toronto.

Hand-drawn fire apparatus and its proud crews were always prominent in parades and other public celebrations. Elaborate decorations in bunting, artwork and flowers were added to the gleam of silver and etched glass company identification lamps and riding lights. At night, torchlight processions saw every fireman carrying his flaming torch.

The Hand Tub Roster

Some of the older cities in the east, such as Montréal and Québec, were in existence long before fire engines were introduced and organized fire companies were accepted as an essential service. In spite of that, when these two cities acquired the services of their first fire engine protection in the 1780s, the much younger cities of Saint John and Halifax were not far behind. It was a case of timing in awareness of fire protection responsibility and the availability of practical engines.

It is noteworthy that at the peak of the hand engine era, about 1855, Montréal had one ladder and nine engine companies, while Saint John had only one engine company less. Québec dawdled, but jumped to eight engine companies after two calamitous conflagrations in 1845 that destroyed 2250 buildings and took 60 lives. One Québec engine company had been installed and maintained by the Québec Insurance Company, probably the only outright insurance brigade in Canada.

Alfred Perry's Union Engine Company once journeyed downriver from Montréal to do battle with a Lemoine engine against the steeple of Québec Cathedral for a £25 bet. After the usual arguments, the local side was declared the winner, splashing to a height of over one hundred and fifty feet.

The Toronto Fire Brigade had acquired four engine and two ladder companies in 1833, a remarkable growth from York's single engine of 1826. These were gooseneck engines, and a program of replacement using piano engines and hose-reels began soon after this. Both Toronto and Montréal virtually abandoned the use of engines by 1861 when more powerful waterworks came into operation. In 1858, Toronto had an authorized strength of one ladder company, nine engine, one salvage and two hose companies. It was probably the largest Canadian fire department in terms of companies in the hand fire engine era.

One Toronto hand engine is famous for its part in driving off rebels from the Don River bridge in the rebellion of 1837. Various modern accounts of this renowned hand tub include a quotation purporting to come from the time of its acquisition by the British American Engine Company. It describes the engine as "a Montréal fore-and-aft tub, more powerful than a piano or a gooseneck engine." In the 1960's the insurance company that donated it tracked it down and restored it from its dilapidated condition. It is now proudly displayed at Black Creek Pioneer Village outside Toronto. Clearly this engine does not in any way match the description. It is, in fact, an American-pattern, modified bedposter engine. Somehow over the years, the description of No.6, the Perry engine, became attached to the "British America" engine. No.6, called the "Provincial Engine," was of the type that won a Great Medal in London in 1851.

Probably the first fire engine in the west was in a part of British North America which is no longer part of Canada. Fort Vancouver was a Hudson's Bay Company post near the mouth of the Columbia River in what is now the State of Washington. Records of the company for 1844 include an exchange of correspondence in which the headquarters of the company in London dickered for the purchase of a fire engine for this major outpost depot on the Pacific Coast. The company files report that "We have also ordered a fire engine for this establishment which will be a great protection, in case of fire, to the large amount of property occasionally collected here."

The final agreement was set with the eminent London engine builder Moses Merryweather early in September 1845, for an engine of 80 to 100 gallons per minute, utilizing 18 to 20 men pumping. It was to have a copper tub or cistern and cast-iron wheels and cost £138 plus extras. The fire engine was to be accompanied by dragropes, two 6-foot suction pipes, six 40-foot brass-coupled, copper-riveted leather hose lengths and nozzles.

The western cities were, as a rule, still too small at the end of the hand engine era to have more than one or two engines. The City of Vancouver was born within the steam age and had no hand apparatus whatever in its history. The Button piano-style engine appears to have predominated in the west.

The Pacific Coast cities started in the firefighting field when the eastern cities were beginning to dispose of hand fire engines, especially the older, smaller machines. Governor Sir James Douglas of Vancouver Island ordered two engines for Victoria in 1858. These were obtained in San Francisco, one a castoff of the Monumental Engine Company of that city, the other a new Hunneman. The first was less than satisfactory, typical of second-hand engines. It was a Baltimore-built Rogers machine, brought out to the coast in 1850 during the California gold rush boom.

The Monumental engine was rather a small one, probably third-class size, with six-inch diameter pump cylinders, and carried the name *Telegraph*. It had been placed in reserve in favour of a larger engine in 1854, then sold to Victoria through arrangements made by George Hossefross, who was active in the Monumental company and for a time was fire chief in San Francisco. Along with the *Telegraph* came a hose cart and five hundred feet of leather hose, the whole lot costing $1600.

The two hand tubs arrived from San Francisco in the steamer *Oregon* on July 28, 1858, and were tested by pumping from a well at old Fort Victoria that afternoon. The *Victoria Gazette* reported:

> The brakes were manned by individuals volunteering promiscuously from the crowd drawn together to witness the throwing the first water by a fire engine in our town, among whom we noticed several old San Francisco firemen. The machines are

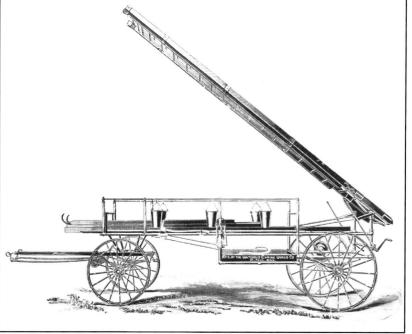

Top: The lineup at Station 2, Court Street, Toronto in the hand-hauled era, including hose reel, engines and ladder cart. The firemen got into trouble hauling their rigs on the wooden sidewalks when the streets were too muddy. (Toronto Fire Dept)

The hand-drawn, hand-raised aerial ladder offered by Waterous Engine Works for village use was a rare item. The extension ladder could be removed and used on the ground. (BHC)

Neptune Hose of Yarmouth, its reel appropriately decorated, is ready for a trip to a big firemen's muster in Saint John. (Nova Scotia Firefighters' Museum, Yarmouth)

rather small, but sufficiently powerful to throw a full stream of water over any building in the town with ease. The prompt manner with which Governor Douglas has acted in this matter is worthy of special praise, and will cause our citizens to feel much more secure and safe in their property.

Actually, the money for the engines was advanced by the Hudson's Bay Company.

Detailed rosters are not recorded in most cases, but an impression of the engines operated in various areas may be drawn. The old towns of the Maritimes owned mainly English bedposters, Hunnemans, Perrys and Smiths, frequently in this chronological sequence. In the province of Québec it was predominantly Perry and Hunneman machines, after the early English insurance models. Following the American gooseneck period, Ontario communities leaned to the Button squirreltails and numerous Perrys. Ottawa and London each operated several Perry engines.

As steam fire engines were introduced in the major cities, small towns usually inherited their hand engines. Those of Saint John, whose careers are better recorded than most, probably exhibit a good cross-section of the fates of such engines. Several were sold to private industries such as the shipbuilding yards where they finished their days providing private protection. One Smith engine was sold to the town of St. Andrews, New Brunswick, where it is still maintained as a showpiece by the volunteer fire department. Another served successively in Annapolis and Bridgetown, Nova Scotia. A third Smith is preserved in Saint John's old Sydney Street Engine House 2, unique in having been built for hand engines and still in use as a fire museum.

The Bradley engine, built in Saint John for adjoining Portland, was sold to a local ropewalk for private protection in 1872. It was subsequently acquired by a veteran firemen's association in Lynn, Massachusetts, in 1897, for competition use. It appears to have been broken up around 1908. Several other Maritime engines also ended their days on the competitive muster grounds of New England.

When Saint John's hand engine companies were disbanded with the coming of steam fire engines in 1864, the city moved to sell the discarded machines for its own profit. The feisty Irish Emerald Company, which had paid $1600 of the $2000 cost of its Smith engine, took exception to this. The members spirited away their engine, disassembled it and hid the parts. Later a deal was made with the village of Tusket, Nova Scotia, the engine smuggled aboard a schooner and delivered to its new owners. When it turned out to be too big for Tusket's needs, the Emerald was traded to a Yarmouth company for a Hunneman. The Emerald came to an ignominious end in the burning of Yarmouth's South End Fire Station in 1899.

San Francisco's first fire engine, locally built in the 1850s, was a Worth side-stroke named "Broderick." It was eventually retired and moved on to provide protection in the British Columbia towns of Yale in 1882, Vernon in 1894, and Kelowna in 1904, where it ended its active days. In 1947, Kelowna returned Broderick to San Francisco for restoration and permanent museum display. A Portland, Oregon, Button engine found its way to Atlin in Northern British Columbia, where it may still be seen.

Thus, for the most part, hand fire engines made redundant by waterworks systems and steamers were passed on to smaller towns, or placed in reserve to slowly deteriorate. Bodies eventually rotted out if not cared for, but the working parts survived. Some Canadian hand fire engines have been restored to working order after many years of neglect, especially under the impetus of the 1967 Centennial Year.

Villages continued to employ hand engines even after 1900. In fact, more modern versions of small, hand-powered pumps for village use were being advertised as late as 1910. Hand hauling of ladder carts, chemical engines, hose-reels and even gasoline powered pumps continued to satisfy the wants of very small communities for another decade or two.

A few of the old-time engines were kept up over the years for parades and muster competitions, notably by the continuing volunteer companies. Some were rescued later from forgotten corners. About a dozen Canadian fire departments are still proudly maintaining hand fire engines today. A similar number are preserved in museums. While the engines turned out by local foundries have disappeared, a number of the Montréal-built Perrys are still appearing in firemen's musters and parades more than a century after leaving the Perry's Craig Street shop.

The era of the hand-tub was one in which the foundations of public fire protection were laid down in conditions of hard labour and crude machines, made tolerable by a spirit of fraternity and competition. While serving their community, the centre of the volunteers' attention was always their pride and joy, their "en-jine." Even today, pride in their gleaming motor apparatus is a significant factor in the volunteers' morale. The later career firefighters rarely had occasion to use hand engines, but today also pay respect to these tools of their profession from yesteryear.

HODGE'S STEAM FIRE-ENGINE.—1840.

A drawing of Hodge's pioneering steam fire engine of 1840, the first in North America.
The rear wheels were jacked up when the engine was used for pumping and served as flywheels. (Ewbank's Hydraulics)

The Steam Revolution

In the first half of the nineteenth century the newly harnessed power of steam was being applied to a growing variety of needs. It was obvious that these should include pumping water onto fires. The increasing size of buildings and the concentration of great quantities of goods in mercantile districts were making it more impractical for the puny water streams of muscle-powered fire engines to cope with city firefighting. More powerful protection was needed against the conflagrations that were now paralysing cities and towns with great regularity. It would be no exaggeration to suggest that the great commercial expansion of Canadian cities in the second half of that century would have been severely hampered without steam fire pumps.

Another factor proved to be of considerable significance in the adoption of the steam fire engine by the municipal authorities of North America. This was the desire to come to grips with the social and political obstreperousness of the large and influential volunteer fire companies. They were a nuisance to the politicians in many cities. The classic example is the case of the famous "Boss Tweed" of Tammany Hall in New York, who started his career of political power as captain of a fire company. Halifax, Toronto, Victoria and other cities in Canada also had major confrontations between authorities and volunteers. The firemen of Montréal were prominent in the Rebellion Losses Bill riots and may be blamed for the destruction of the Parliament Buildings there in 1849.

Firefighting was frequently taking second place to inter-company rivalries, and this would no longer do in maturing cities. However, as long as such large numbers of men were required for manual pumping, it would be too costly to replace them with paid firefighting forces. Clearly, the steam fire engine arrived on the scene to change all this none too soon. The spectacular, smoke belching "steamer" that changed all this was also highly respected as an example of man's mastery over the elements through modern technology.

The first steam fire engine was built by John Braithwaite of London in 1829, from the designs of Captain John Ericcson, later famous for his Civil War ironclad warship *Monitor* and the invention of the screw propellor. The *Novelty*, as the engine was called, was a reasonably practical machine, but was frowned upon by the first chief of the London Fire Brigade Establishment, the otherwise progressive James Braidwood. The fire insurance companies, holding the purse strings, were not enthusiastic either. The pumpermen who were paid for working the hand engines were emphatic in their opposition to any competition.

The *Novelty* weighed 4500 lbs and produced 10 horsepower. Two steam cylinders mounted horizontally drove individual piston pumps to deliver 100 to 150 gpm (gallons per minute) to a height of 90 feet. In weight and capacity this was

Chapter II
The Coffee Pots: Steam-Powered Pumping

A catalogue illustration of the 1870s showing a small hand-drawn Silsby steam fire engine for volunteers. The rotary engine is against the boiler and the rotary pump up front with a small pulsation dome on top. (BHC)

comparable to many hand engines, but the steamer would not tire. It was used at a number of London fires to show its worth. A second, lighter model proved itself by pumping for five hours when the hand engines froze up at a large fire in 1813. But the authorities were still not moved. Braithwaite sold several steamers in other places, but without the endorsement of London and the insurance companies, business languished.

The Mechanics' Institute of New York awakened to the potential of steam in 1840, offering a gold medal for the best steam fire engine design. The prize went to Ericcson for his submission, although the engine was never built. Another entry came from an immigrant English engineer, Paul Hodge, who envisaged a self-propelled machine with a horizontal boiler, and resembling a locomotive or farm traction engine. This fire engine was built on order from the New York fire insurance interests. It performed well on test, but the New York volunteers properly looked upon it as an outright threat, and it was some time before the Pearl Hose Company agreed to man it. However, continued prejudice and hostility soon forced its withdrawal from service. The volunteers of New York had too many entrenched customs and privileges at stake, and opposition to change was too strong.

The interest of the established hand engine builders was nevertheless now aroused and, by the mid-1850s, their experimental steam fire engines were developing into an irresistibly practical tool for firefighting. As the technical problems were mastered, some volunteers increased their resistance to the point of sabotage and violence as the threat to their institutions increased. Others abided by the best interests of their communities, and the determination of the municipal officials prevailed. This was predominantly the case in Canada.

By the early 1860s, satisfactory steamers could be bought "out of the catalogue" and some cities and towns with progressive ideas were making a rapid switch-over to steam. Eventually, some fifty manufacturers in the United States and two in Canada built over 5000 steam fire engines. Canadian production figures are not recorded, but it seems unlikely the total built in this country could have been much over one hundred. The largest number in service at one time, including imports, was about one hundred and fifty engines around 1912, when the automobile pumper invaded the scene.

The first all-professional fire department in North America was installed in Cincinnati with the aid of huge, cumbersome, but workable, self-propelled steamers built by Moses Latta of that city. The first engine was placed in service on January 1, 1853, after trials in which it proved able to supply six hose-streams at once. Alternatively, it could throw a stream of water from a one-and-a-half-inch-diameter nozzle two hundred and twenty-five feet, an incredibly powerful stream for the time.

The *Joe Ross*, as the first engine was called, weighed eleven tons and was mounted on three wheels. Four horses supplemented its two horizontal, outside steam cylinders in hauling it up the steep hills of Cincinnati. It did not much resemble the later engines, with its square, flash-type boiler and tricycle wheels, but it is often considered the first successful steam fire engine.

Various other builders tried to have their individual designs accepted, but prejudice or unsatisfactory performance ruled out many. It remained for more experience and an indisputably practical engine to silence reluctant volunteers and encourage investment by city officials.

Silsby

One company that applied itself early to the fire engine question was Silsby, Mynderse and Company, later the Silsby Manufacturing Company, of Seneca Falls, New York. This firm came up with a powerful pumping engine weighing a comparatively reasonable 9500 lbs. It departed radically from the prevailing reciprocating steam-piston-driven piston pumps by making use of the Holly rotary engine and pump. This system consisted of two interacting cams, rotated in a close-fitting chamber by steam pressure and directly connected by two shafts to a similar pair of cams, forcing water through a second chamber.

This purely rotary motion, instead of a reciprocating movement employing numerous valves, was extremely simple and pulsation-free. A subject of endless salesmen's arguments for many years to come, the rotary pumping engine contributed to Silsby's firm establishment as a leading manufacturer of fire engines. It also strongly influenced pumping apparatus design far beyond the days of steam.

The Silsby horse- or hand-drawn rotary pumping steamer was one of the two American makes that were prominent in the burgeoning field in the 1860s and 70s and helped introduce the steam fire engine to the Canadian fire service. In 1861 a Silsby engine was Toronto's first steamer and the second of any make to go into

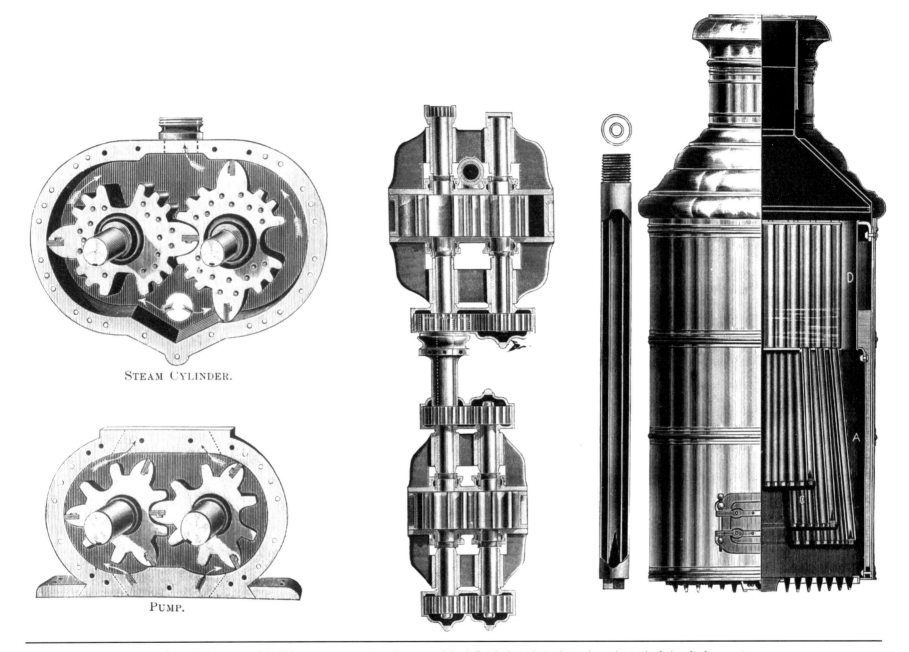

Manufacturer's illustrations of the Silsby rotary steam engine and pump, and the shallow boiler with circulating drop tubes in the firebox for fast steaming. Among the engine's advantages were light weight and simplicity, with few moving parts. (BHC)

service in Canada. Toronto took delivery of another Silsby engine that same year. This company delivered about thirty engines in Canada—a very respectable share of the early market—until the time of its merger with the American Fire Engine Company in 1891. Silsby engines saw service predominantly in the older, eastern centres of Ontario and Québec, near the New York State factory, but customers ranged from Yarmouth, Nova Scotia, to Winnipeg. In the latter case, the engine arrived like the first hand engine and railway locomotive, by boat on the Red River from an American railhead.

The Silsby company used a boiler that featured a number of gravity circulating drop tubes projecting down into the firebox for additional quick-heating surface. These tended to be vulnerable to burnout and leakage if the fire poker was not handled carefully. The type was very successful, however, the Silsby rotary steamer continuing in production for many years, through two company mergers and name changes.

Top: A winter turnout in Montréal at night with the heavy engine on winter runners for the snow-packed streets. A very early flash photo. (John Daggett)

Bottom: The hand-hauled Silsby steamer *Fredericton* was placed in service in that city in 1874. It and its running mate pumped mainly from street cisterns until these were supplanted by a strong hydrant system. (Harold Doherty)

Amoskeag

The other prominent pioneering company was the Amoskeag Manufacturing Company in Manchester, New Hampshire, which built its first steam fire engine in 1859. The name later became Manchester Locomotive Works because of its notable railway locomotive production. The first engine was of the type known as a "mongrel," having two vertical steam cylinders driving a rotary pump through cranks. The frame of the engine consisted of a horizontal, cylindrical tank fastened to the boiler and also served as the boiler feed-water tank and pump manifold. The delivery outlets for hose came out of the front end. The engine weighed a practical 5500 lbs and could raise steam and throw two streams of water 203 ft in the air within seven minutes of lighting the fire. It was sold to the Manchester Fire Department for $3000.

The mongrel pump was not continued; the all-piston, direct-coupled engine

Top: *Albert*, a U-tank Amoskeag with a single vertical piston pump, was originally drawn by hand, but soon converted to horse draught. Its identical mate, *Victoria*, was Canada's first steam fire engine when delivered to Halifax in March, 1861. (Halifax Fire Dept)

Bottom: An Amoskeag engine at work at a fire in north end Saint John. Its fire is burning cleanly, and only the spinning flywheel shows the engine is in action, reflecting a competent operator. The hazards were great in these crowded wooden buildings. (BHC)

and pump were soon adopted instead. In 1860, Amoskeag produced the U-tank engine. In this design, the dual purpose water manifold and frame took the form of a cast, elongated U-shaped pipe. A single, vertical pump was installed, with a single steam cylinder above and the water pump cylinder below, linking through the U with a flywheel on either side. The familiar big brass air chamber— or pulsation dome—now made its appearance on top to cushion the pulsation of the pump.

This 5000 lb engine could be drawn by hand, as was desired by many volunteer fire companies still prepared to manhandle their machines to the fire. For them, horses were a bother, an unnecessary expense—and spoiled the fun. Fredericton, New Brunswick, with its level streets, for example, operated two hand-hauled steamers for some years, one a Silsby and the other an Amoskeag.

Canada's First Steam Fire Engines

The first steamer to go into service in a Canadian fire department was the Amoskeag U-tank engine named *Victoria*, delivered to Halifax in March 1860. It was Amoskeag's No. 20, a hand-hauled engine, and must have proved satisfactory as the Halifax department placed a second one in service the following year, naming it *Albert*.

In 1862 Amoskeag, seeking an even lighter engine, produced the handsome little harp engine, so-called for its cast brass tank frame, a vertical version of the U-tank with a hexagonal cross-section and resembling a harp in shape. In its smallest size, it weighed only 4000 lbs. It was a single-cylinder, double-acting machine, with a fore-and-aft configuration; that is, the single flywheel was mounted crosswise to the frame and inside it. Not to be outdone by rival Halifax, Saint John took delivery of two harp engines in 1863, the third and fourth Amoskeag engines in Canada.

A few more cylindrical- or round-tank engines were built by Amoskeag. One such steamer, apparently the only one in Canada with a double pump, was bought for Saint John's No. 2 Company in 1864. These three Saint John engines, together with a fourth bought in 1874 and a fifth belonging to the adjoining City of Portland, were to fight the long, losing battle against the 1877 conflagration which wiped out more than half of Saint John. At some points the engines did manage to turn the flank of this great, wind-driven fire. Hand engine streams would never have touched it.

One renowned harp engine was Amoskeag No. 121, bought second-hand in Boston by Pictou, Nova Scotia. It had fought the great Boston conflagration in 1872 and had worked for days on end at the Foord Mine pit disaster in Stellarton. Retired in 1931, this redoubtable machine returned to service for the protection of the naval refit wharf in Pictou during the Second World War. It was still workable in the 1960s.

In the late 1860s, Amoskeag introduced engines with solid-bar frames as Silsby and others were doing. The straight-line frame was shortly followed by the crane-neck frame, as in hand engines, so-called because of an arch in the frame behind the front wheels. This enabled the wheels to be racked at right-angles for sharp turns. It also permitted wider frames to accommodate the increasing size of the double engines, mounted in the now common side-by-side piston arrangement.

At this stage of development one can see the basic features and appearance the steam fire engine was to have throughout its era of rapid adoption in the seventies and eighties. At this time, about 1870, Canadian fire departments appear to have had in service about fifteen steamers, according to the limited records available. Nine of these were Amoskeags, of which three were in Saint John, and four were Silsbys, three being in Toronto. The others were Clapp and Jones, and Button engines, also American-built.

Various American steamer makes came into Canada in small numbers, especially before the Canadian Waterous captured the market. This 1883 Clapp & Jones double engine served Hamilton, Ontario, one of a dozen of these engines to cross the border. (Hamilton Fire Dept)

Clapp and Jones

Clapp and Jones's sales were concentrated in Ontario and the engines spread from Sarnia to Québec City. M.R. Clapp left the Silsby firm in the early sixties to develop his own highly successful piston engines in Hudson, New York. The Clapp and Jones engines included some very light, hand-hauled village engines down to 3200 lbs in weight, as well as larger sizes. The later engines featured a boiler with a number of elaborate, sectional, spiral-coil copper water tubes in the firebox. The early boilers were similar to Silsby's, with drop tubes. The pump was a copper-tin alloy and had springless valves and packing-free plungers.

English Engines

After Braithwaite and Ericcson met their cold reception in London in 1829, it was back to the hand engines for British firefighters. Not until 1853, when the Americans were well on the way to perfecting a practical steamer, did the land steam fire engine reappear. Successful work by steam fire pumps on tugs and barges on the River Thames, as well as the American example, pointed the way.

In 1858 patents were taken out for the steam fire engine designed by Messrs. Shand Mason. In spite of the interval, this was not considered a real advance on Braithwaite's engine—and it weighed four tons. However, the London Fire Engine Establishment was now ready to adopt steam, which it finally did in 1860. The hand pumpermen had worked the brakes of their engines to the chant, "Beer Oh! Beer Oh!", but all too frequently would stop pumping to cry, "No beer, no water!" There could be as many as four hundred pumpermen to ply with beer, as was the custom!

The British never did recapture their original lead, as the Americans produced many more powerful, reliable and sophisticated engines. However, it would appear that energetic salesmen managed to leave a sprinkling of the distinctive British engines across Canada. Shand Mason were probably the first when they supplied Montréal's first steamer in 1871. This company also sold Montréal its second engine five years later and supplied engines to Brockville, Halifax and St. Johns, Newfoundland.

Most Shand Mason engines had small vertical, single- or double-piston pumps set against the back of the vertical boiler, and the firebox door was at the side between the front and rear wheels. The double-pump model, adopted as the "London Brigade Vertical," was rated at 350 gpm and had an inclined water-tube boiler. Montréal's second Shand had an unusual triple-cylinder pump located in front of the boiler, much like the typical North American engines. It was rated at 500 gpm and was still in service as late as 1917.

The firm of Merryweather and Sons became a leading British maker of steam fire engines, descended from a long line of hand engine makers, dating from about 1750. Merryweather remained internationally prominent, building automobile apparatus late into the twentieth century. This company built a steamer that was small by North American standards at first, with horizontal, direct-connected, duplex piston pumps. There were some complaints in Montréal that they were not sufficiently robust for the Canadian climate, but three continued in service there for at least twenty years. One lasted thirty years, although not in heavy service. Toronto ordered one in 1895, but was reported to have rejected it on delivery as not coming up to the standards set by the bigger North American engines.

Merryweather engines seeing service in Canada included ones in Victoria, Sherbrooke, St. John's, Winnipeg and Kingston, as well as the three sold to Montréal in 1886. These last three were rated at 500 gpm with 6 x 4 x 8-inch cylinder pumping engines.

Top: A fine example of an Amoskeag double (two cylinder) steam fire engine from the collection of the National Museum of Science and Technology, Ottawa. (BHC)

Right: Detail of the double or two cylinder pump on a Waterous engine with internal flywheel between the cylinder banks. Steam engine is at top and water pump below. The flywheel is run off a Scottish yoke instead of a crankshaft. (BHC)

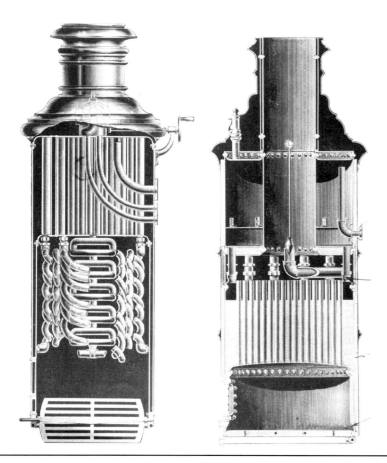

Differing solutions to boiler design are shown in the Clapp & Jones (left) and Button (right) models. The former has water tubes in the large firebox, the latter uses fire tubes and an upper superheating chamber, with a forced draft regulator at the base of the stack. (BHC)

Vancouver's first steamer was a Ronald single, seen here astride a wooden sidewalk, drafting water from a street tank through the large suction hose at the front end. There were no hydrants as yet in this fast-growing city in the 1890s. (Vancouver Fire Dept)

Ronald

Beginning in the early 1870s, when a Canadian city or town was wrestling with the problem of whether to buy an Amoskeag or a Silsby—frequently its first steamer—a determined individual named John D. Ronald would often appear on the scene to make an impassioned plea to buy Canadian.

The Ronald Fire Engine Company (later the Brussels Steam Fire Engine Works Company), he would say, could turn out every bit as good an engine as the Americans. Ronald made no headway with places like Halifax, Saint John and Yarmouth, which thrived on trade with New England and stuck with the products they knew. However, Ronald succeeded in building a satisfactory business and

The Silsby steam fire engine with its rotary-engine-driven rotary pump, was reliable and smooth running with few moving parts. The pump is seen under the seat on this 1880 engine in Yarmouth, Nova Scotia. Steel spoke wheels were regularly used on the Silsby engine. (BHC)

saw his engines in service from coast to coast. It is clear, though, that his product did not grow or diversify significantly, the market being limited and farflung. The Ronald engines were small, and thus suited to small towns. They were similar enough to the American Cole engine to be suspected as a copy.

The Ronald fire engine appeared about 1870 as the Hyslop and Ronald. An engine still preserved in Chatham, Ontario, is believed to have been the first one built. It is a single-cylinder engine and was originally hand-drawn.

These engines were built first in Chatham, apparently, and later in Brussels, Ontario. The names J.D.Ronald Fire Engine Company and Brussels Steam Fire Engine Works were used successively. In later years Ronald steamers were marketed by the Canadian Fire Engine Company of London and referred to as "The Canadian." This company was a distributor, selling various types of fire department apparatus built by Ronald and other manufacturers.

A Ronald village-size engine was displayed at the Chicago Columbian Exhibition in 1893, receiving a gold medal and praise as "the best of its type." This particular engine appears to have been the one later delivered to the City of Regina. The Canadian Fire Engine Company bragged that the Ronald engine was built, with occasional boiler renewals, to last a hundred years. Although long ago retired from service and only lately restored for parade and muster use, several workable engines of this make have made this boast good, the double engine in Winnipeg having done so in 1982.

The distinction by which Ronald engines may be recognized among others in Canada is the fore-and-aft pump configuration, with the single flywheel crosswise to the frame. They are single-cylinder and have suction and discharge connections at the front of the machine, which is always of a straight-frame pattern. The only exceptions seem to be Winnipeg's double fore-and-aft style, a great rarity, and the conventionally cross-mounted double engine built for London in 1904. The fore-and-aft arrangement permitted generous space for the pump within a narrow frame. Thus, Ronald did not feel a need to adopt the crane neck until he built the London engine.

Ronald engines were mostly small to medium in pumping capacity, light and simple, and were directed toward the small-town market. Many larger cities bought one, but it seems there were few repeat orders. Winnipeg and Vancouver were exceptions, each having two on their rosters. Vancouver, a fast-growing city established in 1886, missed the era of hand engines entirely; instead they ordered a Ronald steamer as their first firefighting pump of any kind. This was right after the crude shack boomtown was virtually wiped out in the conflagration of that year.

While Ronald engines were advertised in 1900 as available in village sizes of 300 to 600 gpm and standard engines of 600 to 1200 gpm, there is little evidence that the larger machines were built. Most of the production was for 500 gpm or less.

John Ronald's steam fire engines featured seamless copper fire tubes without, evidently, any elaborate water-tube arrangement in the firebox. Nevertheless, a working head of steam was claimed available in three to four minutes from cold water. In five to eight minutes the engine could throw an effective stream. These engines weighed 4500 to 5000 lbs and were either hand- or horse-drawn. There was no separate boiler feed-water tank, the main suction manifold of the pump being flooded to serve this purpose as well as to prime the pump cylinders.

Like most builders this company used the Archibald roller-bearing wheel and optional rubber-tired wheels. Pumps were of solid brass with German silver valve springs. The boilers were riveted iron, plain, painted, covered with "Russia" iron, or nickel-plated and decorated with brass moulding bands, all to suit the customer's fancy. The usual spun-brass ornamental dome around the smokestack was used.

A builder's photo of small, unadorned Waterous tank-frame engines for small town markets. Pump and steam cylinders are direct coupled without flywheel. This was one of Charles Waterous' first designs (BHC)

Any hopes that Ronald or the Canadian Fire Engine Company had of capturing the Canadian market as their own were dashed by the decision of Charles Waterous to build fire engines. Information on the Ronald operation is rather limited, as is the case with so many dead commercial enterprises. It appears to have faded into obscurity about the end of the Second World War.

Waterous

Charles H. Waterous was a pioneering mechanical engineer who worked on electric motors in New York before making his way to Brantford, Ontario, in 1844. He soon controlled his own engineering firm, C. H. Waterous & Company, builders of sawmill machinery, engines and boilers. From portable sawmills and agricultural traction engines it was but a small step into steam fire engines.

Catalogue drawing of a Waterous hand-hauled tank-frame engine. The main frame of the vehicle is the tubular suction manifold and boiler feed reservoir that was often a feature of earlier and smaller steam fire engines. (BHC)

Steam fire engines and spring-raised water towers produced very respectable elevated fire streams in their time. The technology was very valuable as building heights in the larger cities increased in the late nineteenth century. (BHC)

The *Charles Redfern*, an 1899 Waterous Steam Pumper, was beautifully restored in 1991 by the Victoria Fire Department in British Columbia. (Frank DeGruchy)

New Hampshire-built Amoskeag engines were popular in eastern Canada and were the earliest in service. New Glasgow, Nova Scotia, used this beautifully maintained double, or two-cylinder, craneneck engine, later preserved and proudly displayed in the fire station. (BHC)

Waterous was a late-comer, building his first steamers only in the 1880s, but he had the advantage of a large established organization. At that time, Ronald was making only a modest dent in the Canadian trade enjoyed by American manufacturers. Waterous, too, admonished cities to buy Canadian and must have had an impressive product or lower prices, for he soon took over a large part of the market where Ronald could not. In fact, not satisfied with the potential in western Canada, Charles' twin sons who were in charge of the Winnipeg branch office moved to St. Paul, Minnesota, where they established a fire engine assembly plant.

The American company sold Waterous steam fire engines and later, other types of fire apparatus throughout the United States, remaining in the fire apparatus business long after the Canadian company abandoned it upon the coming of automobile fire engines. Today, the American firm is still a major supplier of pumps to fire apparatus assemblers, some of them in Canada.

The Waterous Engine Works, Limited, as the Canadian company was later called, built a wide range of sizes and styles in steam fire engines, from small hand-drawn village engines up to the largest sizes built. Among the earlier models were small horizontal duplex pumps mounted on a main frame consisting of a steel pipe or manifold. They were reminiscent of the U-tank Amoskeag. In some models, this pipe had an upward kink in it to permit the front wheels to turn more sharply. These lightweight designs catered to hand-drawn village service at about 2500 to 3000 lbs. Later models had straight or, more commonly, crane-neck frames and double-vertical pumps.

The later Canadian-designed and built Waterous steam fire engines were good examples of the peak of development in this type of modern technology, so much admired at the beginning of the twentieth century. In the later, more highly developed Waterous boilers, feed-water was first passed through an isolated section running across the top of the boiler, helping to protect the fire-tube tops from excess heat, then down into the waterleg or jacket around the firebox and into horizontal radial tubes located in the top of the firebox. This design gave the boiler increased heating surface and protected the crown sheet and bottoms of the smoke-tubes from burnout.

With this system Waterous hoped to make it impossible for a poor stoker to damage the boiler, and yet retain the essential quick steaming qualities. In an 1897 test, a second size engine raised five pounds of steam in three minutes from cold water and had seventy pounds in seven minutes. This was enough to get fair hose-streams operating.

The steam fire engine was a complex piece of construction. Waterous boilers had from 110 to 268 upright copper smoke (or fire) tubes in the boiler proper and 48 to 168 radial water tubes according to size. The boiler shells were double-riveted, homogeneous steel plate of 5/16 to 9/16 inch thickness. They were tested to 300 lbs pressure and hammer tested. Most were lagged with asbestos in a jacket of "Russia" iron, sometimes nickel-plated, with nickel bands at the joints.

The pumps in the Waterous engines were solid phosphor bronze castings in which the waterways were always greater in area than the pump cylinders. The 32 pump valves were hard rubber on phosphor bronze springs. At 250 rpm and with an 8- or 9-inch stroke on a piston diameter of $3^{3}/_{4}$ to $5^{7}/_{8}$ inches, various rated capacities from 460 to 1200 gpm were developed. Power was transmitted directly from the steam cylinders to pump pistons of roughly half the diameter through a Scottish yoke and flywheel arrangement.

After about 1900, Waterous Engine Works was the major steam fire engine supplier to Canadian fire departments. Larger cities operated fleets of them. When gasoline-engined automobile pumpers came on the market about 1912, Victoria had four Waterous steamers, Vancouver had five, Toronto five, and Montréal thirteen. Importation of American engines had become rare.

The automobile pumper's arrival abruptly cut off the production of new steamers after a brief period of experimentation and doubts about the gasoline engine's reliability. In both the United States and Canada, 1912 may be taken as the last year in the reign of the steamer. Montréal bought three Waterous engines, its last steamers, in 1911. After 1912, although many of the steam engines in service saw another ten to twenty years of use, it was now the gasoline engine era for fire apparatus. Bolder fire departments and manufacturers

plunged into it. Waterous, in Canada, did not make the transition beyond assembling several trial motor pumpers and hosewagons, then abandoning the field. The American company continued with motor trucks into the 1920s, then became specialists in pumps for other builders' apparatus.

LaFrance

Only a few steam fire engines seem to have been sold in Canada under the celebrated LaFrance name. This company, founded by Asa and Truckson LaFrance, started building fire engines in Elmira, New York in 1875, and quickly made a place for itself in the American market with innovative boiler and engine patents. A series of mergers culminating in 1900 brought in the old names Clapp and Jones, Amoskeag, Button, Silsby, Ahrens and others as the International Fire Engine Company. In 1904 it took the American LaFrance Fire Engine Company name to form the giant that would dominate the United States market well into the era of motorized apparatus and, through its Canadian subsidiary, the Canadian market.

During its first ten years of building steamers, LaFrance exclusively used a rotary gear design, much

Top: *Walsh*, or Engine 3 of the Montréal Fire Department posed with its splendid four-horse hitch at its station on Notre Dame Street. Family of the firemen watch from their upstairs apartments. (John Daggett)

Bottom: The ultimate in Canadian-built steam fire engines. Two of these 1898 extra-first size engines were supplied to Montréal by Waterous Engine Works of Brantford. This is *Nelson*, rated at 1200 Igpm and operated from downtown Station 1 on Youville Square. (John Daggett)

like Silsby's rotating cams. This rotary gear pump's descendants were to become the mainstay of fire department pumping in North America throughout the early motor apparatus era and into the thirties. In the steam age, St. Boniface, Manitoba, and Ottawa each had a LaFrance rotary gear fire engine—the latter still exists. The Montréal Fire Department bought a big 1200 gpm LaFrance piston engine in 1897, the only LaFrance pump of any sort ever to serve in that large department.

Other Makes

A few steam fire engines of other makes were used by Canadian fire departments. They were usually American, but there were two known to have been built by the Burrill and Johnson Iron Works of Yarmouth, Nova Scotia. These apparently successful engines seem to have been typical of double vertical piston types. One was owned by Digby, Nova Scotia, and later, Fairville, New Brunswick. The other is said to have served in both Yarmouth and Sydney Mines. On the other hand, a mongrel, piston-rotary steamer built by the Osborne-Killey Company of Hamilton, Ontario, seems never to have seen service. It was rejected by the City of Hamilton in 1885 on an offering price of $2400.

Halifax included in its roster, in the late 1800s, probably the only Cole engine in Canada. This was the product of Cole Brothers, Pawtucket, Rhode Island, who built some sixty engines between 1867 and 1880. The fore-and-aft pump arrangement and other features were remarkably like that of the Ronald engine. The Button engine, product of the veteran American hand engine builders, also appeared north of the border with its destinctive, short-coupled horizontal pump in Victoria and several Ontario towns. One or two engines by the Minneapolis firm of Nott were probably sold in the Prairies; there is a record of one being tested in Kenora.

Self-Propellers

Some of the earliest experimental steam fire engines were designed to be self-propelled, using the same cylinders used for pumping. On the Hodge engine of 1840, the large traction wheels at the back were jacked up off the ground to act as flywheels when pumping.

None of these machines was notably successful, however, and the necessity for having steam up at all times for immediate response to fires was an expensive complication. Horse- and hand-hauling became the rule. Nevertheless, after the steam pumper became effective and took its established form, Amoskeag, a principal pace-setter, gave some new attention to steam propulsion. The engines were getting ever bigger and heavier. This company built its first self-propeller in 1867, transmitting power from the normal pumping engine to the rear wheels through a chain drive. For this configuration to work, the engine had to be made reversible.

The usual problems encountered in pioneering road vehicles under their own power gave Amoskeag troubles, too. Traction, power-wheel differential on cornering and steering all needed development. The company eventually produced a reasonably practical self-propeller. The Amoskeag differential in the chain drive to the rear wheels was derived from devices used in cotton mill machinery, and very similar to the later gasoline automobile. This machine of Amoskeag's is often overlooked in the history of self-powered road vehicles.

There was little interest on the part of fire departments and, over the years, Amoskeag built only twenty-two of these engines. The first sales came in 1872, when an epizootic disease laid low many horses along the New England seaboard and firemen were obliged to pull heavy engines to fires, including a conflagration in Boston—by hand.

Both New York and Boston bought these self-propelled engines at that time. Later models were very successful and saw long service; they had very large pumping capacities. The principal drawbacks that kept their numbers small were the need to maintain steam while standing in the fire station, and the showers of sparks thrown from the stack while dashing through the streets in excess of 10 mph. Close coordination between driver and engineer was essential to say the least: the former steered and applied the brakes, while the latter handled the throttle from his position on the back platform.

The last self-propeller built, and the only one to serve in Canada was Amoskeag No. 789, sold to the Vancouver Fire Department in 1908. It operated out of Station 1 on Cordova Street. Rated at extra-first size, or 1200 gpm, it was said to have delivered 1432 gpm on test. A pressure of 80 lbs of steam was maintained at all times in the station. This engine was eventually placed in reserve and then removed from service subsequent to upsetting while turning a corner in the early 1930s.

Tactical Operations

In many cities and more small towns the steam fire engine went into service before a piped waterworks system was built and, as a result, the engines were obliged to draw their water directly from rivers, harbours or fire cisterns, as had the hand engines. Such was the case in Vancouver, Toronto, Edmonton and Fredericton, New Brunswick, for example, where wooden underground tanks were installed for them. Even when there was a waterworks system with hydrants, the pressure was usually insufficient for firefighting without the assistance of a steamer. This became the long-term job of the steam fire engine, then the automobile pumper—boosting hydrant pressures to meet the requirements of firefighting streams.

As better waterworks with higher pressures were constructed, some fire departments put aside their steamers as an unnecessary expense and a handicap to speed. They preferred to depend on chemical engines and fast operation with the hoselines connected directly to the hydrants. This occurred in London, which disposed of its two Amoskeag engines acquired in 1867 and 1873, as well as in Toronto, which had been using four steamers, but had none in service in 1895.

The increasing size and height of buildings caught up with these cities and they were obliged to resume the use of fire engines for pumping to hoselines. London re-equipped with the purchase of a Ronald engine in 1904. Toronto purchased six Waterous engines, one Amoskeag and a Ronald as it re-equipped and expanded following a disastrous fire in 1895.

Montréal had installed a powerful waterworks system in the hand engine era, abandoning their use except in the highest elevations on the slopes of Mount Royal. This was just before the advent of the steamer. When other cities took eagerly to the latter in the early sixties, Montréal authorities felt no need to join them. It was not until 1871 that the Montréal Fire Department bought its first steamer, a Shand Mason. It had acquired only this engine and the second Shand until 1886, when three small Merryweathers were purchased to serve the growing areas where the city was climbing the mountainside. With greater heights the hydrant pressures were correspondingly weaker.

By 1900, taller buildings and congestion of combustibles made numerous steamers and powerful hose-streams essential. Thus, as the Canadian metropolis, Montréal eventually operated by far the largest roster of steam fire engines in Canada. In 1919, this numbered fifteen active and three reserve engines, some of them by then motorized with gasoline-driven tractors. Thereafter, increasing purchases of automobile pumpers rapidly cut back this strength.

Normally, in most cities, good firefighting tactics demanded the response of at least one steamer on the first alarm of fire in case strong streams of water were needed in a hurry. But many fire departments,

A brass water trunk at the front of this smaller single-cylinder Amoskeag gave it its nickname of Harp Engine. It was popular in smaller cities and towns. This one has survived many years of service in Pictou, Nova Scotia and in Boston. (BHC)

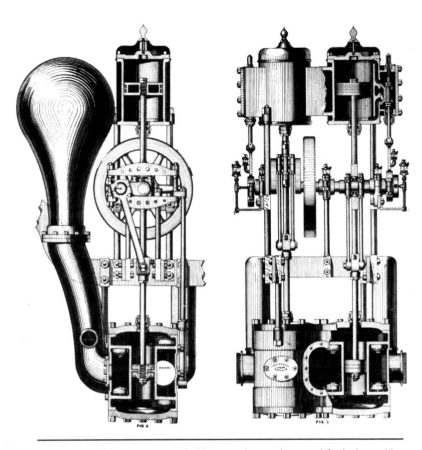

Sectional cuts of the later Waterous double pump, showing the internal flywheel turned by a "Scottish yoke" on the crankshaft. The Waterous fire engine was late on the scene, but the company had a solid background in industrial steam engine building. (BHC)

especially in smaller towns, found it onerous to run out steamers when they were needed only occasionally. As a result, the engine would be kept in reserve in the station and the hose companies worked with direct hydrant streams, except when there was a major fire.

The practice in Montréal after 1900 was for the steamer crew to wait in the station for ten minutes after the alarm had been sounded. If there was no signal that the fire was under control by then, they lit their boiler and responded, assuming that the fire must be serious enough for engine streams. In this way a lot of kindling was saved. Fire underwriters' engineers often complained of poorly maintained engines and of inexperienced stokers in towns where there was a reluctance to use the steamers.

In a few cities, a substitute for maintaining sufficient steam fire engines to control major fires in downtown districts was found in the special high-pressure watermain system, independent of the domestic potable supply. In Canada, these costly systems were installed in Winnipeg and Toronto and used well into the 1980s. Montréal and Victoria utilized systems of watermains overlapping from higher service levels for the same purpose.

In the sixties and seventies, when hose was carried on reels in quantities seldom exceeding 600 ft, one steamer might suffice to supply several hosereels. Later, with hosewagons carrying 1000 ft more of hose, and a need for quick action with pumped hose-streams, steamers and wagons were normally paired as a united hose and engine company. This tactic was important in crowded commercial districts. Outlying fire stations, though, frequently lacked a steamer, depending instead upon direct hydrant pressure streams and chemical engines until reinforcements arrived.

Steamers went directly to a hydrant near the fire and prepared for pumping, while the hosewagons laid off their hoselines. These lines were operated with or without the aid of the engine as fire conditions dictated.

Casual or economy-minded approaches to the use of the steamers in many municipalities is illustrated by the custom in Saint John at the time of the great conflagration in 1877. Although there were three engines in regular service, during the day there was only one immediately available to respond to fire calls. The horses and drivers of the other two would be out pulling gravel carts or doing other city work, often far from their stations and engines. This was just how they were caught when the fateful fire broke out, and there was only one engine quickly on the scene of a rapidly escalating fire.

Firing and Running

An obvious requirement in the design and operation of steam fire engines was the ability to get steam up in a hurry. A few hours' notice was not possible. Boilers were carefully designed and sales competition revolved in large part around quick steaming features. Boiler construction included brass, then copper, smoke or fire tubes. There was feedwater heating by exhaust steam or circulation through the smoke box on top of the boiler, as well as various circulating water-tube circuits right in the firebox.

It was important to protect vulnerable copper tubes and to avoid severe stresses due to rapid, unequal expansion and contraction of the metal. The steam fire engine was a high-performance, hence comparatively delicate, piece of machinery. Most steamers could boast a capability of supplying one substantial high pressure hose-stream at sixty to seventy pounds of steam pressure within four to seven minutes after starting a fire under the cold boiler.

A Montréal Fire Department Waterous engine continues its work, after the horses have been replaced by a Seagrave gasoline-engine-powered tractor. Steam was still highly regarded for its reliability and new pumping engines were a major investment. (John Daggett)

Billows of smoke, sparks and clattering horses hooves thrilled pedestrians when the steamer passed in the old days. These horses on parade have no opportunity to match their ancestors' spirit and dash. (BHC)

Adding to these quick-heating characteristics, many city fire departments employed a hot-water heating boiler in the fire station, usually in the basement, to which the steamer's boiler was connected with quick-release couplings. By this means the water in the engine's boiler could be kept hot all the time. Fire Underwriters' standards called for such installations wherever hydrant pressures were weak and consequently engine-boosted streams were needed for most fires.

The steamer's fire box was laid with shavings, kindling wood in generous quantities and fast burning cannel coal. On leaving the station for a fire call, a wad of oil-soaked waste was ignited and thrown in. Sometimes a metal cap covered the top of the smokestack with a chain from the cap to the ceiling. The cap kept the heat in the boiler while it was connected to the station heater. Also, any smoke was thus bottled in until the engine moved out the door and the chain pulled the cap off.

It was sometimes recommended that the whole firebox be stuffed with kindling. This was calculated to raise a near-working head of steam by the time the engine arrived at the fire. Then coal, or sometimes wood, was added. A thin fire on the grates was best, with large lumps of dust-free coal, preferably cannel or a good grade of soft coal. Ash fell through the grates directly onto the street, and care was required to avoid setting fire to the wooden wheel spokes as ash and clinkers collected during a long fire. A small washdown hose was often fitted to the pump for the stoker's use.

Considerable skill was required to fire the steam fire engine well because of its small firebox and a boiler designed for maximum heating surface with a small volume of water. It took a very good stoker to keep an engine working steadily at top capacity. A common fault was allowing steam pressures to run higher than necessary. The stoker was normally under the supervision of the engineer, but not always. The two had to double at one another's jobs during meal hours.

Copper was the standard material for boiler fire tubes in later models because of its rapid heat conduction. These models had ingenious tube layouts that picked up the maximum amount of heat and protected areas that were subject to burnout from excess heat. There were horizontal boilers in the early experimental models, but the vertical fire tube was universal from an early date. An exception among production steamers was the Ahrens, descended from the pioneer Latta type, whose deceptively ordinary-looking boiler shell did not house the usual fire-tube-pierced pressure chamber. Instead there was only a peripheral water jacket and an open interior filled with water tubes under forced circulation. It was like a modern water tube boiler.

Each steamer was equipped with pressure gauges for water and steam, a water sight-gauge and cocks, safety valves, boiler feed pump and a stop valve for controlling the induced forced-draft effect of the engine exhaust in the smokestack. A whistle was customary, sometimes used as a warning in traffic, but more often signalling for more coal at a long fire. An oilcan with a long spout, a shovel and a poker were the essential tools. A couple of oil lanterns hung where they lighted working areas. From two to four running lamps and frequently an elaborate company identification light provided safety markers when under way at night. The identification light was mounted on top of the air dome, its etched glass panels carrying the company number, and often pictorial artwork.

When working at a fire, with the forced draft of the exhaust steam belching out the stack like a steam locomotive in a rapid, pulsing beat, showers of cinders flew about. Neither stoker nor steamer engineer, nor underwriters' test engineer would be so foolish as to expose a good hat or suit to this hot fallout. Spark-proof garb was the rule, made usually of rubberized fabric.

The rear platform of the engine accommodated a small quantity of coal, enough to keep the engine going until a fuel wagon arrived. This would occur soon after it was known that there was a working fire under way. The engine horses were always unhitched immediately, taken around the corner by the driver and hitched to a lamppost. In winter they would be moved to a nearby fire station as soon as convenient. The driver then returned to the engine to act as stoker for the engineer.

In smaller fire departments the steamer team might be needed to fetch the fuel wagon. Bags of coal were dumped out to make a pile on the street alongside the working engine. The engineer was,

Builder's photo of a large LaFrance double engine with rubber tires, showing the detail of the later "perfected" steam fire engine. It has the more common two flywheels mounted outside the double (two-cylinder) engine. (BHC)

of course, licensed to handle steam boilers. The title "fire chief" comes from the old appellation of chief engineer, used in the days of steam- and hand-pumping engines.

Steamer engineers aimed at having enough steam on arrival at a fire to supply at least one hose-stream as soon as the lines were connected and in position for use. In one large Canadian fire department, competition among the engineers to get into operation first was almost as keen as among the earlier volunteers. Some canny engineers, it is said, stole an advantage by throwing lumps of resin in with the coal. The intense heat of the flaming resin gave them a head of steam in a hurry, but the practice was hardly conducive to long boiler life. In fact, it is alleged, when some town authorities were slow in replacing their steamers with motor pumpers, the decision was deliberately forced upon them by a liberal dose of resin in the coal supply. Boiler tubes aged rather suddenly under this treatment.

The reciprocating action of the pistons caused the working engine to dance up and down on its wheel springs. In the larger ones, particularly, lockout devices were fitted to stop the action of the springs. These were set before starting the pump. The steamer still tended to drift about from vibration while working, and

The LaFrance engine of the Montréal department at work at a fire downtown. The engineer, stoker and helper wear spark-shedding caps, the forced draft producing a rain of hot cinders around working engines. (BHC)

chafing blocks were attached to the discharge hose where it met the pavement to reduce wear on the cotton jackets. Depending upon the balance of the movements, some engines bounced more than others—the Silsby and LaFrance rotary engines least of all, of course.

The operating steamers were a haven of warmth on the scene of a winter fire. A useful ancilliary service they supplied was thawing out ice-covered equipment, and a small steam line from the boiler was provided for this purpose. In Montréal, noted for its long, cold, winter fires, the steam fire engine was referred to as the *cafetière*, or coffee pot. In later days, engines in Montréal usually did carry a coffee pot. The steam-line, poked into the pot, quickly produced a scalding and welcome brew.

The pumping abilities of steam fire engines were proclaimed about as vaguely as those of hand engines for a time. "Throwing a stream from a nozzle of specified diameter for specified horizontal and vertical distances" satisfied both the seller and purchaser. An ability to throw water to the top of the tallest church steeple in town clinched the deal. Examples of this kind of achievement as a test were recorded in the local newspapers. A Silsby engine in Stratford,

The latest of several steam fire engines to be restored to working order by local fire departments, *Charles Redfern*, Victoria's 100-year old, Waterous Second Size shows her form, both function and beauty. (Frank DeGruchy)

Ontario, in 1875 delivered a stream of water 200 ft high from a 1 1/8-inch nozzle at the end of a 1000-ft line of 2 1/2-inch hose. Another engine at Smith's Falls, Ontario threw water 263 ft horizontally from a 1 1/4-inch nozzle.

The engines were eventually rated much more precisely according to volume discharged against a head of 100 lbs per square inch and designated by "size." The size tended to vary with the manufacturer and it was not until after 1900 that, through efforts of the American National Board of Fire Underwriters and the National Fire Protection Association, some standardization was introduced. The following classes of size and gallon capacity are from the Waterous company and the National Board, using US gallons:

Size	Waterous	NBFU
Extra First	1200 gpm	1100 gpm
First	1000	900
Second	800	700
Third	600	600
Fourth	460	500

Working up a sweat on the daily exercise run in downtown Montréal. The fine team of Engine 1 at the gallop along Youville Square near their station. (BHC)

Village steamers were pulled by hand, or by horses if any happened to be handy. One horse might do, but a team was the rule. In small places, horses might be borrowed from the town's public works wagons as needed or, as in the hand engine era, commandeered from a passing delivery cart.

Larger engines in heavy city service were frequently pulled by a three-horse team, especially in hilly places and where winter snows were heavy. The big extra-first size steamers of Montréal used a four-horse hitch. Ordinarily, when other apparatus was switched from wheels to winter sleigh runners, the heavy steamers were not. However, in cities with very heavy snowfall, like Montréal and Québec, runners were used. Rollers mounted in a floor track permitted the runners to move easily across the station floor. Sleighs and runners had to be hurriedly changed for wheels if a sudden thaw melted the packed snow on the streets.

Driving a big steamer weighing several tons through busy city streets called for special skill. The manual brakes on the rear wheels and the efforts of the horses on slippery cobblestones made quick stops and turns a dicey proposition. Many an engine came to grief by dropping its wheels into the streetcar tracks and losing control of its destiny to the trolley line. This sometimes resulted in a collision or the upsetting of the engine on a turn.

Some of the smaller and less well-built steamers of the earlier designs, as well as those subjected to heavy service, required replacement by a later generation of engine. By and large, however, most engines lasted from twenty to forty years, until their retirement in favour of gasoline-powered pumpers. Boiler overhauls were made, of course, and it was not uncommon for an engine of one make to be re-boilered by another maker or a local boiler shop. The 1876 Silsby engine of Saint Jean, Québec, for example, was re-boilered with an improved-pattern LaFrance boiler.

Surrender to Gasoline Power

The steam fire engines in Canadian fire departments passed into reserve as gasoline-engined automobile pumpers replaced them during the period from 1912 to 1930. In newer, expanding cities

like Vancouver, new stations to cover new districts received automobile engines not only for the advantages of the internal combustion engine doing the pumping, but also for the rapid travel that was possible over long distances. Some steamers were fitted with motor tractors to prolong their lives. Motor apparatus builders supplied special four-wheel tractor units and two-wheel, front-drive attachments for this purpose.

Steamers pushed into reserve usually deteriorated quickly and were soon scrapped. Scrap metal drives in two world wars claimed some. Often, the steamer's value for thawing ice was remembered and some engines ended their days thawing frozen hydrants and storm drains for the water and sewerage departments, stripped of their fittings and looking decidedly less glamorous.

Like antique automobiles, some steamers put into reserve were left in forgotten corners until they acquired a recognized historical value. Today there are at least twenty-five steam fire engines still in existence, being maintained in various states of preservation and restoration in Canada. Fifteen of these are being kept by municipal fire departments for parade and display purposes. A few have been restored to working order and are licensed for operation.

There can be no doubting that, in fifty-odd years of evolution, the steam fire engine became a highly developed and efficient tool for a difficult and demanding service. The steam engine was a reliable and flexible power source matched to the available pump tech-

Top: A Waterous steamer at work presenting a typical scene—a pile of coal dumped alongside, guard plates to protect the wheel wooden spokes from hot ashes, a stoker tending his fire and a man possibly brewing a bucket of coffee with the steam line as was the custom in Montréal. (BHC)

Bottom: Canada's only self-propelled steamer and the last built, this 1908 extra-first size Amoskeag of the Vancouver Fire Department was rated to pump 1200 gallons per minute, very respectable by any standard. Brakes and throttle were controlled by the engineer from the rear. (Vancouver Fire Dept)

Their days numbered in this 1913 picture, a finely matched three-horse hitch draws its Waterous engine smartly through the streets of Vancouver. The firemen sorely missed their horses and the work of caring for them after they were gone. (Vancouver Fire Dept)

nology. Attempts to tie these well-tried pumps to the gasoline engine will be seen to have produced much frustration, however.

A steamer from Québec City officially clocked ninety-six hours of continuous pumping at the Port Alfred pulpwood fire in 1927 before being withdrawn because of burned out grates. This was by no means the record among steamers. A Calgary engine worked continuously for a full week at the Burns packing plant fire of 1913 in severely cold weather—a probable Canadian endurance record.

Intelligent fire chiefs could hardly be blamed for reluctance to throw out the steamer when the first temperamental automobile pumpers came on the scene. What converted them finally was speed of response over the growing distances within cities, and lower operating costs.

The steam fire engine is now looked upon as a picturesque and romantic piece of technology. It was regarded in its prime as an awesome example of man's genius. In 1896, the *Handbook of Steam Fire Engines* described it as "the Hercules of the 19th Century."

As is to be expected, the technology of the steam fire engine first came into Canada from Britain and the United States. But Canadians put their own stamp on the device with their own improvements and even shipped it back across the border in what the Canadian manufacturer asked one to believe was a condition "improved to the limit of improving."

When Montréal adopted horses and fulltime staff in the 1860s, two hand reels were coupled together in this effective rig pulled by one horse with four men riding. They are holding their tools: hydrant wrench and cutoff, axe, playpipe and whip. (BHC)

As late as 1860 the fire departments of Canada's principal cities were still in the incongruous position of propelling their emergency vehicles to fires by hand. Although the streets were full of horses pulling carts, wagons and carriages of every description, the firemen, like their American brethren, still trotted about with their engines and reels at the end of a long hauling rope. They spurned the use of horses except when there was deep snow or mud.

This situation existed in considerable part because the volunteers did not want to give up the glamour and pride of place in conveying their equipment by might of their own muscle. The city fathers were happy to go along with this because, after all, a horse cost at least fifty dollars to buy and still more to feed. It would also be a problem to look after it without full time firefighters in the station. In the early 1850s the members of the Montréal Hook and Ladder and Hose Company bought a horse on their own to speed up their responses, only to be called spendthrift by the authorities, who declined to feed the animal.

When the sixties arrived, however, the picture was changing. The cities were growing larger and more spread out, and the runs to fires were longer. Fire apparatus was getting heavier, too, especially with the introduction in this decade of the steam fire engine. At 4000 to 9000 lbs the early hand-hauled steamers were in most cases soon given up to horse power. In a flat city, on the Prairies for example, steamers might be hand-hauled, but it is a wonder there was any attempt to operate the steamers without horses in some of the hillier places like Québec or Halifax. In small towns, especially, it became a matter of using a horse if one could be found when needed.

Again, the sixties saw the introduction of the first paid firefighting forces. The full time firefighters were a small fraction of the number of volunteers they replaced and were unable to pull the apparatus by hand. Greater efficiency and speed were demanded of these small paid forces as well. Their heated, manned fire stations were also suitable for the maintenance of horses.

Hose-reels

The light, hand-drawn, two-wheeled hose-reel of the volunteers was converted or replaced by a heavier one having a driver's seat and, usually, a back step that enabled a crew of four to ride. The less common four-wheeled reel was similarly modified. In a few cases the old hand-pumping engines were modified for horse draught, but for the most part, in the cities, they were fairly quickly supplanted by the steamers or strong hydrant pressures.

In Montréal, a paid driver and a horse-drawn reel were installed in each station in 1860. Steamers were not required as hydrant pressures were sufficient without their assistance. The Montréal Fire Department developed an ingenious and unique *dévidoir double*, or double reel. It had four wheels and comprised simply two volunteer-

Chapter III

Horse Power: Carts, Trucks and Wagons

In addition to their steam fire engines, the Silsby Manufacturing Company of Seneca Falls supplied some Canadian cities with fine four-wheel hosereels, hand- and horse-drawn. This Toronto reel is horse-drawn. (Toronto Fire Dept)

Late in the age of horses pumps powered by gasoline engines appeared in this form in small towns, an alternative to the steam fire engine. (BHC)

A Montreal hosewagon as it was in service in an exhibit by the fire department. Two hoselines could be laid at once. (Exhibit at Man and His World)

style reels joined together and pulled by one horse. Four men could ride on this rig. The department acquired a great reputation for the speed of their attack on fires after more full time firefighters were added in 1863, but this speed was mainly due to the lack of need for pumps. Without the complication of heavy steamers, hoselines were rapidly laid out by the double reels directly from the hydrants. Eight fire stations covered Montréal in this fashion in 1860.

When heavier apparatus came to the smaller towns that could not afford the luxury of full time firefighters and horses, one option was to contract with local carters to provide horses whenever there was a fire. Larger places might use the town's public works horses and their drivers to pull the steamer, or on a step higher, they might maintain fire department horses and drivers, but use them on street maintenance work during the day. Montréal firemen operated the street watering carts this way for a time. These practices delayed response times to fires, but helped keep the horses in good physical condition. Unlike Montréal, which always had its own horses, the Toronto Fire Department long had a contract with a local firm to supply horses and drivers. In 1891 the city took them over.

The simple horse-drawn reel, reasonably enough, was often the product of a local carriage factory, unlike the complex steamer. There were, however, some elaborate reels, such as Toronto's four-wheelers built by Silsby, the American fire engine supplier. Sleigh mounted reels were substituted in winter. City reels carried up to 1000ft of hose and generally two branch-pipes or nozzles, as well as axes, lanterns and small tools. The reel was particularly suited to carrying the heavy leather and unlined rubber hose in use before 1880, because the hose was not subjected to sharp bends. More flexible hose would be flaked in folds in the successor hose carts.

The reel laid out hoselines easily and these could be rolled up again quickly for the return to the fire station. A rewinding crank was usual, as well as a brake for controlling the reel's speed when laying out hose. A disadvantage of the traditional hose-reel vehicle that led to its demise between 1880 and 1900 was its lack of ability to carry sufficient personnel, hose and miscellaneous equipment for the increasingly sophisticated firefighting operation.

The Hose Wagon

After the introduction of the more flexible cotton-jacketed rubber-lined hose, now standardized at $2^{1}/_{2}$-inch diameter, the reel hose-tender began to be replaced by a conventional high wagon, similar to a delivery cart. The hose was flaked in the body so it would pay out smoothly at the back, and this is essentially the way most hose is still carried, in the accordion, "U" and flat load styles. This fact does not discourage the many lay people who still refer to fire apparatus as fire reels, even a century later.

The hose wagon could be built with larger hose capacities and the body divided various ways so that more than one line could be laid at once. Short ladders, the soda-acid hand fire extinguisher, minor tools and equipment were added, making these vehicles relatively self-contained. In city service the larger hose wagon was pulled by two horses and carried a thousand or more feet of hose. In smaller places, light, single-horse wagons had a capacity of only 500 or 600ft of the now common double-jacketed cotton, rubber-lined hose. Hilly Saint John was criticized by the insurance underwriters for restricting their single-horse wagons to 500ft of hose instead of using two-horse teams.

In common with other fire apparatus after 1900, the better quality hose wagon was equipped with solid rubber tires and the popular Archibald patented roller-bearing wheels. In winter, sleighs with bodies similar to the wagons were substituted or the wheels of the wagon were removed and runners put on. This switch could be accomplished very quickly when a heavy snowfall came or a sudden thaw removed the snow cover. The axle was jacked up and the wheel-nut and wheel

When the heavy winter snows arrived, the sleigh-mounted hosereel took over. No. 4 on Chaboillez Square in Montréal sported this elaborate one with fancy dashboard. (BHC)

removed, the runner was then slipped onto the axle in the wheel's place. When sleighs or winter runners were used, a "floor truck" or string of rollers was frequently provided to ease them across the floor to the doors. In other cases, snow was shovelled onto the floor for the runners to slide on. Of course, in the days of horse-drawn vehicles, a hard packed snow cover was retained if possible on the streets for the sleds and sleighs that made up vehicular traffic in winter. Plowing to bare pavement would not have been helpful.

Large fire departments paired steam fire engines and hose wagons as a single firefighting company, a closely coordinated unit referred to simply as an engine company. After 1890, some big city hose wagons were fitted with large-calibre fixed nozzles or turrets able to deliver greater streams of water supplied by two to four lines of hose. Some larger calibres of hose also came into use. These gave the engine company of the period heavy-duty firepower when working on fires in the larger combustible buildings.

Example of a superior quality hand-hauled, double soda-acid chemical engine as used by villages and large industrial plants in the first half of the twentieth century. (BHC)

Hose wagons were most frequently supplied by local builders, although by the turn of the century, more highly specialized and elaborate wagons were being built by the fire apparatus manufacturers. Many of them were the established steam fire engine builders. Some were imported, but most in Canada seem to have been Canadian.

Chemical Engines

Even after the invention of the powerful steam fire engine and the installation of comprehensive waterworks systems, there was still a notable gap in the firefighting arsenal. What was needed was a way of striking at the small fire with great dispatch, or at very least a means of holding the advance of an incipient blaze until the bigger guns were ready. Fires are almost always escalating situations and a rapid initial attack is essential.

Alternatives for plain water, effective though it undoubtedly was, occupied the attention of many. From a number of ideas to miraculously extinguish fires, one invention had a profound effect on firefighting, even though its supposed superiority over water was eventually discounted. From Paris, in 1864, came the idea of mixing sulphuric acid with a solution of

Top: Larger, double hosebed wagons with two horses came into use in larger cities. This plain wagon (no chemical tank) has just laid two lines of hose while a fair maiden leaps into a lifenet for an early movie scene in Montréal. (John Daggett)

Bottom: A Bickle or *Canadian* model combination hose and chemical wagon of the Hamilton Fire Department shows the increasing load of ancillary equipment carried as operations became more sophisticated, especially in the larger cities. (Hamilton Fire Dept)

Horses were unhitched during major fires for other duties like hauling coal for engines, or simply taken away from the noise and excitement. (BHC)

The Toronto Fire Department museum set up this rare example of snap or swinging harness. One horse is hitched while the other stands under its harness with the split collar open. (Toronto Fire Dept. Museum)

baking soda and water inside a pressure vessel. The quantities of carbon dioxide generated in the reaction provided a powerful pressure to expel the water through a hose.

It was long believed by the fire service, and a source of argument for many years, that the bicarbonate of soda and carbon dioxide expelled with the water gave the stream greatly increased fire killing power. This was eventually disproved by research. Regardless of the merits of this argument, the pressure of the reaction in the soda-acid extinguisher was a boon to firefighters, giving them a stream of water from a small self-contained device, the smallest versions of which they could carry in their hands.

About 1870, the Babcock Manufacturing Company of Chicago was producing two- and three-gallon capacity soda-acid hand extinguishers. Numerous fire departments fitted their hose wagons with "Babcocks," as they became widely known. The Montréal Fire Department is recorded as having installed them in each fire station in 1873. By about 1900, this fire department had forty-three of these hand extinguishers as well as two large horse-drawn chemical engines. Others were not far behind. The "first aid" or incipient fire-handling means had arrived. The hand- or horse-drawn cart,was referred to simply as "the chemical."

Babcock and others produced large soda-acid units in capacities varying from 30 to 60 gallons per tank. They were mounted on special carts made for the purpose and fitted with $3/4$-inch diameter hoselines. These horse- and hand-drawn chemical engines, comprising one or two tanks, were an immediate success. Sensational "stops" on small, but threatening fires were now possible. A crew of two or three with a chemical cart regularly headed off or killed fires before the big hose was connected.

The Holloway Company of Baltimore was also prominent as an early chemical engine supplier to Canadian fire departments, having started production in 1873. Among the makes seeing action in Canada, Holloway, Babcock and Champion were the most common during the horse-drawn era. All three were absorbed into the American LaFrance Company which continued production of them all. The earliest chemical engines had vertical cylinders, but later the horizontal style predominated.

In addition to the separate chemical cart carrying 30 to 100 gallons, one or two small soda-acid tanks began to be fitted on hose wagons and ladder trucks. This merging of functions resulted in their being designated simply as "combinations." When the hose wagon became motorized, the chemical tank continued to be part of its equipment in many cases until superseded at the end of the 1920s by a tank of plain water that fed a pump powered by the vehicle's engine.

The soda-acid chemical engines and hand-carried extinguishers were very simple to operate. They consisted of a cylindrical tank designed to withstand high pressures with a glass or lead sulphuric acid bottle suspended inside, just below the access cap. The main tank was partially filled with a solution of water and bicarbonate of soda, while the acid bottle was capped with either a loose-fitting lead stopper or an externally turned screw plug.

The hand extinguisher was simply turned upside down, releasing the acid into the solution, and the carbon dioxide that was generated expelled the water through a small hose. The large vehicle-mounted tank had a shaft with paddles running through it and an external crank for stirring and mixing the solution. In the Babcock, the acid bottle was suspended on this shaft so that turning the crank dumped the acid. In the Champion, the whole tank was rotated to invert the fixed acid bottle. Carbon dioxide gas from the reaction forced water, soda and carbon dioxide bubbles out through the $3/4$-inch rubber hose and through a nozzle of $3/8$-inch diameter. The 200 or 250ft of hose was coiled in a basket or rolled on a small reel.

Tarpaulins, mops, brooms and buckets were carried on ladder trucks or on salvage wagons where provided. This rig, similar to a plain hose wagon is from the volunteer Salvage Corps and Fire Police Company 2 in Saint John, New Brunswick. (Saint John Fire Dept)

Naturally, once the acid was "dumped", the whole tank had to be exhausted, hence the frequent installation on chemical carts of two small tanks in preference to one big one. It allowed the commitment of only half the available capacity if desired, as well as the capability for recharging one tank while still feeding the hoseline with the other.

Fire apparatus with chemical tanks always carried a spare bottle of acid and a bag with a measure of soda for recharging. A fitting on fire department chemical engine piping permitted the connection of a $2^1/_2$-inch hose into it from a hydrant supply. The small chemical hose could thus continue to be supplied after the tank was exhausted. The connection was convenient, too, for flushing and recharging the chemical tank on the spot.

The chemical tank was most often made of copper, the cheaper ones of lead-lined steel. Seams were riveted and the tank tested to 350 or 400 lbs pressure. The horse-drawn chemical cart, sometimes on two wheels, more often four, consisted largely of a steel frame with no body—only the tanks, seats, rear step, hose and equipment baskets. As a result, they were comparatively light and even delicate in appearance, gleaming with well polished copper and brass; altogether machines of some beauty. Regrettably, only one appears to have survived in Canada—the *Acadia* of the Halifax Fire Department, now in the Nova Scotia Firefighters' Museum in Yarmouth.

The acceptance of almost magical extinguishing powers in the chemical engine eventually boomeranged on those fire chiefs and municipal officials who failed to maintain adequate backup in large-capacity hoselines. Used reasonably, the soda-acid chemical engine and hand extinguisher greatly improved the performance of public fire departments. The latter also found a large scale function as first aid extinguishers for use of the occupants in buildings. Malfunctions, largely due to poor maintenance, caused their phasing out in the 1960s. With their copper and brass well polished they are now ornamental collectibles.

After 1900 hand-hauled chemical engines were often the sole firefighting device installed in small villages. It was the 30- and 40-gallon, two-wheeled engine that gave Robert S. Bickle, later a major Canadian apparatus builder, his start in 1907. He made hundreds of sales, mainly in the Prairie provinces, then many more to the government during the First World War.

Numerous Canadian cities and towns purchased Babcock, Holloway or Champion chemical engines on carts. Toronto's double engine, bought in 1884, together with the upgraded waterworks system, apparently so improved the fire fighting record that complacency set in. A combination hose and chemical unit was added in 1892 and, over the objections of the fire chief, the steam fire engines were retired. A rude awakening came in 1895 with the inferno that destroyed the *Globe* newspaper building, when the department was unable to muster sufficiently powerful water streams.

Montréal acquired a large Holloway double engine in the early 1890s for work in residential districts, as did many cities where hydrants were few or weak. This one was too heavy for the outlying dirt streets and was traded for two single-tank machines. Neither of these two big cities committed itself heavily to the chemical engine, however, two units being a relatively small number in such large apparatus rosters. Ideally, there should have been sufficient machines for prompt response to fire alarms in all districts.

Some cities achieved this goal. Among those better equipped before the automobile era, when the combination became almost universal, were Edmonton with five chemical carts, Winnipeg with six chemical carts and seven combinations, London with one and four, Ottawa and Hamilton with six and four combinations respectively. Many other cities and towns operated one or two chemical engines, but at least as many more never realized their value during

The Champion-Babcock

Chemical Tank

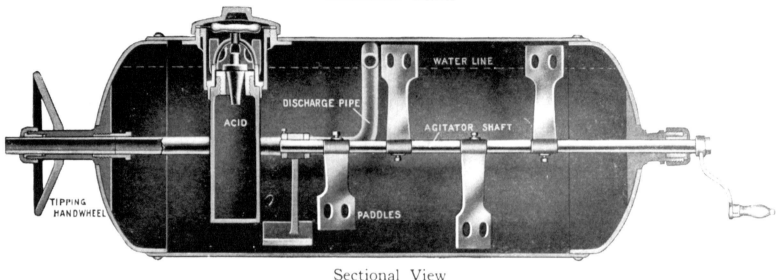

Sectional View

Diagram of the Champion soda-acid chemical tank as eventually refined by American LaFrance. The soda and acid reaction simply provided carbon dioxide to expel the tankful of water.

the horse-drawn era. Their only weapon was the heavy $2^{1}/_{2}$-inch line with 1- to $1^{1}/_{4}$-inch nozzle, although a few used devices like the Decarie nozzle, which had an optional $1/_{4}$-inch outlet.

The general trend during the approximately four decades of horse-drawn chemical engine service in Canada was away from the straight chemical cart towards a combination with the hose wagon, or occasionally the ladder truck. The builders of fire apparatus in Canada mounted various proprietary chemical tanks on their vehicles. The Bickle Company appeared to use several makes, and it is not certain whether they also manufactured some themselves. The Waterous Company built some, but not very many. In all, there would appear to have been in the neighbourhood of one hundred plain and combination chemical engines of the horse-drawn period in Canada, according to the 1918 Grove Smith survey of fire departments.

After petroleum products proliferated in the latter 1800s, the invention in 1909 of Foamite was the predecessor to a variety of modern synthetic foams, and proved a useful firefighting tool. It was like the soda-acid extinguisher, but with the addition of a licorice derivative to produce a lasting mass of bubbles that floated on burning, flammable liquids. In 1927, the LaFrance Company took over the Foamite Firefoam Company and its associates. It was a sufficiently important product that the company changed its name to American

LaFrance and Foamite Corporation. The Canadian subsidiary was named LaFrance Fire Engine and Foamite, Limited.

Ladder Trucks

Taller buildings required longer ladders, and the older single-piece, solid-beam type gave way to trussed beams and extension ladders. The Bangor ladder, a trussed beam extension ladder with supporting tormentor poles, was introduced widely by the 1890s. It and its many imitators made it practical to manually raise ladders of 50 to as much as 65ft.

When the larger cities and towns turned to horses and paid fire-fighters the hook and ladder truck grew bigger and heavier, and carried more equipment and longer ladders. In addition, the light ladder cart of the volunteers acquired shafts for horses, a driver's seat, running boards and mud guards.

When more and longer ladders were adopted, the Montréal Fire Department, using Seagrave ladders, refitted many single-horse trucks to two-horse teams. Because of the trucks' increasing length, tillers for steering the rear wheels were added. On the other hand, the heavy pull-down hook of an earlier and more desperate fire-fighting age had shrunk to a light pike-pole used mainly for pulling down ceilings.

Increasing sophistication in the firefighting operation caused an expansion in the duties of the ladder crew to include rescue, smoke ventilation, overhaul, salvage of contents and other support duties at the fire scene. Loaded with as much as 200ft of assorted manually raised ladders, the larger ladder truck became known as the city service truck. In accordance with the terminology of the horse-drawn period, the term "wagon" was applied to the smaller hose and auxiliary vehicles, while the ladder vehicle was always referred to as a "truck." These terms are still widely used in fire service parlance.

Ladder trucks, being comparatively simple vehicles, like hose wagons, were built by local carriage works to meet communities' needs—until they became too complicated. Specialists, including the old established hand and steam fire engine builders, arose as trucks with Bangor type ladders, tiller steering, chemical tanks and aerial ladders came into use.

The names of those who manufactured city-service ladder trucks have not been so well recorded as those who built steamers and aerial ladders, nor are their products as easily recognized by appearance. Trucks built by such American manufacturers as Seagrave, LaFrance, Pirsch, and Gleason & Bailey were imported in apparently modest numbers. Many were built under the names of Canadian firms such as R.S. Bickle of Winnipeg, Fire Equipment Limited of Montréal, John D. Ronald of Brussels, Ontario, and the Canadian Fire Engine Company of London. In most cases however, the basic vehicle would be supplied to order for these firms by general carriage builders. One of the most prominent was Ledoux-Jennings in Montréal.

The Aerial Ladder: Cable and Windlass

The unprotected, combustible interiors of buildings made interior firefighting more difficult and dangerous than in modern structures. Thus there was greater need for an external approach to upper floors. Even using the trussed extension ladder with supporting poles, a 50-foot wooden ladder was heavy enough to require a five- or six-man raising crew, while a 65-footer was a backbreaker.

Before 1880, inventive minds were seeking means to provide a mechanically raised ladder able to reach beyond these limits. At first, various sorts of extension ladders were mounted on trucks and elevated by winches and levers to make it easier on the muscles of firemen as well as ensuring a solid base of support. These ladders suffered the common fault of being rigidly fixed along the longitu-

An example of the fully developed city service ladder truck with tiller steering and carrying a full suit of trussed ground ladders. Three ladders are of the Bangor extension type having stay poles and range up to fifty feet. (Alex Sprenger)

dinal axis of the vehicle, which had to be lined up exactly toward the point the ladder had to reach. There was no horizontal rotation or training of the ladder on the truck.

One such early ladder, and the first of the sort in Canada, was the Skinner ladder of the Montréal Fire Department, acquired in 1873. It was one of several built to the design of an American, George Skinner. The solid-beam extension ladder was an impressive 84ft long and was raised from the horizontal by a block and tackle and windlass which shortened the telescoping frame of the truck. This levered the ladder upward against two pivoting arms while pulling the front and rear wheels together. It performed at the St. Urbain Street fire disaster of 1877 and remained in service for some years, operated by a crew of six.

Montréal's Skinner ladder inspired other attempts and this fire department was notably receptive to inventors in this experimental period. Using a windlass and cables, and pivot arms like the Skinner, but without the telescoping frame, a unit called the Dorval ladder was placed in service in the late 1800s. It featured a primitive turntable, a 75-ft ladder and served for some years.

Pursuing the same principle of levering the ladder upward against pivoting arms with a windlass, a Montréal fireman named Rodrigue Colleret patented a design in 1891 which covered a 105-ft, three-section ladder, incorporating a turntable with a levelling device for hilly streets. A Colleret ladder was built within the fire department, under the inventor's supervision, and placed in service at Station 16.

The Colleret ladder appears to have been the longest successful mechanical ladder then in use in North America. It was taken to an international congress in London, England, in 1896, where its Montréal crew won various competitions. A similar ladder seems to have been built for the Montréal fire department by a local carriage firm named Langevin, bringing on a series of patent infringement suits by Colleret. He lost, finally, in 1901, but the day of the simple, manually powered aerial ladder was nearly done anyway.

There would be one more strictly manual cable-and-windlass-aerial ladder, although it was mechanically more advanced. It was the effort of the American Gleason & Bailey Company, brought out in 1895 and called the Dederick ladder. The only one to come into Canada was sold to the Ottawa Fire Department. The Dederick and all other ladders elevated solely by muscle power suddenly became obsolete in 1902, the spring-assist ladder seizing their place.

Hayes and Babcock Worm Gear Ladders

The most successful of the all-manual-raised aerial ladders, in terms of proliferation among North American fire departments, were cranked up with a worm gear mechanism. Generally conceded to be the first successful aerial ladder is one designed by Daniel Hayes, a former New York fireman. He built the first one for the San Francisco Fire Department on patents taken out in 1868. It could extend to 85 ft and was elevated by a hand crank on a long horizontal worm gear. The Hayes ladder's breakthrough was its ability to rotate on a turntable mounted on the truck frame. It was able to train to the side of the truck and be pointed precisely toward any objective. The Hayes was a solid-beam ladder and came in lengths ranging from 65 to 85 ft.

Hayes licensed several manufacturers to build his aerial ladder truck and it soon appeared in considerable numbers among larger fire departments. Montréal, Saint John and Vancouver are known to have had a Hayes ladder each. The ladder trucks carrying Hayes ladders had a tiller steering wheel at the rear, and the tillerman's position was located under the projecting end of the ladder—a unique arrangement by which the type may be easily recognized. The single raising gear was turned by a crank attached at the front end of the truck and it was necessary to unhitch the horses before the ladder could be raised.

Chemical 2, *Micmac* speeds along Argyle Street past City Hall in Halifax while pedestrians appear duly impressed. The fire department had two such units in 1910, each carrying two 60-gallon tanks. (Halifax Fire Dept)

The Hayes patents were purchased by American LaFrance of Elmira, New York, in 1883, all subsequent production being turned out there. This would include all Canadian deliveries with the possible exceptions of one for Montréal, purchased in that year, and the Saint John ladder mounted on a Waterous truck.

A strong competitor for the Hayes ladder was that of the Fire Extinguisher Manufacturing Company in Chicago, who now made the Babcock chemical extinguishers. This company's Babcock aerial ladder, introduced in 1887, differed from the Hayes in being elevated on two vertical worms driven by hand cranks at the side of the truck. The ladder was made with a truss-type lower section and mounted lower on the truck. This permitted the tillerman to sit above the ladder where he had a better view. Toronto's first aerial ladder was a Babcock, purchased in 1888. Montréal and Vancouver also had one each of this type.

The Waterous Engine Works of Brantford, the leading steam fire engine builders in Canada, sold a number of unique hand-drawn aerial ladder trucks to small towns. These had an extension ladder of up to 50-ft length, elevated on the truck with a screw or worm gear, but had no turntable. The ladder could also be removed from the truck and raised without mechanical assist. It is not certain whether these were built in the Canadian plant or only at the associated American factory.

Spring-Assist and Spring-Hoist

Manual raising gear for aerial ladders had its limitations. It was slow, when the need for greater speed, particularly for rescue, was obvious. The horse-drawn vehicle, however, had no power source applicable to the problem. Compressed air was tried with some success in the United States by the American Fire Engine Company and was used to "repower" a number of Hayes ladders. It was not widely adopted, however, possibly due to fears of running out of compressed air.

The breakthrough came in a simple concept from the F.S. Seagrave Company of Columbus, Ohio, in 1902. Frederick Seagrave had started building ladders for orchards in Detroit in 1881. He later applied his skills to fire service ladders, producing the widely used Seagrave trussed-beam ladders. Progressing into the building of fire apparatus in Columbus, his company came up with the spring-assist raising mechanism for aerial ladders.

This simple device comprised large concentric coil springs that maintained a pressure counter-balancing the weight of the ladder. When a single hand-screw crank, much like Hayes's, was turned to elevate the ladder in its bed, the compressed springs carried most of the load. Lowering the ladder was also easy; the springs compressed again without effort if a couple of men sat on the outer end of the ladder while it was cranked down. The ladder was still rotated and the fly section extended by hand cranks, relatively easy operations. The trussed wooden lower section of the ladder was later succeeded by a solid beam with steel trussing rods along the top.

The first primitive ladder truck in Windsor, Ontario pictured in 1892 was doubtless locally built. It had tiller steering at the rear, and carried a few simple solid beam ladders. (Windsor Fire Dept)

Spring-assist was rapidly adopted in similar designs by other manufacturers, the older types becoming obsolete overnight. American LaFrance, which had been producing the Hayes, Babcock and Dederick ladders, the principal ones on the market, introduced their version in 1904. It featured a large toothed-gear segment attached to each beam of the ladder and a gear train leading to the two cranking wheels. It was very successful.

However, LaFrance soon modified the principle and started the competitive race over again. Their new ladder mechanism was called the spring-hoist and most of the spring-type ladders in service over the years were of this type. It featured two sets of powerful springs more heavily compressed than those in previous models. On the release of a brake, the springs were set free to throw the ladder upward to an almost vertical position within several seconds. The hand cranks were then used only for final adjustment into the precise position required and for cranking down.

The spring-hoist ladder was so fast and so simple to maintain that it was still preferred by numerous fire departments a decade after it had been succeeded generally by the all-hydraulic steel ladders.

Top: A small service ladder truck of about 1920 ready for delivery to Ville St. Pierre, Québec by Fire Equipment Limited, Montréal. Winter runners were quickly interchangeable with wheels on the axles when the snow cover on the street melted, as it often did. (Gaston Tremblay)

Bottom: Used in the City of Fredericton, New Brunswick, until the late 1930s, this ladder truck is unusual in its two hosereels mounted under the frame and its battery operated headlights. It was one of the last horse-drawn fire vehicles in the country. (Fredericton Fire Dept)

A fine team of greys pulls Ladder 9 through the narrow streets of Upper Town, Québec where tiller steering was invaluable. The horses' harness is the special split-collar, quick-hitch style that became universal in the fire service. (Service Incendies Québec)

Top: The American-designed Skinner aerial ladder was one of the first to see successful use. The truck had a frame that telescoped to lever the 84-foot ladder vertical with a windlass. Montréal had the only one to see service anywhere.

Bottom: One of several local Montréal aerial ladder designs to be used in the era of manually raised ladders was the windlass-operated, turntable-mounted, Langevin three-section ladder, seen here with a two-wheel hosereel. (BHC)

As it was, the spring-hoist ladder—built of two sections in solid or laminated Douglas fir with hickory rungs and steel reinforcing rods—reigned supreme until 1935, long after the disappearance of horses from most fire departments. Second World War production priorities also contributed to the slow replacement of the spring-hoist.

From all indications the Seagrave model sold best in Canada among the spring-hoist aerial trucks of the horse-drawn period. In 1901 W.E. Seagrave, son of the founder of the American firm, moved across the border to establish an assembly plant in Walkerville, Ontario. A number of the trussed spring-hoist ladder trucks appear to have been assembled there, including ones destined for Halifax, Québec, Montréal, Toronto, Windsor, Winnipeg, Regina and Vancouver. Aerial ladders became standardized on lengths of 65, 75 and 85 ft, always in two sections. European ladders, because of narrower streets, were built in more compact designs of four or more sections.

Because of their weight, aerial trucks were normally rigged for a four-horse hitch in Canadian fire departments. Most departments were satisfied with one aerial, being content with the plain city-service ladder trucks for their other ladder companies. Taller buildings tended to be concentrated in the central core then. Even Montréal, in 1904, had only four aerial trucks, against eleven of the city-service type.

A rapidly raised and trained ladder of greater lengths than was previously possible, was only part of the aerial's value. Its ability to stand alone without leaning on a building permitted the direction of an elevated stream of water into upper floors or over a roof without having to approach the fire too closely. A "ladder-pipe" nozzle and hose was commonly attached to the underside of the lower section of the ladder, becoming a valuable tool as structures sprouted higher every decade.

Water Towers

During the time that the aerial ladder was being developed to provide ladder access to higher buildings, thought was being given separately to the need for elevated streams powerful enough to cope with large fires at high levels. The aerial truck's ladder-pipe had been introduced in the mid-1880s, but it had a somewhat restricted capacity and reach.

Experimental "portable standpipe" devices were being tried and, in 1885, about the same time that the ladder-pipe appeared, Fire Chief Hale of Kansas City produced a practical mobile water tower. It was similar to an aerial ladder, but was built of telescoping pipe on top of which a large, controllable nozzle was mounted. It was elevated by hydraulic power from the hoselines that supplied the nozzle.

The Fire Extinguisher Manufacturing Company, builders of the Babcock aerial ladder, produced the Champion water tower, a widely used model. Its telescoping pipe was raised by the same twin worm gear mechanism as was the Babcock ladder. Seagrave similarly adapted their highly successful spring-assist ladder mechanism to water towers in 1907 and LaFrance followed suit.

The water tower was capable of supporting a considerably heavier stream of water than the wooden aerial ladder—even two streams—at heights of 50 ft to as much as 85 ft. As a result, large cities with numerous multi-storey combustible buildings prone to vertical firespread found the water towers a desirable addition to their firefighting rosters. Smaller cities could not justify maintaining such highly specialized apparatus.

In Canada, four was evidently the total roster of water towers. Winnipeg and Montréal each had a Seagrave tower while Toronto and Montréal each had a Champion. Because of the nature of their job, standing before a burning building heavily involved with fire, water towers were frequent victims of falling walls. Montréal's 1893 Champion, a 75-footer, was wrecked in 1898 and a new Seagrave replaced it. But the Champion was later repaired and retained in reserve. The Seagrave was ultimately motorized and continued in service until the 1940s, as were numerous American towers.

Auxiliary Vehicles

Along with the basic firefighting apparatus, horse-drawn fire departments utilized other vehicles in support. As a general rule, the protection of goods from smoke and water damage was a function of the ladder company. A few fire departments, however, operated separate salvage wagons for this purpose. In either case, the equipment carried included waterproof covers, scoops, mops, sawdust canvas bags and other paraphernalia. Montréal set up the first of a number of separate salvage companies in 1872, expanding to three before motorization. Smaller departments operated salvage wagons where there were volunteer salvage companies in existence. A good example is Saint John, where two such companies operated with their own wagons. A typical salvage wagon was a high cart like a hose wagon, but with compartments and enclosed equipment spaces instead of a hose box.

During the volunteer era in the cities, the chief officers were expected to get to fires on foot as their men did, and when the first paid departments were set up with horses, little thought was given to any change. The chief walked if he did not catch a ride on one of the apparatuses when it turned out. As late as 1869, Chief Alexander Bertram of Montréal maintained his own personal horse in fire headquarters, even using it as a substitute for the department's own apparatus horses if one of them was sick.

Eventually, buggies and sleighs were supplied for chiefs. The horses used were often long-legged, capable of extra speed and endurance. In the larger cities, senior chiefs had long runs to make to supervise at fires. Relief horses were sometimes required, pony-express style, to keep them mobile.

Fuel wagons, perhaps converted old hose wagons, were needed to keep the steamers supplied with coal as they worked. Of course, small towns had arrangements for supply by other municipal vehicles or private suppliers. General utility carts, also used for exercising the apparatus horses, were also maintained. At the peak of the horse-drawn era, Montréal, the largest city, had twenty-two buggies, six fuel wagons, and three salvage wagons.

The Manufacturers

Horse-drawn fire apparatus of the simpler types was built by both local carriage makers and the fire apparatus specialists. The Montréal Fire Department eventually built most of its numerous city-service ladder trucks in its own maintenance shops. The more complex aerial ladder trucks, steamers and chemical engines were manufactured by the specialists.

The Waterous Engine Works, Canada's largest builder of steam fire engines, also appears to have built hose wagons, ladder trucks and chemical engines. They seem to have used only the Hayes aerial ladder. John D. Ronald, the other steamer builder, built—or had built for him—some hose wagons and ladder trucks, both hand and horse types.

Fire Equipment, Limited, was founded in Montréal in the early twenties by Joseph Tremblay, a former chief of the Montréal Fire Department. They built, with the assistance of carriage builders, a number of horse- and hand-hauled ladder trucks and hose wagons.

Although the W. E. Seagrave Company built a number of the popular Seagrave aerial ladder trucks at Walkerville as early as 1902, its principal business before closing its doors around 1920 was the assembly of early motor fire apparatus, including tractors for converting horse-drawn equipment.

In 1912 at Sorel, Québec, Charles Thibault was mounting hand pumps on sleighs and building other light horse-drawn apparatus for small communities. This was a small business, but eventually his son Pierre would make Thibault, for a time, the most prominent name in Canadian motor fire apparatus.

An emerging manufacturer after the turn of the century was Robert S. Bickle, who had started the assembly of hand- and horse-drawn chemical engines in Winnipeg in 1907. Previously he had been a concert singer with his wife, a member of the American Obenchain-Boyer fire apparatus manufacturing family. His business on the Prairies prospered with the sale of hundreds of hand-drawn chemicals. He supplied Winnipeg, Calgary and other western cities with numerous horse-drawn wagons and ladder trucks, then started selling them imported automobile apparatus as well. After his two-year-old factory proved too small, Bickle moved to Woodstock, Ontario. There he reorganized and eventually, with his two brothers, became a leading manufacturer in the motor era. Founded as R. S. Bickle Company, the name was later changed to Bickle Fire Engines Company.

The "Hayburners"

In the beginning, any delivery-cart horse might be taken on by a fire department to pull the light

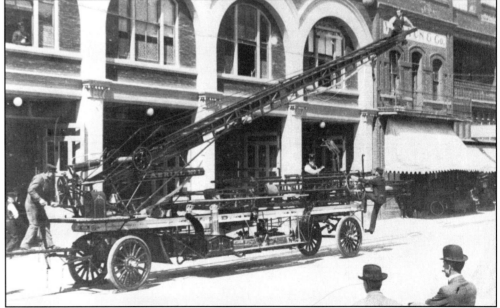

Top: The American Hayes was the first widely accepted aerial ladder and was built by various manufacturers. This 65-footer was built by Waterous for Toronto. It was turntable mounted and cranked up on a worm gear. The tillerman sat under the ladder. (Toronto Fire Dept)

Bottom: The Seagrave spring-assisted aerial ladder of 1902 revolutionized mechanical ladder design. *Victoria's* aerial is seen being cranked down, compressing the raising springs with the aid of a man's weight at the top. The spring housing has "Aerial No. 1" written on it. (Victoria Fire Dept)

reels and wagons of the day. Such unfortunate animals usually suffered the wearing of harness twenty-four hours a day, and probably got their principal exercise pulling a street sprinkler or snow plow.

The firemen too were on duty continuously, living in the station with only occasional days off. Men and horses became buddies in this hard life, the horses beautifully groomed and cared for and well versed in their duties. Some old-time firefighters would swear that their horses could count the strokes of the alarm bells and thereby knew to what street location they should respond. For most of the horse-drawn era, fire alarms were sounded on station tower or church bells and were heard by apparatus crews and chiefs out on the road, as well as men off duty or out at meals.

Fortunately for the horses of later years, harness sores became largely a thing of the past when the quick-hitch, snap-harness was invented. It was introduced in St. Joseph, Missouri, in 1871, and had reached Montréal by 1883. By this time, heavier apparatus and the workload in the bigger cities demanded a special horse. Strong, fast animals were sought. New horses were engaged on probation, like the men, to see if their personalities were suited to the job. They were then trained to response procedure alongside a veteran until they would respond "like an old fire horse."

The stables were located across the rear of the apparatus room, the horses' individual stalls opening immediately to the rear of their assigned apparatus. Since they came out on their own and passed alongside the apparatus to stop in front of it for harnessing, the horses were normally trained as right- or left-handers, always working in that position to avoid confusion.

Windsor, Ontario in 1910 had an early Seagrave aerial truck, assembled in adjoining Walkerville by W. E. Seagrave Limited. The main ladder beams were trussed, later solid or laminated. The two spring housing cylinders are visible on the turntable. (Windsor Fire Dept)

The second water tower of the Montréal Fire Department was this 75-foot 1905 Seagrave spring-hoist type operating out of Station 1 in the heart of the old financial district. It was later given a motor tractor to extend its life. (BHC)

When an alarm sounded on the fire alarm telegraph system and the bells rang in the station, an automatic release device unlatched the stable doors. The spring-loaded doors flew open and the horses trotted out to their places in front of their rigs, standing under the harness suspended from the ceiling. The swinging harness was already connected to the wagon tongue or shafts and the wagon. Its T-shaped suspending frame hung from the ceiling on counter-weighted or spring-loaded ropes. When the driver gave the harness a tug downward and released the T-bar, the harness came down over the horses' backs and the bar retracted up out of the way. Closing the split collar around the horses' necks and snapping the reins to the bits completed the hitching.

Keen international as well as local rivalry developed in this act of hitching. The record finally reached an ultimate limit in the area of $2^{3}/_{4}$ seconds. For the most part, the turnout of horses was as fast as that for automobile apparatus. The horses were invariably in position under the harness waiting for the firemen when they came down the slide-pole from the dormitory at night. When the time came for horses and early crank-started motor apparatus to compete, odds were even as to who would arrive first to nearby fire locations.

A restored Silsby four-wheel hose carriage. These had a brake to control the unwinding of the hose and crank to take it up again. (BHC)

Horses were exercised regularly with a jaunt around the neighbourhood. This exercising run and the work of attending to their horses were greatly missed by the firemen when their stations were motorized. Large stations needed many horses, Montréal's No. 7 having fifteen at one time.

By far the largest roster of horse-powered firefighting vehicles in Canada was that in Montréal. Due to the absorption of a number of suburban fire departments, the peak actually was reached some years after Montréal had begun to replace some of its horse-drawn units with motor vehicles.

In 1919, there were forty-five fire stations in Montréal. Operating from them were eighteen steam fire engines, forty-nine hose wagons, seven aerial trucks, thirty city-service ladder trucks, two chemical engines, a water tower, five salvage wagons and six fuel wagons. Eight of these vehicles had gasoline engines, the rest were powered by two hundred and thirty-three active and thirty-five reserve horses. A veterinary hospital was maintained at one station with a staff of four veterinarians.

Response to an alarm in the congested downtown "Old Montréal" district must have caused a minor traffic jam of fire apparatus alone. Just before motorization, the first-alarm assignment was seven hose wagons, three engines, four ladder trucks, a water tower, a salvage wagon and three chiefs. Toronto reached its horse-drawn peak about 1912, when it had one hundred and twenty horses, fifty-five horse-drawn vehicles and twenty-one seldom used winter sleighs. The first motor truck arrived that year.

Some cities converted from horses rapidly, Vancouver, Victoria and other western cities taking the lead. Significant inroads upon the fire service's use of horses by gasoline-engined vehicles began around 1910 when some chiefs acquired automobiles—1907 in the case of Vancouver. In spite of a rearguard action by defenders of the horse, the automobile age came in. Victoria's last horse retired in 1919, making it the first sizeable city in Canada to be fully motorized. Large eastern cities and older smaller towns were much slower. Toronto's last horse-drawn rig went out of service at Montgomery Avenue Hall in 1931. It had been kept on because of muddy streets in the northern outskirts.

Montréal's last horses were retired from the outlying Cartierville district in 1936, and Fredericton's ladder truck horses in 1939. Most major fire departments were fully motorized by 1930. The last horses in city fire department service in Canada were in all probability those used until the early 1950s, in the winter months only, in St. John's, Newfoundland. They were handy after heavy snowfalls for operations with sleighs in outlying districts. They were finally replaced by a snowmobile.

The time of the fire horse is remembered by the very few, as an era of romance and excitement which vanished with motorization. It is easy to think of such a period as one of greatly inferior effec-

A closeup of the later LaFrance spring-hoist mechanism which improved on the Seagrave spring-assist. Its powerful springs alone were able to throw the ladder to a vertical position. The improved quadrant and gear controls used for fine adjustment of elevation, extension and rotation are evident. (BHC)

A display of apparatus in Hamilton, Ontario in 1900 represents the usual response to a fire alarm in the downtown areas of many cities. Included are the chief's buggy, a steamer, chemical engine, three hose wagons and a service ladder truck. (Hamilton Fire Dept)

Just arrived on the scene of an alarm in Winnipeg, a Seagrave service ladder truck and a Clapp & Jones steamer await orders from the chief. (Winnipeg Fire Dept)

tiveness, but those fire departments were actually able to bring to bear on fires strong forces of heavy and elaborate equipment, using only "hayburner" power to get it there. This era was one in which Canadian manufacturing entrepreneurs were able to develop facilities to satisfy most of the country's needs in firefighting apparatus, within the technology of the time.

A number of the distinctive AC40 and AC80 Seagrave "buckboards" served in Canada. With an air-cooled engine it was the first purpose-built motor fire truck. This operating 1909 chemical engine in Pasadena, California, extensively rebuilt, is the only example still in existence. (Pasadena Fire Dept)

Self-Propelled Vehicles

The appearance of the automobile had an understandably sensational effect on firefighters and the service they provided. The connection was very quickly made between their tireless speed and power and their rapidity of response to fires; the mobility of firefighting tools and appliances and especially, the power available for pumping.

The internal combustion engine was invented by Daimler in 1885 and the automobile in all its essentials was born in France a few years later. Actually, the North American fire service had had its own self-propelled fire engine capable of sustained travel since 1872, complete with steering, forward and reverse power and rear wheel differential. But the Amoskeag steam self-propeller was highly specialized and hardly able to answer all the needs of a fire department's transport; therefore, firemen observed the struggling infant automobile with considerable interest.

The designers of automobiles tried various avenues in their search for the most reliable and useful form. The fire service followed them through much the same essays in steam, electric and gasoline engined vehicles of varying degrees of usefulness. In addition to adapting available automobile chassis as fire apparatus, they also converted some of their existing horse-drawn vehicles by equipping them with automobile tractors and, because early trucks and gasoline engines were too light for their service, soon settled upon models designed expressly for their needs.

Of the three means of propulsion in competition—steam, gasoline and electric—the first was a familiar friend to firefighters in providing power for pumping water. However, the six or seven minutes available for a steam pumping engine to get up pressure on the way to a fire and while hose was laid out was no longer tolerable in the case of propelling the vehicle to the fire. Maintaining steam in the station between alarms, as in the case of the self-propelled Amoskeag, was costly.

Steam automobiles were eventually brought to a highly efficient form—the well-known Stanley Steamer for example—but by then steam had been bypassed by the fire service. One steam propelled combination hose and chemical wagon was built in the United States, but its success is not recorded. New York City's first fire chief used a steamer car bought in 1902 and the first fire service automobile anywhere was probably a Merryweather steam car in England in 1899.

The first internal combustion engines in firefighting service in North America were the interesting transitional pumping engines built by the Waterous Engine Works Company at the St. Paul, Minnesota, plant and possibly in Brantford as well. These four-wheeled engines were hand- or horse-drawn, but their small rotary gear pumps were powered by a large single-cylinder internal combustion engine.

Chapter IV

Hand Cranks and Hard Tires: First Automobiles

American LaFrance built 168 of these Type 31 two-wheel, front-drive units (13 for Canada) with four- and six-cylinder engines to motorize horse-drawn steamers and aerial ladder trucks in the twenties. Complete trucks were also built in this configuration. None were coupled to steamers in Canada. (BHC)

Lacking electrical ignition, these motors used a platinum glow tube extending into the cylinder, heated with a torch to start the engine. Later, electric ignition was fitted and, ultimately, the original engine was succeeded by the conventional four-cylinder gasoline engine used in automobiles.

These pumping engines were essentially a small-town substitute for the steam fire engine. They appear to have been sold in considerable numbers in the Prairie towns of Canada.

Throughout the turn of the century, 1898 to 1907, these pumps were produced by the Brantford Waterous plant. During the 1920s, the Bickle Fire Engine Company in Woodstock produced a number of similar units using automobile type engines. Fire Equipment Limited and Tremblay Fire Engines Limited, in Montréal built such pumps on two wheels, easily interchangeable between horse, hand and automobile towing. The Montréal-built pumps may be considered the first trailer pumps, ancestors of the hundreds produced for civil defence and army bases in the Second World War.

Commercial Automobiles

For large established fire departments, the first experience with the motor vehicle was the acquisition of a car for the chief. Cities were becoming more spread out and it was an increasing problem for the chief officers to cover their territories by horse and buggy. A few Canadian fire departments obtained automobiles around 1910. These were open roadsters or touring cars, two- and four-seaters, of low power and sometimes, unfortunately, little reliability.

Fire Chief Joseph Tremblay of Montréal said of his new 1910 Oldsmobile, "With this car I can reach fires very rapidly and do my inspection work with the greatest facility. I am most enthusiastic over the efficiency of motor propelled apparatus for the fire service." The following year he recommended the complete motorization of several downtown fire stations and the provision of roadsters for all chiefs.

With the speed and endurance shown by fire chiefs' motor cars, it was soon found that the chief and his chauffeur often arrived at a remote fire scene long before the nearby horse-drawn fire companies. This

Top: J.C.Carlisle, the progressive fire chief in Vancouver, motorized his department early and was driven about his fast-growing city by his chauffeur in this touring car. This experience quickly converted him to the use of motor apparatus. (Vancouver Fire Dept)

Bottom: A McLaughlin tourer in Toronto appears to be part of a manpower "flying squadron". The untiring speed of the automobile was irresistible for normally conservative fire chiefs. (Toronto Fire Dept)

A horse- or hand-drawn Waterous rotary gear pump driven by a single-cylinder glow plug engine for St. Vital, Manitoba, showing the addition of a later option, electric ignition. Such engines were popular in small prairie towns and villages. (BHC)

prompted the carrying of hand chemical extinguishers and even large soda-acid chemical engines on chiefs' cars.

From there it was a small step to switch the lighter chemical and hose companies to motor vehicles. The large touring car could be adapted fairly easily and this was done locally within the fire department as well as by commercial builders of apparatus. It was the beginning of what became known as "commercial chassis" fire apparatus, built on a general-production automobile and truck chassis, as opposed to "custom apparatus," built from the ground up for fire service. Oldsmobiles, Packards, Cadillacs, Pierce Arrows, Fords and other cars were used for hose wagons and combination hose and chemical wagons in many Canadian cities and towns prior to 1920.

Records of the very earliest commercial chassis motor fire trucks are sketchy, many having had a short life due to their unreliability or inadequate power. Because the available car and truck chassis were rather light or slow for emergency response duty compared to the custom type, they quickly lost favour in many fire departments.

Early commercial chassis units were used primarily for hose wagons (the term wagon was retained), frequently carrying a chemical tank. They were also used for auxiliary duties and sometimes as tractors in the conversion of light ladder trucks from horse draught. They ranged across the available makes, from the Pope-Hartford of Westmount, Québec, put in service in 1911, to the Cadillacs of Kelowna, a few years later.

Some large carriage builders tried their hand at automobile fire truck manufacture and Montréal's first fire truck, in 1912, is one example. It was built by Ledoux Jennings Company of that city on a Gramm chassis. Like many such trials, it was not a success due to design weakness. Its big Herschel-Spillman engine wound up in the fire chief's motorboat! It was only with the development of reliable trucks capable of some speed, such as those produced by Mack, Reo, White, Gotfredson and G.M.C., that acceptable heavy-duty fire apparatus could be built on the commercial chassis.

Electric Trucks

Electric power for heavy motor vehicles was becoming well developed in the first decade of the 20th century. Many believed its attributes of simplicity and reliability, as well as the lack of noise, smell and risk of explosion, would enable it to triumph over the internal combustion engine.

By 1910 electric trucks driven by a motor in each wheel and fed by heavy banks of batteries were becoming fairly common as delivery vehicles on the streets of some big cities, and several manufacturers were turning them out. Their operating record was good and they performed well in snow, but their weaknesses were low speed and poor hill-climbing ability.

The first automobile in a North American fire department is thought to have been an electric chief's car in San Francisco in 1901. Prior to 1910, British and German fire brigades were using electric trucks in considerable numbers—before they were being considered seriously for heavier apparatus in the United States. Perhaps the European first-aid escape vehicles outran horses on the medium-to-long responses usual there, but on the shorter runs common in North American cities, horses often proved faster than the electrics.

The self-contained battery supply was not particularly suitable for firefighting service. Batteries suffered from the jarring of solid rubber tires on rough pavements and could become run down at inconvenient times for an emergency vehicle. At such moments, boys on bicycles are said to have beaten them to a fire. As a result the gasoline-electric drive became the favoured configuration for electric fire apparatus.

The Couple-Gear Freight Wheel Company of Grand Rapids, Michigan became the principal supplier of electric drive vehicle chassis to fire apparatus assemblers. The Webb Company of St. Louis, Missouri was a major user. Couple-Gear equipped about fifty chassis, mainly for aerial ladder trucks, in the United States and Canada, the majority with gasoline-engine-driven generators. In the US, battery-electric and gasoline-electric tractor units were used to convert horse-drawn steamers and aerial trucks. New York's last major order for steam fire engines included electric drive tractors.

No electric drive tractors are in evidence as having been in service in Canada, but the Couple-Gear drive as used by Webb saw service on some aerial trucks. A 1919 Couple-Gear aerial ladder truck was used by Saint John for many years, but its poor performance on the city's steep hills caused it to be restricted to second line service for much of its career. Webb Couple-Gear aerial trucks were on the rosters of the Vancouver, Calgary and Medicine Hat Fire departments, and possibly elsewhere, apparently giving satisfactory service in the flatter cities for many years. Some appear to have had electric ladder-elevating motors, others were simple spring-hoists. Calgary's 1911 model cost $13,000.

If one of the electric motors mounted in each of the four wheels of the Couple-Gear truck failed, as they did, it could be cut out and the truck run on the other three. The gasoline engine and genera-

tor were located in the middle of the chassis. A typical Webb-electric had a Midwest four-cylinder T-head engine of 60 hp, direct-connected to a 12.5-kilowatt, 100-volt generator feeding a 3.5 hp motor in each of the four wheels. A street railway crank type of controller was used to apply power in driving.

American LaFrance and Seagrave also built gasoline-electric aerial trucks, but apparently not for any Canadian customers. All of the electric aerials had tiller steering at the rear. Poor acceleration, top speed and hill-climbing ability in the face of the superior performance of the direct gasoline-engine-powered automobile doomed the electric truck in fire service.

The Custom Chassis

When the major fire apparatus builders first considered the use of gasoline engined vehicles they found the available chassis too light and under-powered for the major firefighting functions. At 40 to 60 hp, they were unsatisfactory for driving large pumping equipment or for use as tractors to pull formerly horse-drawn steamers and aerials. After some study, most of the major fire apparatus specialists turned to building their own complete

Top: The hosewagon and chemical engine being admired at a fire chiefs' gathering are from the 1907 order of three Seagrave air-cooled, 55 hp vehicles by the City of Vancouver. They were probably the first motor fire trucks in Canada and the first custom models in North America. (Vancouver Fire Dept)

Bottom: The Seagrave AC40 double chemical engine with 55 hp air-cooled engine is a year older than the Amoskeag self-propelled steamer in this Vancouver picture, but in 1908 steam was still the only reliable means of pumping. (Vancouver Fire Dept)

In 1912 American LaFrance delivered two flared body Type 10 motor hose wagons to Vancouver. They still run on their four-cylinder LaFrance engines, finely restored, though the original solid tire wheels are gone. (Frank DeGruchy Photo)

vehicles, including engines. They had, after all, been building the almost equally complex steam fire engines. The fact that their production was small by later standards was not of great significance then.

Seagrave's Hose Wagons

The first of the production-line custom chassis fire apparatus models to go into service was the "buckboard" style produced by the Seagrave Company of Columbus, Ohio, so-called because of the appearance of its front end. It was the original cab-ahead fire truck. This quite successful vehicle was first produced in 1907. It had a four-cylinder, 55 hp air-cooled engine behind the driver's seat and sold for around $5000. Company records show that the first three of these Model AC53 trucks off the Columbus assembly line went to Vancouver, BC.

Top: This Pope-Hartford hose and chemical combination of the Westmount, Québec, fire police department was the first motor apparatus in the province in 1911. The body and chemical tank were later moved to a more durable LaFrance chassis. (Westmount Fire Dept)

Bottom: In Kelowna, British Columbia this 1916 Cadillac hose wagon, plus a second one obtained two years later, motorized the fire brigade, making it a strictly Cadillac operation. (Kelowna Fire Dept)

All the leading manufacturers were involved in the struggle to match the gasoline engine with the available pumps in order to produce a suitable replacement for the steamer. The Seagrave Company had not been a steamer builder and, while working on this problem too, went ahead with producing the buckboard to satisfy its established market for chemical engines and hose wagons.

Many fire departments were looking for just these pieces of apparatus. They could see a great advantage in having motorized hose and chemical units, and particularly a combination of the two, for speed in the initial attack on fires. The heavy pumpers and aerial trucks could then be a little slower.

The three Seagrave "autos" Vancouver purchased in 1907 were probably the first automobile firefighting units of any kind in Canada, certainly the first custom type. Even the two chemical engines and the hose wagon following them in 1909 seem to have been a little ahead of any other recorded motor apparatus. Vancouver was undoubtedly the first Canadian city to leap unreservedly into the switch to automobile fire apparatus, thanks to its sagacious, longtime chief, John C. Carlisle.

A number of other communities ventured into the motor apparatus picture in 1911. There were the experimental units like Westmount's Pope-Hartford combination and Montréal's Gramm-Jennings, as well as more Seagraves. Two buckboards went to each of Kamloops and Victoria, one to Saskatoon, one to Toronto (Hall 8) and possibly there were several others of that vintage. Prospects must have looked good to Seagrave, for that year they set up the assembly plant in Walkerville, Ontario, and commenced production of horse-drawn aerial trucks and the buckboard AC40 motor apparatus under the name W. E. Seagrave, Limited.

In 1912 the dam burst and the days of the steamer and horse-drawn apparatus were clearly numbered. Seagrave marketed a heavier, six-cylinder Model AC80 on the same chassis. This air-cooled engine had a $5^3/_4$-inch bore and 6-inch stroke, developing 80 b hp (brake horsepower). It was rated as able to tow a steamer, which fit in with the proposals of some fire chiefs, as in Victoria and London, to use hose and chemical combinations for normal responses to alarms, but to tow out the steamers from reserve if needed for big fires. In this year Seagrave also introduced a tractor with its engine forward, while both Seagrave and LaFrance finally offered practical gasoline powered pumping engines.

Vancouver and Victoria each bought two of the new engine-forward Seagrave tractors and two more of the smaller vehicles. Québec also ordered two of each and Montréal bought a big air-cooled tractor for its No. 20 steamer. Toronto bought two more buckboard combinations.

The first Seagrave automobile hose wagons and chemical engines were somewhat like horse-drawn apparatus in their basic lines. They had a straight frame, wagon-like body and the driver's seat up forward, shielded by a flat, buckboard dash. The engine most used was the four-cylinder, air-cooled type, mounted under and behind the seat. It is said to have "dieseled" somewhat; that is, it continued running after the ignition was turned off because of excessive heat in the cylinders. In extolling the virtues of their product, W.E. Seagrave took pains to point out that it was "not merely an assembled touring car."

The big, boxy, engine-ahead units were better suited for tractor service and, with the introduction of a water-cooled engine, could power the company's first pumping engines and new production models of tractor aerial ladder trucks. Some of the big tractors had air-cooled engines, like those in Vancouver and Montréal, but most others in Canada seem to have been water-cooled. In some a huge four-cylinder engine with $7^3/_4$ x 9-inch cylinder displacement producing 97 hp was installed. Others used a six-cylinder power plant said to be a water-cooled

A 1921 Type 75 LaFrance (625 gpm) triple combination with soda-acid tank that saw long service in various stations in Saint John, New Brunswick. The overhead ladder mounting was unusual at the time. (BHC)

Small towns like East Angus, Québec, often depended heavily upon quick results with their soda-acid hand extinguishers and 30-gallon tanks. This double chemical model was built by Joseph Tremblay's Fire Equipment Limited, about 1920. (Gaston Tremblay)

Vancouver's Webb Couple-Gear gasoline-electric drive aerial ladder truck with its 85-foot electric assisted aerial ladder. A streetcar type motor controller stands in front of the driver's left hand. Seriously under-powered, these trucks were slow, especially on hills. (Vancouver Fire Dept)

rebuild of the air-cooled engine. All of these vehicles had solid rubber tires and hand crank starting. Hand throttles were used when driving, no foot accelerator being provided at first. The purchaser could have electric or acetylene headlights.

The First LaFrance Car

American LaFrance started producing automobile hose wagons in 1909 at their Elmira, New York, plant, using a modified Simplex four-cylinder engine while the development of their own was going on. The first vehicle—or "car" as they called it—was a combination hose and chemical wagon delivered to Lenox, Massachussetts, in 1910. It was said to be still in running order more than fifty years later. A unit of this model demonstrated to a convention of fire chiefs that year its ability to travel at fifty miles per hour. It bore a remarkable resemblance to the Maxim automobile and may well have borrowed its engineering.

In 1912 LaFrance introduced its own four- and six-cylinder, water-cooled T-head engines. The first pieces of LaFrance motor

Vancouver's 75-foot spring-hoist aerial ladder is pulled by a 1912 90-horsepower Seagrave AC90 tractor. The round opening in the front is for the blower of the air-cooled engine. (Vancouver Fire Dept)

apparatus delivered in Canada were two, 1912, Type 10 hose wagons sold to rapidly growing Vancouver. These earliest trucks had the LaFrance four-cylinder engines and hand crank starting. They featured a 5$\frac{1}{2}$-inch bore and 6-inch stroke, the cylinders cast in pairs and bolted to the engine's aluminum base. Lubrication used the Pedersen system, having oil reservoirs mounted between the cylinder blocks feeding a combination of a splash and pressure pumped supply to bearings and cylinder walls. There was an oil sight feed and a feed regulator on the dash. Both dry and oil clutches were available. The six cylinder engine, with the same cylinder blocks as the four, was rated at 100 hp at first, 105 hp later on. The four was 70 hp.

The first LaFrance apparatus of the motor age came to Canada as the result of the Vancouver Fire Department abruptly shifting its loyalty away from Seagrave with the order to LaFrance in 1912 for two plain hose wagons and a chemical engine. This was the start of a fleet of LaFrance apparatus that would make up almost the entire roster in this fire department from the twenties to the sixties. Fire departments frequently demonstrated this kind of long-term loyalty to one make of apparatus.

In Canada, only a few steam fire engines were motorized and then with four-wheel tractors. In the United States the Christie two-wheel unit with four cylinder, cross-mounted engine was common, along with those of LaFrance and others. (BHC)

The specifications of the first Vancouver hose wagon, shipped from the Elmira plant on November 23, 1912, stated it weighed 6000 lbs unloaded, had a 140-inch wheelbase, hose capacity of 2000 ft, Dayton Airless tires and the LaFrance, four-cylinder, 70 b hp engine. The carburetor was a Wheeler and Schebler updraft with float feed. Ignition was Bosch high tension, 6-volt, dual coil and magneto. It had Pedersen force-feed lubrication, a Hele-Shaw 29-plate oil clutch, Rushmore Prestolite acetylene headlights and an Uncas flywheel driven siren.

Also in 1912 suburban Point Grey, later absorbed by Vancouver, bought the first LaFrance motor ladder truck, a Type 14 city-service truck. A number of other places bought LaFrance hose wagons and chemical combination wagons in the next two years, including Toronto, Edmonton, Nanaimo, Nelson and Stratford.

The American LaFrance Fire Engine Company had appeared at a Canadian fire chiefs' convention just prior to the First World War. When Canadian orders picked up rapidly in 1914, LaFrance were persuaded to consider establishing an assembly plant in this country. This they did in 1915, erecting a plant in West Toronto and incorporating under the name American LaFrance Fire Engine Company of Canada, Limited. They were soon busy with the assembly of pumpers and tractors from American parts. One of their first contracts was for the conversion of three Toronto aerial trucks from horse-drawn to front-drive tractor attachments. George Fox, an office boy in short pants hired on the opening of the plant, worked his way up the ladder to become the long-time president of the Canadian operation. He was a popular and effective ambassador for the company. Another well known employee was the colourful William "Billy" Latter, for many years the Canadian delivery engineer and trouble-shooter in the field. It was said that some fire chiefs bought LaFrance in order to have a visit from Billy.

Bickle and Webb

Robert Bickle had moved into the motor age through the expedient of importing the apparatus of the Webb Company in St. Louis, supplying western fire departments with a number of these. Before the First World War, Calgary in particular, built up a fleet of Webb apparatus consisting principally of hose and chemical wagons on Webb touring car-sized chassis with four-cylinder engines. Calgary started buying automobile apparatus in 1908 and, by 1913, had eight vehicles supplied by Bickle, including an electric aerial and two Webb pumpers. These were piston pumpers, rated at 750 USgpm, installed on a 90 hp chassis and sold for $10,000.

Bickle moved from Winnipeg to Woodstock, Ontario in 1914, became Bickle Fire Engines Limited and commenced the assembly of fire apparatus himself on a variety of commercial chassis. In 1915 he left the business in the hands of his brother Russell and brother-in-law George King, but returned on the death of the latter in 1919.

Tractorization

Tractorization was the conversion of horse-drawn apparatus to gasoline engine power by the simple expedient of replacing the horses with a truck tractor under the front end. This was a preferred course in the case of the more costly aerial ladder trucks and steam fire engines. Many commercial chassis were too light to handle a heavy steamer and it fell to the custom units of the apparatus builder to do the job. These took the form of four-wheel tractors with a fifth wheel connection or a two-wheel front end unit bolted to the frame of the truck.

The first motorized apparatus in Montréal was a LaFrance steamer converted using a Seagrave air-cooled tractor, while Toronto had a Seagrave aerial truck fitted with a LaFrance tractor. Seagrave sold a number of tractors of conventional design on four

The horses were being muscled aside by this Seagrave AC80 hose-wagon about 1913 at Montréal's Station 1. It worked in conjunction with a tractorized steamer pulled by a similar air-cooled unit. (John Daggett)

wheels. Their 80 hp tractors pulled steamers in Vancouver and Victoria, but were more often used to convert aerial trucks of their own make.

LaFrance delivered six conventional four-wheel tractors in Canada, but there were also six of their unique two-wheel, front wheel drive conversion units supplied in the tractorization era. Using the regular four- and six-cylinder engines, these self-contained packages were simply bolted onto the frame of a ladder truck or steamer and it was ready to drive away. The resultant vehicle was a four-wheeled, front drive truck with steering at both ends in the case of the aerial. It could thus travel crab-wise and was quite maneouverable considering it often carried a two-section, 85ft ladder and had a wheelbase of around 380 inches. These machines were rated at only 25mph. Toronto tractorized its three aerials in 1916.

Comparative success for the LaFrance front-drive conversion unit led to its widespread use by the company as the propulsion part of new aerial and service ladder trucks. These were sold over a period of some years to Halifax, Westmount, Toronto, London, Ottawa, Sherbrooke, and Vancouver. Toronto eventually had seven city-service ladder trucks of this type. The last was delivered in 1931. The only one built by the company in its later Master series, it still appears as a parade piece.

The lighter horse-drawn ladder trucks were sometimes converted locally with commercial trucks, especially in smaller communities in the 1920s. Québec and Montréal went this route and maintained them for many years. Until the end of the 1960s, Montréal was still using more than twenty formerly horse-drawn ladder trucks, many of them on their third or fourth four-wheel tractor and themselves remodelled almost beyond recognition.

This was a remarkably economical means of maintaining apparatus in service. It had been predicted by Chief John Kenlon of New York in 1912 as the best way to operate all types of fire apparatus.

One of Winnipeg's earliest motor trucks, a snub-nosed Gramm plain hose wagon at Station 1.
The Canadian Gramm was favoured at first, but was later outclassed by the competition. (Winnipeg Fire Dept)

He had in mind particularly the thought that gasoline engines were unreliable and that it would be helpful to change tractors in a few minutes when they broke down. Unfortunately, the practice, where followed, also tended to perpetuate out-dated firefighting equipment, notably so in Montréal in the fifties.

The Pumping Engine

Most steam fire engines had used piston pumps, their reciprocating motion nicely matched to the reciprocating steam engine. The rotary pumps of Silsby and LaFrance were popular as well,

Small towns operated many small commercial chassis home-built or -assembled pumpers and combination hose wagons like this one that served Otterville, Ontario with its small rotary pump. (BHC)

another case of similar drivers and pumps. Finding drive trains for steamer pumps that would allow gasoline engines to function efficiently as the driver was a problem that occupied fire apparatus builders' engineers for some time. Automobile engines were slow turning and had to be of very large displacement and great weight when substantial power was required.

The available automobile chassis could not reasonably be adapted to heavy pumping duty in the order of 700 to 1000 gpm, especially if the rotating motion of the engine had to be converted into reciprocating motion for a piston pump. In addition, a wide range of pump pressures and volumes had to be met, demanding great flexibility from the engine-pump team. Steam was almost infinitely flexible, but the automobile engine produced maximum power within a narrow speed range.

The Waterous Engine Works in St. Paul had successfully matched a small rotary gear pump to large gasoline engines in their horse-drawn unit for small towns. Simply placing one of these coupled units on an automobile chassis gave them the first automobile pumper in the United States in 1906. The following year, this veteran steamer builder built the first motor pumper in which the pump was driven by the same engine that drove the vehicle. The chassis was their own design and the engine was enormous. The pump was a four plunger, V-form piston model of 600 gpm capacity.

Both of these Waterous vehicles were similar to steamers in that their sole function was pumping. In 1908, The Webb Company of St. Louis built the first combination of a larger capacity pumping engine and a hose wagon, the form virtually all succeeding engines would take. It had a rotary pump mounted across the centre of an Oldsmobile chassis. Several Webb rotary and piston pumpers were sold in Western Canada, including two in Calgary rated at 700 gpm and one in Edmonton.

A number of companies struggled to adapt the piston pump to the automobile, without lasting success except for the Ahrens-Fox Company of Cincinnati. Using a modification of their well tried steamer pump geared through cranks to the front end of their truck engine, this company arrived at a workable combination of piston pump and gasoline engine in 1912. It was one that, with a little further modification, they would stick to, with loyal buyers, into the 1950s. It was impressive looking with its big up-front air dome and it is still a favourite with old apparatus buffs today. It was rare in Canada.

American LaFrance studied the pump question for some years before presenting its choice in 1912—a machine equipped with a rotary gear pump. The first one went to San Antonio, Texas. It was the prototype for several thousand essentially similar pumpers this company was to contribute to the motorization of Canadian and American fire departments. Halifax, the first Canadian city to buy a steam fire engine, also appears to have led the way with motor pumpers, ordering a LaFrance Type 12, 600 gpm triple combination apparatus in 1912. This was the famous *Patricia*, delivered in February of 1913 and virtually demolished four years later in the Halifax explosion.

By 1912, many fire chiefs were committing their departments to motorization through tractorization of heavy units, thus gaining the tactical advantages of speedy motor hose and chemical wagons. However, the difficulties the manufacturers were having in supplying them with an effective pumping engine gave them reason to be cautious in this area.

The question of reliability was brought to a head in September, 1913, at the convention of the International Association of Fire Engineers (IAFE) in New York. Eight manufacturers subjected their pumping engines to a twelve-hour endurance test, drafting water from the Hudson River. There were pumpers representing the various lines of development being pursued—Seagrave centrifugal, LaFrance rotary gear, Ahrens-Fox front-mounted piston, Nott rotary and Waterous four-cylinder single-acting, and some two- and three-cylinder piston pumps by Knox, Robinson and Luitweiler. Four machines dropped out of the contest and others had temporary shutdowns, but the gruelling test established the growing ability of motor pumpers to perform.

Three years later, another twelve-hour test under the sponsorship of the IAFE pitted the Seagrave centrifugal and the Ahrens-Fox piston pumps against rotary gear, piston, and centrifugal engines entered by American LaFrance.

These pumpers could now demonstrate that the well designed automobile pumping engine had arrived. Once its reliability after twelve hours had been proven, all interest turned to the detailed results, with calculated efficiencies and ratios of water pumped to pump weight. These were closely scrutinized and advertising capital made by the manufacturers where possible. The fact was that,

The first gasoline-engined vehicle in the Amherst, Nova Scotia, Fire Department, a commercial chassis combination hose and chemical truck. The chassis appears to be a Jeffrey. (Amherst Fire Dept)

although the positive displacement pumps showed higher efficiencies than the centrifugal, the economies were really of little significance to a service such as firefighting.

While LaFrance developed and marketed all three leading types, it was the rotary they promoted although the tests held in 1916 saw the highest efficiency marks go to the LaFrance piston pump. The reason for this decision was the rotary gear pump's smallest bulk and weight per gallon pumped. All the pumps performed at engine speeds in the 900 to 1400rpm range. Pump capacity ratings were 700 to 1000 USgpm.

Arguments over the relative merits of the three types of pump were to occupy the advertising pages for many years. Seagrave would extol the centrifugal and LaFrance the rotary. The piston pumps fell by the wayside early, except for the front mounted Ahrens-Fox, which, becoming highly developed, acquired a modest but devoted long-term following. Eventually all companies would

Calgary's roster of motor fire apparatus before the First World War was comprised almost entirely of Webb vehicles, supplied by R. S. Bickle of Winnipeg. At right are two piston pumpers and an electric-drive aerial ladder truck. (Calgary Fire Dept)

produce centrifugal pumps and the positive displacement type disappeared from the market, but not until the centrifugal version had been considerably refined and its engines substantially improved in power and speed.

Ahrens-Fox Pistons

The first Ahrens-Fox pump was a modification of the company's double (two-cylinder) steamer pump, but the wide range of operating pressures and volumes demanded in fire service—which the steam engine could meet—gave the gasoline engine difficulties. The problem was resolved by Ahrens-Fox through the provision of two independent banks of two or three pump cylinders on parallel crankshafts. Cylinders on the two banks had slightly different displacements. Shifting the "major" and "minor" banks into gear either separately or together gave the required flexibility in pump output for a narrow effective range in engine speed with best torque.

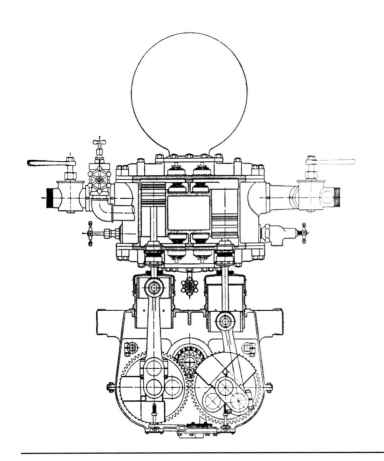 

Ahrens-Fox managed to mate their four- and six-cylinder piston pumps to the front end of their own gasoline engine, to provide the only sustained production motor piston pumpers in North America. Only four were sold in Canada, however. (BHC)

American LaFrance tried all three of the competing pump types for use with gasoline engines. This is their piston pump with two cylinders. At left is the transmission and crankcase. The large air dome at the top dampens pulsation in the hoselines. (BHC)

With a pump weighing up to 2000 lbs mounted on the front end, the Ahrens-Fox engine was naturally front-end heavy. It often seemed that the front end was halfway through an intersection before the driver could see what was coming on the cross street. However, the location of the pump was very handy when it came to hooking up the hoselines and the piston pump could not be beaten for drafting water at a high lift. Dirty water, on the other hand, was hard on the valves and cylinder walls of such a pump.

The Three LaFrance Pumps

The first centrifugal pumps were bulky and they had large, slow speed impellers operating in several stages. The first LaFrance and Seagrave models were similar in this respect, having two double impellers on a single shaft to pump in four stages. LaFrance marketed theirs (Winnipeg had two), but publicly stated their objections to its high power requirements, its bulk and the difficulty in accommodating it on a chassis. They felt it was not suited to the wide performance requirements and turned at the excessive speed of 2000 rpm, double that of the engine. The efficient, combination, parallel-series pump of the 1930s was considered earlier as a solution to the performance range problem, but was dismissed as an undesirable complication.

LaFrance also produced a piston pump for fire apparatus, but did so, again with serious reservations. A substantial gear ratio was necessary, this time a reduction to about 250 rpm for ideal pump piston speed. The necessary double train of reduction gears, additional crankshafts, valves, crossheads and pins were deemed a serious drawback. A big company with considerable resources, LaFrance nevertheless solved the problems to produce a heavy, bulky, but efficient piston pump mounted amidships for anyone who wanted one. In the end, few did.

In any case, the extensive studies begun as early as 1902 by the LaFrance company called for the endorsement of the rotary gear pump. Other rotary pumps, including the predecessor LaFrance, the Silsby steam-driven models and the Northern pump, had complex impeller shapes and sometimes gibbs or vanes to form a seal and prevent water slippage.

The LaFrance motor apparatus pump, on the other hand, had two plain spur gears turning against one another. At first these two gears were different sizes, but soon two identical eight-toothed gears were adopted. One gear was driven from a transmission box on the main drive-shaft and the other directly from the first. The gear teeth did not contact the pump casing and there were no gibbs. An oil seal was applied when developing a vacuum for drafting. Two gear ratios were available in the pump transmission, one for high volume at low pressures and the other for low volume at high pressure. The earliest pumpers were provided with only one gear ratio, but the addition of the second improved their range of performance.

The gear pump's attributes were respectable efficiency over a broad range of outputs, few parts, low weight and bulk, and a reasonable 500 rpm, about half the speed of the engine. On a LaFrance pumper, the drive shaft between the engine and the road transmission passed through the pump transmission where the pump shift lever disengaged the driveline and engaged the pump. This was done without benefit of declutching.

Canadian fire departments in great numbers accepted the LaFrance arguments and the rotary gear pump reigned supreme as the predominant type until the thirties, when it was replaced by the parallel-series centrifugal pump, driven by higher speed engines. A few rotary gear pumpers placed in service prior to 1920 were still in very good working order fifty years later. Some were held in reserve, ready to help protect their communities.

LaFrance produced rotary gear motor pumpers ranging from 350 to 1200USgpm For a time they built a larger model of 1400 gpm as well. It was introduced in 1915 and used an enormous Sterling 225 b hp, T-head engine. There were six cylinders of 7-inch bore and 8-inch stroke. Only Vancouver and Lachine, Québec, purchased pumpers of this Type 15 in Canada, although the same engine and pump combination was also used in the Toronto fireboat built in 1922. During this rotary gear period, the regular engines were gradually boosted to as much as 150 hp for driving the 1200 gpm model.

The Seagrave Centrifugal

The Seagrave Company, without any background in piston or rotary pumps for steamers, took a completely fresh and apparently unbiased approach. They chose the centrifugal pump, something new to the fire service which was looked upon with suspicion for some years to come—with help from LaFrance salesmen.

The first Seagrave automobile pumper was built in 1911 and put on the market the following year. It had a Gorman three stage pump and a new water-cooled engine. The air-cooled type was impractical for pumping where high engine speed was required while the truck was standing still. The pump on the Seagrave engines produced in the first several years was mounted at the rear of the chassis, hose compartments being arranged on either side. Pumpers of this type were used in Montréal, Windsor, Calgary and Regina. They were delivered in the years 1913 to 1915, then a new model was brought out. After brief use of the Gorman pump, Seagrave began installing the Manistee four stage pump, coupled with their own design of four- and six-cylinder T-head engines. The earlier pumps had been bulky and sat high on top of the chassis. With the Model F pumper, introduced in 1915, a new pump, based on the Manistee, was set down in the frame and located amidships. This model was to be the basic pumper Seagrave built, with progressive modifications, for almost two decades—just as LaFrance had stood by their successful formula of 1912.

Seagrave built pumpers in capacities ranging from 350 to 1300 gpm and designed both two- and four-stage pumps for different needs. The regular all-bronze pumps were used on the

---

Top: The American LaFrance centrifugal pump design. It was bulky and required the engine speed to be geared up to a much higher pump impeller speed. Some were sold and saw good service, but the company was not satisfied with it. (BHC)

Bottom: The original LaFrance rotary gear pump with its large and small gear impellers. This was the pump the company recommended and their choice for mass production. Performance flexibility was achieved with two gear ratios. (BHC)

larger models, an iron pump for the smaller ones. The four stage pump had the road drive-line running through the pump, concentric with the pump shaft. The pump shift lever located on the side of the truck at the pump operator's position declutched the engine and shifted the drive from road to pump shaft. It also actuated the small rotary-gear priming pump as needed.

Bickle and Northern

At this time, a number of American general pump manufacturers produced pumps for automobile fire apparatus manufacturers. As the basic design questions were settled, rotary pumps proved popular for their simplicity and small size. When the very first automobile pumper was built by Waterous and sold to Wayne, Pennsylvania, the Hale Motors Company, whose partners were volunteer firemen, had the job of maintaining it. They soon developed their own ideas on pumpers and decided to build fire apparatus themselves. Their business grew and, like Waterous, although they eventually stopped assembling complete apparatus, remained important suppliers of pumps to Canadian and American builders.

The Northern Pump Company was an early supplier of a successful rotary pump to pump builders. Hale took over their pump and the Hale Northern rotary pump

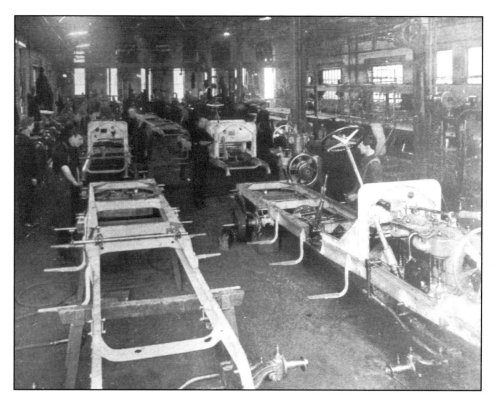

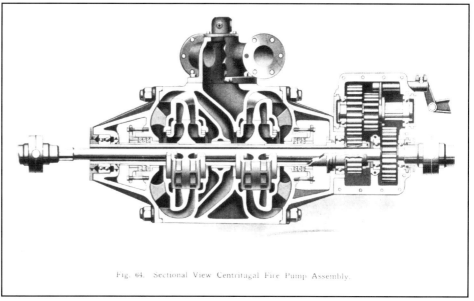

Top: Production line for the first American LaFrance motor fire apparatus models in Elmira about 1913, showing both four- and six-cylinder engine chassis under assembly. (BHC)

Bottom: Sectional view of the first successful centrifugal fire apparatus pump, a four-stage Seagrave design consisting of two double impellers on a single shaft, concentric with the vehicle's drive shaft. (BHC)

LaFrance Fire Engine & Foamite, Ltd. and fire department personnel at the acceptance drafting test of one of the Toronto Fire Department's first pumpers, around 1920. The department operated 14 LaFrance gear pumpers. (Toronto Fire Dept.)

became the standard component for the Bickle Fire Engine Company in its assembly of commercial chassis pumping engines in Woodstock. Bickle eventually built Northern pumps in their own plant. The Bickle Northern rotary pumps were similar in operation to those of LaFrance, the most important difference being the internal one of impeller design. The Northern impellers had four lobes fitted with gibbs instead of toothed gears. Bickle mounted pumps on a variety of early chassis including Chevrolet, Federal, Ford, Fisher Fast Freight, Republic and Ruggles, as well as four wheel trailers for villages.

Waterous

The Waterous Engine Works Company in Brantford, Canada's major steam fire engine builder, turned out one or two motor pumpers, possibly a few others, then abandoned this field. One pumper was built for Brantford in 1917, the other was delivered to Toronto in early 1915 and was similar to the St. Paul plant's production. It is probable that these two were assembled from parts made in St. Paul. The Toronto engine was rated at 800 gpm, apparently using a four-cylinder pump, and was the city's first motor pumper.

The American offspring, now grown up, continued building motor fire apparatus late into the 1920s before deciding to specialize in pumps alone. The Canadian firm, possibly daunted by the activities of LaFrance and Seagrave in Toronto and Walkerville, did not really get into the motor age with fire apparatus. For them, fire apparatus had been only one part of a large production that included agricultural, road-building and sawmill steam machinery.

Joseph Tremblay

In the first decade of automobile apparatus production in Canada, or about 1912 to the early twenties, horse- and hand-drawn apparatus was still being produced for small towns and villages. One small manufacturer's production exemplified this mixture of types particularly well in its short lifetime.

Joseph Tremblay had been the police and fire chief of the municipality of St. Cunegonde when it was absorbed by the City of Montréal. In a meteoric career with the Montréal Fire Department, Tremblay rose to become its chief and then director of public safety. Forced to retire early—in 1918—because of politics, he soon turned with his three sons to the manufacture of firefighting equipment. His firm, Fire Equipment, Limited, was located in Montréal and most of its carriage and heavy body work was sub-contracted to a local carriage firm. In 1923, the business was reorganized as Tremblay Fire Engine Company, continuing on much the same lines until the end of the decade.

Tremblay produced horse-drawn hose wagons and ladder trucks, motor pumpers, and hose and chemical trucks assembled on Pierce Arrow and other chassis. His most notable product was gasoline-engine driven pumps on two-wheeled trailers. Tremblay appears to have been the first builder of the light two-wheeled trailer pump in North America. Descendants of this device were built in large numbers during the Second World War.

Pierre Thibault

Around 1920, Tremblay produced a few pieces of automobile apparatus for which the body work was done by one Charles Thibault of St. Joseph de Sorel. Some forty years later Thibault's son Pierre and Pierre's nine sons had built the family carriage shop and foundry into Canada's largest fire apparatus manufacturer, supplying an international market. In the twenties, however, Thibault seems to have done only occasional fire apparatus work. Some of this was in collaboration with Watson Jack and Company of Montréal, major producers of forestry fire pumps. Pierre took over

A hose and chemical combination truck built for Waterous in 1917 for Brantford, Ontario. The Canadian Waterous company had only a brief flirtation with motor fire apparatus, possibly using the American company's components. (Waterous Engine Works)

the family business and moved to Pierreville in the late twenties, becoming seriously interested in fire apparatus manufacturing. The depression slowed his plans.

The Early Chassis

When pneumatic tires were adopted for automobiles and light trucks they were not accepted as reliable enough for heavy fire apparatus. The need for a high degree of reliability, and probably the spectacular explosion of a pneumatic tire at a fire chiefs' convention were behind this reluctance. As a result, the leading fire apparatus builders did not adopt them as standard equipment on their own chassis until the mid-twenties.

As a consequence, the bone-jarring solid rubber tire was a part of fire service operations for many years. These tires included the Dayton Air-Less, said to have been developed specifically for fire vehicle use. This tire had a hard outer layer of rubber with a softer inner core. With age, water penetrated to the core through cracks, causing deterioration and chunks of rubber to fly off the spinning wheel. Another common patent tire was the Sewell Cushion wheel. They all made for a rough ride on rough streets, particularly cobblestones, numbing the drivers' hands with vibration, and could be treacherous on ice or wet pavement. Snow chains were sometimes worn for much of the year where there were muddy side streets. To maintain steering, chains were even worn on one or both front wheels.

The principal makes of fire apparatus, like most heavier trucks of the time, utilized a chain drive from a differential jack-shaft to each rear wheel. Only rear wheel mechanical brakes were available. LaFrance had internal and external shoes on the rear wheel drums for the hand and service brakes respectively. Seagrave differed in having the service brake act on a drum on the jack-shaft.

With two-wheel mechanical brakes the rule into the latter twenties, control of these four-ton vehicles demanded skill and anticipation on the part of the driver. Right-hand drive was also adhered to during this period.

Tactics with Motorization

Tactically, motorization of fire departments meant increased striking power. Speed of response was greater for the increasingly long runs resulting from the urban sprawl of for-

Top: The Seagrave WC96 pumping engine of the Regina Fire Department working at a fire, showing the pump location and wide body needed to accommodate hose. (White Estate)

Bottom: The Waterous Company built this large piston pumper for the Toronto Fire Department, the pump mounted under the hosebed. (Waterous Engine Works)

In 1914 Regina boasted this Seagrave motorized strength at headquarters, A spring-assist aerial with AC80 tractor, two AC80 hose and chemical cars, and a Type WC96 centrifugal pumper. All have air-cooled engines, except the pumper. (Regina Fire Dept.)

merly compact cities. The automobile age was in part the cause of this expansion. Hose and chemical combinations arriving quickly at the scene of an alarm greatly enhanced the fire department's ability to knock down fires while they were still small and permitted the rapid call for reinforcements if the fires were too far advanced. The combination wagon was in some cases referred to as a scout or a reconnaissance vehicle.

Motorization made it possible to reduce the number of fire stations in many older cities, although it took the Depression of the thirties to bring this about. Savings in manpower were also made, but it appears they were usually negated by reductions in working hours or the loss of members to the army in the First World War. Heavier loads of hose and other equipment could now be carried, although there would be moments when firefighters would wish for the return of their horses as smooth treaded, solid tired trucks bogged down in heavy snow.

The speed of response by automobile apparatus prompted the adoption of the "flying squadron" or squad company in some cities. Operating from a central station, a crew of firefighters on a piece of light apparatus, or even with a car, responded to all alarms over a wide area to bolster the personnel of the regular companies. These manpower pools were ordinarily composed of firefighters selected from among the other companies. A common reason for organizing the flying squads was the shortage of manpower during meal hours. Before the introduction of two platoons, or shifts, which took place mainly between the end of the First World War and the end of the Second World War, firefighters were on duty continuously for three days or up to a week but they got off to go home to meals in groups.

At such times the on-duty strength in the stations was as little as half the normal number. The flying squad helped counter this weakness and in some cases was only in operation during these hours.

Today's rescue squads are descended from these flying squads, and also function as personnel pools supplementary to regular companies in most career fire departments. They counter a deficiency in full time members, especially for aerial ladder companies, which are rarely fully staffed.

The most significant tactical development in apparatus was the combination of the pumping duties of the steamer, the hose-laying capacity of the hose wagon and the first aid firefighting of the chemical engine into one vehicle. The majority of pumping engines built in the motor age have performed all these functions, and thus are called triple combinations. The remainder simply lacked the chemical tank, which might be carried on a hose wagon, or, as in Montréal, no need was felt at the time for a hose-stream intermediate between hand extinguishers and those fed from a hydrant.

The considerable saving in operating a triple combination engine instead of three separate vehicles brought with it a tactical disadvantage. Where the steamer had proceeded directly to a hydrant to pump while a hose wagon ran about laying out its hose, the triple could not commence to hook up to the hydrant until after its hoselines were laid. Also, once the pumper was committed to pumping, it could not easily be moved for other functions.

These problems were overcome in some large American fire departments by equipping individual engine companies with a motor hose wagon in addition to a triple combination pumper. This was referred to as a two-piece company; it has disappeared in recent times with further tactical evolution. Many fire departments expected one large pumper to do the pumping for several hose companies, much as they had in the case of the steamer. Montréal and Ottawa did this on a large scale for many years. Generally, though, the triple combination was left to be a jack-of-all-trades. Eventually it was the essential, frequently the only, vehicle in each fire station. It was rated at 500, 750 or 1000USgpm and carried 1000 to 1200ft of 2½-inch hose. The light commercial chassis pumpers in small towns commonly carried a pump of 350 to 500 gpm capacity.

The aerial ladder remained much the same as in the horse-drawn era, still spring powered and ranging from 55 to 85ft in length. Hand-raised ladder complements on trucks consisted of eight or ten wood trussed ladders of from 10 to 60ft and totalling about 200ft. This was much greater than today, reflecting the necessary emphasis on accessing upper floors of burning buildings from the exterior at the time. Miscellaneous tools and equipment increased in variety and quantity with the additional carrying capacity of ladder trucks, but enclosed compartments were rare. Everything either lay in a basket or was clamped onto the running boards or the outside of the body.

The Change-Over

With the appearance on the market of reasonably reliable motor fire apparatus, its attributes of speed and economy were undeniable. Firefighters had had some reservations about its reliability, with justification, and were desolate on losing their equine brothers-in-arms. Nevertheless, there seems to have been little serious foot-dragging on the part of the fire service, as there had been on the advent of steam fire engines, for example. Motor apparatus was more economical to operate, and capital cost appears to have been the main factor in the prolonged conversion period from about 1920 to 1930.

Some cities converted rapidly to the gasoline engine, notably in the West. It was a period of expansion for many municipalities, with new fire stations to equip. Calgary bought nine Webb units between 1908 and 1913. Moose Jaw, enjoying a boom in 1914, purchased an

Delivered at the same time as Vancouver's 1912 hosewagons were two 1913 LaFrance combination chemical and hose "cars" for Nanaimo. Both Type 10s are still operating, one fully restored. (Frank DeGruchy)

R. S. Bickle used a variety of commercial chassis for light fire apparatus. This example from Revelstoke, BC, is a hose and 30-gallon chemical wagon on a 1923 International chassis. (Frank DeGruchy)

aerial ladder truck, a city-service ladder truck, one pumper and two hose wagons at once. Edmonton bought eight pieces of apparatus in 1913 and 1914. In both cities these were all LaFrance models. By 1914, booming Vancouver had placed in service thirteen pieces of motor apparatus of Seagrave and LaFrance manufacture. Victoria was fully motorized in 1919 with a collection of Seagrave, Nott, Kissell and Knight-Thomas trucks, the first sizeable city to accomplish this in Canada. It should be observed, however, that much of this early motor apparatus in the West was not purchased to replace horses, but to meet expanding protection needs.

The eastern cities were slower. Some would buy one piece of motor apparatus and evaluate it for a few years before buying one or two more. Some bought at a slow, steady rate until the conversion was complete. Halifax ordered its Type 12 LaFrance pumper *Patricia* in 1912. It was not until 1917 that a second LaFrance pumper was bought. This was on the way to the city on the fateful morning the *Patricia* turned out for the fire in the ammunition ship *Mont Blanc* in the North End. A few minutes later, the proud *Patricia* was a shattered wreck, along with a substantial part of the city. All but one of her crew were killed, but *Patricia* survived, was rebuilt and served for many more years.

Winnipeg, Toronto and Montréal were typical of the major eastern cities that purchased motor fire apparatus steadily over a decade or more to accomplish their conversion from horses. The Grove

Many attempts to adapt commercial chassis for use as fire engines failed. This 1914 LaComb Commer Car with rear-mounted pump in Prince Albert, Saskatchewan did not last long—less than a year. (Prince Albert Fire Dept)

Smith report of 1918 noted that the one hundred and four fire departments in places over 5000 population had acquired twenty-six pumpers, sixty-four combination chemical and hose wagons, thirty-three plain, twenty-eight ladder trucks and sixty-five auxiliary vehicles and automobiles. This was a substantial investment in, for the most part, a scant seven years. Before 1920, LaFrance had sold seventy-eight of their custom fire trucks in Canada and were well on their way to domination of the market during the years of motorization.

It was quite a jolt for many a driver, long experienced in handling horses, to bid farewell to his old partners and have to make friends with a motor vehicle. This was a snorting, noisy, nerveless beast, one that had to be controlled by an array of switches, pedals and levers, unable to understand verbal commands. Early instruction manuals clearly reflected the fact that operating motor vehicles was quite alien to most of the men who would be assigned to handle and care for them.

The firefighters made the transition with professional aplomb, not the uproar with which many of the early volunteers had greeted change. At first the driver might yell, "Whoa!" before putting his foot on the brake, but he soon became proud of his mastery of the new technology that was assisting him in the fight against fire.

The Westmount, Québec Fire Department was once entirely LaFrance equipped. From left are a 1917 Type 40, four-cylinder hose and chemical with wooden body from the earlier Pope-Hartford apparatus, a 1927 Metropolitan pumper and a 1915 Type 19 pumper. (Westmount Fire Dept)

Custom Designs Predominate

The period from 1910 to 1920 saw the first tentative moves for motorizing the horse-drawn fire department grow into full confidence in the gasoline-engined firefighting vehicle. Reliable motor vehicles and an adequate successor to the highly developed steam pumping engine had proved themselves when tested, and on the job.

The use of the available commercial truck chassis had proven reasonably successful in the case of lighter apparatus such as the popular combination hose and chemical wagon, light ladder trucks and auxiliary vehicles. But for the heavier apparatus—the aerial ladder truck, the larger capacity pumping engine and tractors for horse-drawn steamers—success had come primarily with the use of the specialized custom chassis built by the apparatus manufacturers themselves. It was the choice of fire chiefs in the larger places and willingly supplied by the builders. The chiefs also liked the extra reliability features such as dual ignition. For the majority of cities and towns in Canada, custom motor fire apparatus was becoming the mainstay of their fire operations, although they were frequently supplemented by the lighter, commercial chassis units.

In Canada before 1920, custom apparatus meant W.E. Seagrave in Walkerville, Ontario (now part of Windsor), assembling components largely imported from the Seagrave Company in Columbus, Ohio, or the American LaFrance Fire Engine Company in Toronto, using components manufactured by their Elmira, New York parent.

The Seagrave Type F apparatus, introduced in 1915, and LaFrance's original 1912 motor apparatus line, both refined by a few years' development and experience, became stabilized in their essential designs. Heavy-duty apparatus purchased by Canadian fire departments through the 1920s was thus mainly Seagrave or LaFrance, chain-drive, with a big six cylinder T-head engine and a series-centrifugal or rotary gear pump. Even the four Ahrens-Fox pumpers delivered in Canada differed in basics only in having the front-mounted piston pumps. Bickle also met with some success using the Gotfredson chassis before producing their own heavy chassis in 1928.

In the first half of the decade, solid tires and two-wheel brakes were the rule, then pneumatic tires were made standard and, eventually, at the end of the twenties, left-hand drive and four-wheel brakes were adopted. Although there were exceptions, windshields were rare and enclosed cabs virtually unknown. Winnipeg and its suburb, St. Boniface, were the first in Canada to order windshields on custom apparatus, in 1922 and 1923, a reasonable move in their climate.

On the whole, the twenties were a period that saw little in the way of important design change in major fire apparatus, although there were numerous small modifications. Limited production, of course, ruled out frequent change without good reason. It was bad enough that each fire chief

Chapter V

Time of the T-Heads: A Successful Formula

The first of 15 Seagrave Type F pumping engines to serve Montreal undergoes acceptance pumping tests in 1921. Director Chevalier watches. In the driver's seat is mechanic Raymond Pare, who later headed the department for twenty years. (Eric Sprenger)

Quebec Lower Town was protected in the twenties by this Seagrave apparatus, a spring-assist aerial with AC80 air-cooled tractor and a 1923 Type F1060 triple combination pumper, at Station 5. (Service Incendies Québec)

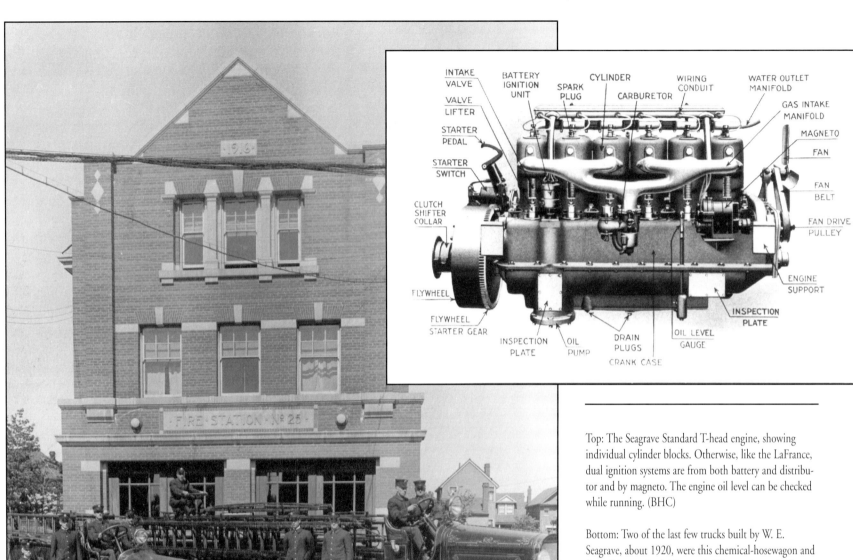

Top: The Seagrave Standard T-head engine, showing individual cylinder blocks. Otherwise, like the LaFrance, dual ignition systems are from both battery and distributor and by magneto. The engine oil level can be checked while running. (BHC)

Bottom: Two of the last few trucks built by W. E. Seagrave, about 1920, were this chemical-hosewagon and front-drive service ladder truck. They and two similar pumpers for Winnipeg had six-cylinder, 80 horsepower engines. (Toronto Fire Dept)

At an age of about twenty-five years, a veteran Montreal Seagrave F shows her mettle on a service drafting test on the Lachine Canal. These Montreal pumpers had no chemical or water tank for small streams. (BHC)

wanted pet options incorporated into his vehicle; fortunately, options were possible because each vehicle was built only after an order had been received. The major manufacturers stuck with their successful formulas, which provided communities with generally competent service.

In the area of commercial chassis-mounted vehicles, with particular emphasis on the small town market, the all-Canadian Bickle Fire Engines Limited, were busy turning out all the basic types of fire apparatus based on the customer's choice of chassis, except aerial ladders. The general motor truck manufacturing industry made steady improvements during the twenties in engine power, speed, load capacity and such refinements as four-wheel brakes, semi-cabs and windshields. Nevertheless, with custom chassis apparatus setting the styles and conservative fire chiefs desiring maximum accessibility, even existing doors and cabs were usually removed.

Bickle carved out his market in the field of lighter hose and chemical units, service ladder trucks and small capacity pumpers in the 350 to 60 gpm range. Chassis makers included big names like Ford Model T, GMC, and many others now long gone such as Ruggles, Menard-Maple Leaf, Republic and Reo. The last was particularly popular in the Speedwagon model. The Bickle company

One of three Ahrens-Fox pumpers in the Hamilton, Ontario Fire Department pumps at draft. The six individual cylinder blocks are visible under the hood, raised here to improve cooling. The six-cylinder pump placed a great weight on the front end. (BHC)

also approached the custom chassis class with the regular use of the big Walkerville-built Gotfredson truck as the basis for a large pumper. A number were sold in Ontario, rated at 600 to 1000 gpm with Buda, Waukesha or Sterling engines. Toronto had five Gotfedson-Bickle pumpers of 1000 gpm as well as a city-service ladder truck.

Bickle also continued production of two- and four-wheeled trailer pumps for village service. They apparently turned out mostly the latter, using their own smaller gear pump with either the Ford or the larger Northwestern engine.

The market for custom fire apparatus began to show a clear geographical division between Seagrave and LaFrance after the for-

To market a large pumping engine, Bickle used a number of the Gotfredson truck chassis with some success, including this one at Paris, Ontario showing the trademark wings on the back end of the body. (BHC)

mer's initial success in the West before the First World War. The division became well established in the twenties, the province of Québec becoming Seagrave territory and the rest of Canada going to LaFrance. The reason was essentially one of salesmanship. By 1930 however, Bickle also had become a recognized custom apparatus builder, invading both territories.

The Model F Seagrave

One of the most successful and well engineered of the American custom fire apparatus models was the Seagrave Model F, introduced in 1915 and continued for almost twenty years. Some were imported into Canada and others were assembled in Ontario.

The ladder apparatus in the Westmount Fire Department's all-LaFrance roster in the twenties were a 1925 Type 14-6 city-service truck and Type 31-6 spring-hoist, 75-foot aerial truck with front drive and tiller rear steering. (Westmount Fire Dept)

Their main attributes were the fine Seagrave engine, the centrifugal pump and their high-quality design and workmanship.

The Seagrave Company managers were far-sighted in their first venture into pumping apparatus when they committed themselves to the centrifugal pump, the first to do so. While all others promoted the positive displacement pump, Seagrave saw the virtue of the centrifugal pump's simplicity and few wearing parts. The only major moving part was the pump shaft with its two or four impellers. The only friction surfaces were in the two main bearings located outside the pump which were easily lubricated.

With this pumper model Seagrave pioneered the installation of a closed-circuit heat exchanger to use water from the pump for auxiliary cooling of the engine. This avoided possible contamination of the regular radiator coolant. A single gear ratio handled all ranges of pressure and volume in pumping and the road and pump gearshift levers were linked to prevent improper engagement of either.

In addition, the Seagrave pump was the first to be fitted with a pressure governor to regulate surges in pressure. A rise in the pressure at the discharge of the pump triggered an immediate cutback of the throttle by means of a pressure actuated control. This prevented an excessive jump in pressure on other hoselines when one was shut down suddenly—a danger to the firefighters holding them.

In the 1920s, Seagrave was using its two-stage pump for intermediate capacity ranges and the bigger four-stage bronze pump for the largest, 1300 gpm, size. A light economy-model pumper called the *Suburban*, likely designed to meet competition in the commercial chassis field, had the small four-stage iron pump rated at 350 gpm. It was driven by a 70 hp Continental engine.

The Seagrave *Standard* engines, built in their own factory, were distinctive in having individual cast iron blocks for each cylinder. They were bolted to the main engine base. The T-head configuration, with intake valves on one side and exhaust valves on the other, allowed for generous valve sizes. The engines had $5^{3}/_{4}$-inch bore and $6^{1}/_{2}$-inch stroke. Four-cylinder engines delivered 70 hp and the six produced 130 hp. The *Giant Standard*, at 1720 cubic inches, produced 180 bhp to drive the 1300 gpm *Metropolite* model pumper. The T-head engines of this era turned slowly, around 1000 rpm, hence the large displacements. At these low speeds torque was high.

The Seagrave engines had a seven-bearing crankshaft and a dual lubrication system with pumped feed to the bearings and splash troughs under the connecting rods. Seagrave claimed the engine could run safely even with clogged oil lines. A sight feed was provided on the dash to allow the operator to check on the operation of the lubrication system. A float oil level indicator was provided on the engine, registering sump oil level while the engine was running the pump.

The exhaust camshaft could be shifted slightly with a lever on the dashboard, bringing into contact a supplementary set of cams that prevented the valves from closing fully. This compression release permitted easier cranking by hand if needed. Both high tension magneto and Delco 12-volt battery ignition systems were provided, each with its own set of sparkplugs. Gasoline was gravity fed to a Schebler or similar updraft carburetor. Controls included manual choke, carburetor gas setting, hand throttle and foot accelerator.

In pumping engines, the three-plate disc clutch was supplemented by a clutch lockup which could be engaged during long pumping jobs. In most cases, Seagrave used the chain and sprocket drive extending from a differential jackshaft to the rear axle. A Timken worm drive was also an option. The transmission had three speeds forward, and an interlock with the clutch prevented shifting of the gears without depressing the clutch pedal. Service brakes acted externally on drums located on the jackshafts, hand brakes internally, on the rear wheels. Wooden spoke or steel disc wheels were available.

Distinctive features of the Seagrave F pumper show on a 1930 unit under restoration: individual cylinder blocks, truss rods and engine inter-cooler cylinder under the truck frame, and rear brake drums mounted on the jackshaft. (Eric Sprenger)

On both pumpers and ladder trucks the truck frame made use of lengthwise truss rods and turnbuckles like a railroad car for increased rigidity. A pumper weighed between 9000 and 12,000 lbs and its wheel base ranged from 159 to 180 inches.

Seagrave had done quite well in Canada with its pioneering air-cooled, engine-powered "buckboard" hose wagons and chemicals, as it had in the supply of big tractor units during the pre-First World War years. The rosy prospects for its Canadian affiliate company in Walkerville, based on this headstart, did not anticipate the powerful competition to come. For some reason LaFrance captured the fancy of the fire chiefs when it started production in Toronto in 1915. About 1920 the W.E. Seagrave

A catalogue drawing of the LaFrance chassis of the T-head era, with its triple-block, six-cylinder engine, under the seat rotary gear pump, integral transmission and differential gear case, and chain drive to the rear wheels from a jackshaft. (BHC)

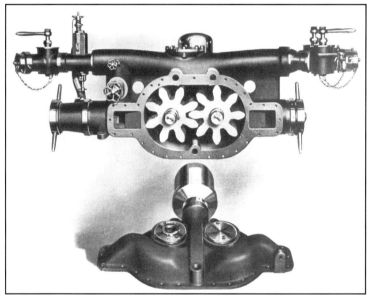

The LaFrance rotary gear pump of the mid twenties. The first gear was driven by the engine, and drove the other. Excess pressure was relieved by recirculation through a spring-loaded relief valve or a manual churn valve, at left. (BHC)

Company folded, and for some time thereafter deliveries were made from Columbus.

In the era of the T-heads, Seagrave had comparatively slim sales in most of Canada. The 1929 city-service ladder truck of the Moncton Fire Department seems to have been the only representative in the Atlantic provinces. Few were sold in the West, old customers having deserted Seagrave when LaFrance came into the market. Winnipeg bought a pumper in each of 1919 and 1928, and had a 75ft aerial truck. Hamilton had pumpers of 1000 gpm bought in 1917, 1921 and 1923.

It was in Québec that Seagrave had its loyal fans—or best salesmen. The Montréal Fire Department purchased a Seagrave air-cooled tractor in 1912 and for nearly forty years thereafter bought no other make of custom apparatus, except for three Magirus aerial trucks and a few LaFrance and Bickle tractors for ladder trucks. This department bought two of Seagrave's pioneering 1912 model centrifugal pumpers with 1200 gpm rear-mounted pumps. Montréal picked up another of the 1000 gpm pumps on absorbing the Maisonneuve Fire Department. Throughout the 1920s, this

The Ahrens-Fox piston pumper of the Kingston, Ontario Fire Department was one of only four to serve in Canada. They were assembled by Bickle Fire Engines Limited in the latter 1920s to compete with the big trucks of Seagrave and LaFrance. (BHC)

largest of Canadian fire departments phased out its steam fire engines, and replaced them with a fleet of 1200 gpm Seagrave Type F pumpers without chemical or booster water tanks, buying a pair of them nearly every year. Before it was discontinued in the early thirties, the Montréal Fire Department had fifteen of the Type Fs on its roster at one time and they formed the backbone of its firefighting force into the 1950s. Five Seagrave tractor aerial ladder trucks and several tractors for other trucks were also added during this period.

Québec City and some other cities in the province had one or two Type F pumpers and aerial tractors. After the end of the T-head line a few years later, Seagrave launched a renewed assault on the Canadian market, to give this company a wider share of the national market.

The face-to-face pumping contests of the hand engine and steam fire engine eras were long gone in this modern age, but one final great competition was to take place. LaFrance did not accept the Seagrave monopoly in Montréal without a fight. Strong representations in the early part of the twenties finally brought the city to accept a contest between LaFrance and Seagrave pumping engines.

Top: Early four- and six-cylinder engines under assembly in the American LaFrance factory in Elmira, New York before the First World War. This company had long-established expertise in steam engines and pumps. Seagrave did not. (BHC)

Bottom: A 1000 USgpm Type 12 triple combination engine just turned out of the LaFrance assembly plant at Weston (Toronto) for London, Ontario. By 1926, the day of solid tires and chemical tanks as standard equipment was nearing an end. (LaFrance Fire Engine & Foamite Ltd)

Halifax Fire Service maintains this fine example of the Bickle company's own custom fire truck, introduced in 1928. The Bickle generally used engines by Waukesha, but in a few cases used the Ahrens-Fox. The pump was a rotary type of their own. (BHC)

Top : Regina received this Type 94 LaFrance plain city-service ladder truck, together with a hose wagon and pumper in 1928. The truck is an early option to the standard chain drive of the day. Winnipeg had this option on some pumpers. (LaFrance Fire Engine & Foamite Ltd)

Bottom: Refinements with the fine Master 200 Series LaFrance included four-wheel brakes and left-hand drive. This 1931 triple combination with 840 gpm rotary gear pump had its windshield installed much later, in the 1950s. (BHC)

Both companies delivered pumpers and the match was held on the bank of the Lachine Canal. As in almost all past contests of this sort, it ended in an argument. Although the two machines had the same rating, the Seagrave delivered so much more water, as measured, that there were accusations of juggling with the outlet valves when the readings were being made. At any rate, the LaFrance bid for Montréal's favour was rejected. Their pumper was later sold to the Town of Brockville, where it served faithfully until 1968.

Bickle and Ahrens-Fox

Doubtless in an effort to counter their deficiency in the area of heavy-duty, specialized, custom apparatus in the mid-twenties, Bickle Fire Engines made an arrangement with the Ahrens-Fox Company of Cincinnati to assemble their apparatus line for sale in Canada.

The evidence suggests that either Canadian fire departments did not share the enthusiasm of the numerous "Fox" devotees across the border, or that possibly the price of these fine quality, well built pumpers was too high. At any rate, only four Ahrens-Fox piston pumpers were sold in Canada, the first to Kingston in 1924, and three to Hamilton in 1926, 1928 and 1930. Two of these have been preserved. They carry the name Canadian Ahrens-Fox.

The Canadian-built Foxes were Model N, with the Ahrens-Fox 110 hp, six-cylinder engines. These were typical of the large displacement T-head power plants, having $5^1/_2$-inch bore and 7-inch stroke, displacing 998 cubic inches. The cylinder blocks, which earlier had been cast in pairs like the LaFrance, had become single like Seagrave's. The piston pump, coupled to the front of the engine, had four cylinders. At capacity rating, with all cylinders working, the pump operated at 320 rpm and the engine at 1300 rpm. Bigger models rated up to 1300 gpm had a six-cylinder pump.

These piston pumps were fairly efficient, achieving flexibility as they did through the operation of the pump cylinders in two independent banks of slightly different displacements. At pressures over 140 psi only one bank was used, with a consequent reduction in volume delivered. However, the pumps were a massive 2100 lb load on the front end of the vehicle, they had many working parts and were unable to make use of incoming pressures from hydrants. Wear on many friction surfaces and vibration were additional drawbacks they had in common with other positive displacement pumps.

Developed from the company's steam pumps in 1912, the piston pumps were phosphor bronze. They used cluster valves and circulated engine cooling water through heat exchanger coils inside the pump suction manifold. In addition to cooling the engine while pumping, the coils provided heat for the exposed pump in freezing weather. The pump had its own crankcase with an independent lubricating oil system. Individual control levers at the front of the pump were used to mesh the gears of the two pump crankshafts with the engine as needed.

In addition to the four piston pumpers, Bickle also assembled some pumpers with the Ahrens-Fox chassis and engine coupled to Bickle rotary pumps. Kentville in Nova Scotia and Pembroke and Ottawa in Ontario bought such units. Some service ladder trucks were also built with Ahrens-Fox engines and components. Hamilton, London and Galt each had one of these. Most of these trucks could easily be identified by the headlights mounted high on the radiator shell and the far forward position of the front axle, both being features designed for the accommodation of front-end piston pumps.

The Custom Bickle

Bickle soon stopped marketing Ahrens-Fox engines but, making use of some of the body patterns, finally achieved the important status of custom fire apparatus builder, introducing its own models

LaFrance produced a number of modest price pumpers like this Type 99 for Pictou, Nova Scotia using a GMC chassis, between 1928 and 1930. Although the driving position was on the left, pump controls remained on the right side for some time. (BHC)

just before 1930. The heavy-duty Bickle chassis was produced from 1928 to 1938, and was designed by Vernon Bickle King, nephew of Bob Bickle. It bore a strong resemblance to the Ahrens-Fox from which it was derived, but utilized the 160 hp, six-cylinder Waukesha engine and the Bickle rotary pump, derived from the Hale-Northern. Rated at 800 gpm, the pumper was called *The Canadian*, although its ancestry was definitely American. A *Special Canadian* with a 200 hp Waukesha engine was produced, rated at 1000 gpm, and the smaller *Volunteer*, *Underwriter* or *Chieftain* could be selected to deliver in the range of 350 to 800 gpm. All of these were rated in Canadian gallons.

The borderline between custom and commercial fire apparatus has always been unclear because no assembler manufactured every component of his vehicle. In the Depression of the thirties, all builders were intent on covering every aspect of a weak market and this resulted in the manufacture of some economy and half-custom models. Bickle produced a number of 500 and 600 gpm pumpers on some hybrid assemblies that came from various sources.

With a snap of the latch the ladder flies up under the power of its big coil springs. Crew at the control pedestal raise the 1930 75-foot LaFrance ladder on a Type 31 truck at London, Ontario. (BHC)

The company also attempted to market the American Pirsch wooden, hydro-mechanical and the German Magirus mechanical aerial ladders at this time, with very little success. Montréal and Québec each purchased a 100ft Magirus aerial ladder on a Bickle chassis from them.

Before building their own chassis, Bickle struggled with the limitations of power in the commercial chassis of the twenties. The Ford T was only 20 hp and could carry a pump of only 200 gpm. Even the bigger Ruggles had only 55 hp and was not up to heavy pumping jobs. The cities had little interest in small pumping engines.

Bickle custom pumpers became widely distributed across Canada. From Vancouver to St. John's, the 1000 gpm size with 80 gal cylindrical booster water tank (replacing the chemical) was most popular. A number of large, quadruple combination pumper-ladder trucks were supplied on the Bickle chassis, notably for towns in Québec. Toronto had four Bickle hose and booster units.

Ubiquitous LaFrance

By far the largest American fire apparatus manufacturer in the early part of the twentieth century was the American LaFrance Fire Engine Company of Elmira, New York. It gained this position by virtue of a number of major take-overs and mergers. Most of the principal hand engine and steam fire engine builders and their descendants in the United States wound up in LaFrance. The company withheld its debut in the motor apparatus market until it had carried out extensive development work. Then LaFrance offered the fire service a practical, rugged and reliable product. It eventually was sold worldwide. As a result, this basic 1912 model needed no major redesign for many years. Instead, it evolved slowly until the thirties when completely new pumps and engines were adopted.

The original LaFrance T-head, six-cylinder engine of 100 hp was modified and reworked in several versions to achieve power plants that suited various needs up to 140 hp. These engines were in many ways similar to the Seagrave, the salient difference being the casting of the cylinders in pairs, like the earlier Ahrens-Fox, rather than individually. LaFrance engines weighed about 1650 lbs.

As on the Seagrave engine, there was a cylinder compression release cam to make hand cranking easier, the cam control lever being up front under the radiator. All custom fire trucks of this era had the engine crank permanently mounted and held disengaged by a spring. Both splash and pressure lubrication were installed and there was a float-type sump level indicator on the engine. Like most motor fire apparatus, and many automobiles of the period, a Boyce MotoMeter thermometer was integral with the radiator cap. To cool the engine while pumping, water was bled from the pump into the radiator, causing it to overflow. Consequently antifreeze was not used.

Gasoline feed on LaFrance engines was by gravity to a Stromberg, float-feed, updraft carburetor. Dual ignition from magneto and distributor coil supplied two sets of sparkplugs on the pumpers. Ladder trucks had only one set of plugs.

The gearshift and clutch control features of Seagrave were not provided in the LaFrance. With the road transmission to the rear of the pump shifted into neutral, the pump shift lever could be placed in any of the three gates for volume (low ratio), high pressure (high ratio) and out of gear. The pump gears were meshed with the slow-turning drive gear without benefit of declutching.

As in the Seagrave, chain drive for the rear wheels was favoured for its ease of repair on the road. Worm gear drive was available but rarely seen. The original service and hand brakes operating respectively on the outside and inside of only the rear wheel drums were continued until the advent of the Master series apparatus with four-wheel brakes.

Originally a Vancouver pumper, this 1920 Type 45 LaFrance 840 gpm rotary pumper gleams in its original white and brass finish, now with the Surrey, British Columbia Fire Department. (Frank DeGruchy)

To avoid over-pressure in the LaFrance rotary gear pump, as in all such positive displacement pumps, there were a churn valve (a simple manual bypass from the discharge side back to the suction side) and an automatic relief valve. The latter was a spring-loaded bypass operated on a pressure differential at a pre-set pressure. The original LaFrance relief valve was later superseded by the bigger Ross relief valve and some of the older pumpers were refitted with these. The various sizes and types of LaFrance apparatus of this era were designated by "type" numbers. The basic engines used and the primary function of the apparatus determined the number, but the assigning of numbers for sales purposes was somewhat at odds and confusing. The biggest regular model was the Type 12 fitted with the 885cu.in, six-cylinder engine rated at 120 hp at 1300 rpm It weighed 9950 lbs and had a 161-inch wheelbase. This model was used for 1000 US gpm pumpers. Type 75 had the same engine rated at 105 hp and it drove the 750 gpm pump. Smaller still was Type 38 with a 573cu.in. engine. Type 40 was the four-cylinder model, but it had a 590-inch engine and the same horsepower as the Type 38. It was shorter with a 140-inch wheelbase.

During the twenties LaFrance lagged behind Seagrave in the introduction of changes aimed at maintaining a contemporary appearance. Other than a switch to drum headlights in 1922, no obvious change in overall look came until 1927, when the radiator and engine hood line grew larger with the Metropolitan Series. It was only in 1929 that a moderately different looking model, the Master Series, was introduced. Much was the same, but there were some significant and overdue changes. Along with cast steel wheels replacing the wooden spokes and new rounded-off fenders, there were four-wheel brakes, left-hand drive and pumps enclosed in the body.

The Master Series marked the climax of the T-Head engines, chain drive and gear pumps for LaFrance. All of these features were still included, with the power of the engine at its maximum of 140 hp. There was still no sign of a cab, doors or a windshield to protect the crew, unless ordered as an extra, and these options were rare. Within the next few years, however, under this same external shell, the mighty V-12 engines would go into action.

This last series of the LaFrance first-generation apparatus, despite its lack of personnel protection, was an excellent machine that gave good service to a number of Canadian fire departments. Most of these machines were replacements for earlier discarded trucks, but a few were still taking the places vacated by the last horse-drawn apparatus. In Montréal, they were used to tractorize ladder trucks of the horse-drawn era, in Victoria they replaced old light-weight commercial chassis units, and elsewhere they met the expansion needs of cities. The last front wheel drive aerial ladder trucks were two of the Master Series sold to Shawinigan Falls and Verdun in Québec. The latter, like some other front drive trucks, was later converted to four-wheel tractor operation to gain a new power plant and better manoeuverability.

On right hand drive pumpers, the pump operating position had been on the right, where the hand throttle, spark advance and other engine controls were within reach from where the operator stood on the ground. With the change to left hand drive the operating position was not changed, so an auxiliary throttle was added, permitting adjustment of the engine speed while pumping.

The first LaFrance fire apparatus and its salesmen must have impressed Canadian fire chiefs and their bosses. They gave this company the lion's share of the business from the time Vancouver bought the first hose wagons in 1912 and Halifax received the first pumper in 1913. By 1930, LaFrance had delivered one hundred and eighteen pumpers, thirty-three hose wagons, fifty-five ladder trucks and twelve tractors for ladder trucks, claiming ninety per cent of Canadian fire departments as their customers.

In many parts of the country any other make was considered a curiosity. Halifax, Saint John, Toronto, London, Winnipeg, Edmonton and Vancouver, as well as many smaller places, used LaFrance apparatus exclusively, or almost so, until after the Second World War when the market became more open and other manufacturers appeared on the scene.

The Depression delayed replacement of the older units until the war cut off delivery of new vehicles. It was in large part, therefore, fleets of vintage LaFrance, rotary gear, T-Head pumpers, some over thirty years old, that held the firefighting front until postwar production caught up. LaFrance apparatus of the teens and twenties were still operating in a few fire departments in the late 1960s, and in a few cases, units of this age are still on the roster for parade purposes.

LaFrance produced some economy models on commercial chassis to meet the small town purse as other manufacturers did. One of the more notable was their Type 99, a 500 gpm pumper using a GMC chassis. The company also built a few of their own lower priced custom chassis models using the Buda engine.

Although both Seagrave and LaFrance produced four-cylinder engines in their T-head lines, these were very few in number as far

Early Seagrave spring-assist and spring-hoist, tiller steering aerial ladders were kept running by the Montréal Fire Department for as much as forty years by virtue of a periodic change of tractors like this GMC model. (BHC)

One of the last spring-hoist ladders to go into service in Canada was this 1936 LaFrance Series 400 at Windsor, Ontario. Both LaFrance and Seagrave grouped the manual ladder controls on a pedestal on the turntable in their last models. (LaFrance Fire Engine & Foamite Ltd)

as Canada was concerned. There may have been none of the Seagraves in Canada—as far as the records show. The first LaFrance machines in Canada, the three LaFrance hose wagons of 1912, had four-cylinder engines, as did the first ladder truck in Point Grey. It would appear that a large part of the company's earliest production was in the smaller engines. This can be explained by the high proportion of hose wagons to pumpers.

Only the smallest of the pumpers, usually of 350 gpm capacity, used the small engine, and in Canada these were concentrated in the Maritimes. Fairville, New Brunswick, Wolfville, Truro and New Waterford, NS had them. There were several other hose wagons and six of Toronto's fourteen front-drive ladder trucks that had four-cylinder engines. A disproportionately large number—at least five—of the LaFrance four-cylinder pumpers and hose wagons are still operable, including two of the pumpers mentioned above.

Aerials and Chemical Tanks

The spring-powered mechanism for raising the aerial ladder, invented by Seagrave in 1902, and soon improved by LaFrance, had proven so satisfactory that the introduction of the internal combustion power plant on the ladder truck did not bring any immediate move to harness this power to "the big stick." Not until the introduction of multi-section metal ladders in the mid-thirties would engine power be applied on any scale for this purpose. Older spring-hoist aerial trucks were simply tractorized and new motor-propelled trucks used the same ladders. Four-wheel tractors had the advantage of providing additional stability for the ladder through partial jack-knifing of the tractor added to the use of ground-jacks.

Similarly, the soda-acid-solution chemical tank was still satisfying the need to nip small fires in the bud. Many still believed that the soda

A good part of the business for Tremblay Fire Engine Company and Fire Equipment Limited of Montréal was trailer pumps. These two with Darling gear pumps and wide treads for lumbering roads were for the Québec government forest protection service. (Gaston Tremblay)

solution or the entrained carbon dioxide in the stream made it more effective than plain water. Most pumpers were, therefore, still fitted with a 30gal or 40gal chemical tank, although it had long been feasible to substitute a tank of water in connection with the main pump.

About 1930, the chemical tank rapidly began to fall out of favour. Instead of a superior extinguishing medium it was now seen as an unnecessary expense and a messy nuisance. Tests by Underwriters Laboratories had disproved the supposed benefits of the soda solution. In addition, the small tank capacity was an unnecessary limitation.

Some chemical tanks were simply piped into the pump on older pumping apparatus and filled with plain water, but most were replaced with a larger tank for water. This was generally a rectangular tank of 80 or 100gal set into the front end of the hose body. Combination hose wagons were fitted with small, power take-off pumps to supply their small first-aid firefighting streams. The word "chemical" was now replaced by the word "booster" when referring to the ¾-inch hose and water tank. As early as the mid-twenties Seagrave was offering a cylindrical 80gal booster water tank on new vehicles. Bickle followed this style, the tank shape being distinctive of their apparatus. LaFrance hewed to the rectangular tank.

Tremblay and Trailer Pumps

The principal product of Joseph Tremblay's Fire Equipment Limited, changed to Tremblay Fire Engine Company in the twenties, was the line of two-wheeled trailer pumps. The Tremblay trailer pump was quickly adaptable from hand to horse to automobile hauling and was sold in considerable numbers to villages throughout Québec. It was also used by the Québec government for forest protection and by industrial plants. For winter operation, sled runners were supplied.

These pumps were of the rotary type in 200 to 600 gpm capacities, built by the Darling Brothers foundry in Montréal. The engines ranged from small Continentals to large Waukeshas. Some smaller pumps could be carried by four men, and a pioneering lightweight forestry pump was powered by a small Peterboro outboard motor. It could be carried on a man's back.

In the very modest number of self-propelled fire department pumpers turned out by this company, the Northern rotary pumps were installed. The chassis included light trucks and touring cars built by Packard, Chevrolet, Ford and Pierce Arrow. A number of hose and chemical combinations were also built by the Tremblays.

Built to Last

One of the salesman's key points in selling custom chassis fire apparatus before the Second World War was always the availability of replacement parts—promptly and virtually forever. The apparatus manufacturers were aware that fire vehicles did not accumulate mileage fast. A few hundred miles a year was normal for even a relatively busy fire company. They often did not respond to emergency medical and other non-fire calls, nor did they have today's high level of training and prevention work. Using commercial chassis components, fire departments had a problem with vehicles long outliving the manufacturer's stock of parts.

With few model changes, and by manufacturing most of their own product, the custom builders maintained a good supply of parts for even the oldest of their T-head apparatus right into the post Second World War era. Such service deteriorated rapidly after the war as the result of corporate takeovers, more frequent model changes and increasing costs.

With parts growing scarce or expensive and having apparatus with many hours of serviceability left, fire departments resorted to cannibalization. Frequently fire department mechanics kept some

Montréal's Station 34 covered the muddy streets of developing pre-war Notre Dame de Grace with a little Ford hose and double chemical, apparently a Tremblay assembly. (BHC)

of their old units going by taking parts from similar units. Sometimes it was possible to substitute other parts; for example, the Toronto Fire Department installed Ford engines in some of its front-drive LaFrance ladder trucks. Many attempts were made to update old apparatus that refused to wear out, but was not up to modern performance standards. Air or vacuum brakes, modern headlights and windshields were the most common examples of such modifications.

An interesting example of cannibalization occurred in Saint John, New Brunswick. The department had operated a service ladder truck and two pumpers of the LaFrance Master Series, and had acquired a third similar pumper on amalgamation with suburban Lancaster. Through cannibalization, the weaker of these units were sacrificed to keep others going in order to maintain an emergency apparatus reserve. The number was finally reduced to one pumper still in service. Eventually another pumper was put together using parts from all four machines to provide an example of this model for the National Science Museum's collection.

On apparatus built to last indefinitely, a good paint job was essential. Up to twenty-one coats of paint were applied to the custom apparatus and carefully hand finished. Gold leaf was frequently used in elaborate decorative work, especially on some Seagrave apparatus.

Operators were admonished by maintenance manuals to take great care in cleaning and preserving the finish. The dangers of ammonia-laden dust from dirt roads frequented by heavy horse traffic were pointed out in one manual. Trucks were regularly washed underneath, including tires, on their return from every run. On the continuous duty system, a piece of fire apparatus had one regular operator, with a substitute only intermittently. These operators came to tend their engine with the same jealous devotion as they had a favourite horse.

At fires, the big LaFrance and Seagrave pumpers, having no mufflers, worked with a mighty roar under full load. In winter, the small stream of cooling water piped into the exhaust manifold came pouring out of the exhaust pipe in a great cloud of steam, often obscuring the pumper from view completely. A T-head LaFrance pumper in Alaska once worked continuously for thirteen days. Another, from Chicoutimi, Québec, was logged as pumping without relief for ninety-six hours at the 1932 Port Alfred pulpwood blockpile fire. Working with the LaFrance for the same period was a small Bickle pumper from Québec City.

Motor Pumper Standards

At the International Association of Fire Engineers (IAFE) conventions of 1911 and 1912, the performance tests on pumping engines had been made at net discharge pressures of 120, 200 and 250 psi. By 1913, a standard test procedure had been put together and the following year the National Fire Protection Association (NFPA) adopted a recommended performance standard for pumpers. The IAFE, the NFPA and the National Board of Fire Underwriters (NBFU) all cooperated in these efforts to standardize tests and specifications for automobile pumpers.

The standard test of 1913 called for prototypes of all new pumper designs to pass an endurance pumping test of twelve hours at draft. Performance requirements were set at nominal capacity against a net head of 120 psi, fifty percent of capacity at 200 psi, and one-third at 250 psi. The National Board set up a testing service based on these requirements and made the service available to all comers. Canadian tests followed these standards and in view of the American design of most of the pumps, used the same requirements.

A standard fire stream from a hose was defined as a flow of 250 US gpm and the rated capacities of pumps were standardized for the most part on multiples of this unit, i.e., 500, 600, 750, 1000 and

1250 gpm. There was a good deal of confusion over transpositions into Imperial gallons and, much of the time, US gallons were used in Canada. Not until 1953 was real standardization of gallonage figures achieved in Canada under Standard B89.3 of the Canadian Standards Association (CSA) and a national free testing program organized by the Dominion Board of Insurance Underwriters (DBIU), later the Canadian Underwriters' Association (CUA).

End of the Era

The limited production of the original custom chassis motor fire apparatus models, made more costly still by individual modification demands by purchasers, tended to act as a brake on frequent design changes. This, together with the custom engines' successful performance, caused the design process that existed between 1915 and 1930 to remain relatively static

As time went by, the design and development of new engines strictly for the limited fire apparatus field became unworkable. The big displacement T-head engines of LaFrance, Seagrave and Ahrens-Fox had been required as a result of the inadequacy of other engines available prior to the First World War. By 1930, it was fire apparatus engines that were becoming the poorer performers. Similarly, chassis features like four-wheel brakes and cab protection for the crew were not being offered. Some of this backwardness in fire apparatus design must, however, be blamed on the conservative fire chiefs' preference for open apparatus. They wanted the visibility and easy access they had had with the horses.

Replacement of the essentially pre- First World War engines with higher speed, higher powered engines was certainly overdue when LaFrance and Seagrave finally produced them. The fact that both companies based part of their range of new engine models upon purchased, proprietary engine designs was a sign that the small production, specially designed and produced fire apparatus engine was on the way out. Other manufacturers, including Ahrens-Fox, moved directly to proprietary gasoline engines like Waukesha and Hall-Scott with minor fire service modifications. Bickle stayed with Waukesha. All were still gasoline fuelled.

The time was right for a switch to centrifugal pumps by LaFrance when the new apparatus engines and power-operated aerial ladders were introduced. All of these changes would come in a rush in the mid 1930s, but the bark of the mufflerless T-head would be heard in the land for years to come, for in the rugged mechanical simplicity of it there was no trace of planned obsolescence.

For one generation the passing of the steam fire engine was lamented for the loss of romance and spectacle in the fire department. In the eyes of the sentimental, the galloping horses and the billow of smoke from the gleaming stack had a poor substitute in the automobile fire engine. Not surprisingly, it was a similar story for the next generation who had grown accustomed to the mechanical bucking bronco—the snorting motor pumper of the early motor age. With its flying front fenders, big sad-eyed headlights, most of its plumbing completely out in the open, and the crew sitting high on top and clinging to the sides, the apparatus of the teens and twenties had its special appeal, too.

It was an auditory experience to hear the old T-head LaFrance turn out on a run. Engagement of the starter gear on the flywheel made a clear ringing, like a bell. The engine barked, spat and back-fired through the open four-inch exhaust as it warmed up, then turned into a deep-noted roar as the engine or truck moved off the floor and turned into the street. The hand-cranked siren and the 40lb locomotive bell were hardly needed when the driver accelerated, the blast of the exhaust scattering dust and loose gravel as he felt for the right speed for the tricky shift between gears. Anyone within two blocks knew the T-head was under way.

Fire Equipment Limited of Montréal supplied this double chemical combination hose wagon on a Packard truck chassis to the Town of Montréal West about 1920. (Gaston Tremblay)

The St. George, New Brunswick firemen equipped with this home-grown Ford-powered fleet in 1928 must have found fires in buildings like these a considerable challenge. (BHC)

New Fire Hose

For about fifty years riveted leather hose had served fire departments well, if properly cared for. It was considerable work, taking care to dry out the leather and then rub it well with tallow and neatsfoot oil every time the hose was used. Even the full-time firefighters found it a bother. The volunteers with their ill-heated shacks for fire stations frequently left hose to harden and crack. But leather hose was a known quantity and when well cared for lasted as much as twenty-five years. On the arrival of steam fire engines, however, the higher pressures caused a menace from flying rivets and bursting hose.

With great joy all round a suitable rubber hose was brought onto the market, soon followed by one with a circular-woven cotton jacket to strengthen and protect it. The jacket, eventually to become a double one, appeared in the late 1870s. Even the most cautious skeptics soon endorsed the new hose and leather gradually disappeared. North American fire departments almost all settled upon a $2^1/_2$-inch-diameter hose with screw thread couplings. Alas, they did not adopt the same thread.

In the middle of the twentieth century considerable effort was made to standardize the $2^1/_2$-inch hose threads. Under the stimulus of cold war civil defence planning, each province adopted a thread convenient to itself. Québec was first, in 1927, but made little effort to change any of the other threads existing across the province. A massive change-over was carried out in Ontario in the early fifties. The many variants remaining across the country have been a hindrance to mutual aid among fire departments when there are major emergencies, although close neighbors usually had compatible threads. In the United States however there is large-scale standardization of the $2^1/_2$-inch threads. Border towns carry adapters as that arbitrary international line has never had much significance when it comes to fire departments helping one another out.

Brass was long the material used for hose couplings, as it was for nozzles, playpipes and other hose fittings because of its good resistance to abuse, its ease of casting and machining. Unfortunately it was heavy. With male and female screw threads, the two ends of a standard length of hose differed. It was necessary to get them the right way around or use double connectors to join them. European fire brigades had long used universal quick-connect couplings and these are only now in growing use in North America, notably on the 4- and 5-inch supply hose that has recently come on the scene on a large scale. The official adoption of metric or SI units of measure has been largely cosmetic as far as hose and fittings dimensions are concerned.

Traditional $2^1/_2$-inch-diameter, cotton, rubber-lined hose came in 50ft lengths weighing 50 lbs and up per length. Modern jackets with synthetic fibres and thinner linings reduced both weight and bulk, while hardened aluminum alloy couplings brought a further weight reduction. For a long time hose couplings had pin lugs to provide a grip for wrenches, but after years of snagging when dragged around corners, a snag free, rounded-off lug supplanted them in the 1950s.

As a part of the modern fog stream methods of water application on fires, introduced in the fifties, came the large scale use of lighter, more mobile attack lines using $1^1/_2$-inch hose. Used as pre-connected lines from ever larger booster water tanks, in many fire departments this size gradually replaced the smaller 1-inch booster hose. By the eighties there would be other sizes of hoseline, $1^3/_4$ and 2-inch lines added as progressive fire chiefs innovated more freely. These smaller sizes permitted easy movement within the confines of a building and thus eased personnel shortages. Since pumpers are better positioned adjacent to the fire building with these methods, large diameter hose, mostly 4-inch, has been carried to provide an adequate supply from a hydrant to the pump.

In the 1920s, most ladder trucks were of the city-service type and carried only hand-raised ladders. This LaFrance unit for the Kelowna Volunteer Fire Department was a combination with a small pump. (Frank DeGruchy)

This larger hose is a product of the age of synthetics, made of rubber having the reinforcing jackets imbedded within it.

Breathing Apparatus

Ever since firefighters have had the use of hoselines enabling them to enter smoke filled buildings to ferret out the seat of a fire or perform rescues, they have risked death from the blinding, noxious and frequently lethal products of combustion. Fires in Hollywood movies use clear gas flames and little smoke so the audience can see the action. What firefighters see most of the time is a wall of smoke. They frequently crawl on the floor trying to see under it, feeling their way through the murk.

The worst and omnipresent danger is carbon monoxide, called the silent killer, since by itself it is colourless and odourless, giving no warning of its presence. The age of plastics has added to the peril with its new poisonous gases and thick volumes of greasy smoke residue that clog delicate human lungs.

It is natural that many efforts have been made throughout the time of interior firefighting to devise means for firefighters to breathe safely in smoky atmospheres. Many crude devices are recorded, but the technological breakthrough for reasonable success had been lacking until fairly recently. Miners and divers shared in the same quest and in the resultant developments in breathing apparatus for alien atmospheres. The approach was made from two directions. On the one hand the attempt was made to filter the objectionable gases, vapours and solids from the air, and on the other to provide a self-contained supply of breathable air to accompany the firefighter.

Various hoods, leather or fabric bags and a facepiece were put forward by inventors throughout the late 1800s, but they were impractical or useful for too short duration. Methods of supplying fresh air through a hose were not much better, and added the hindrance of managing the air hoseline. Eventually, a system similar to that of a deep sea diver's hardhat was reasonably successful and was carried by some fire departments for use in special situations where the hose was not too great a problem.

The filter approach occupied much the same period of development and longer. It usually involved a facepiece and had various means of filtration, from a simple water soaked sponge to charcoal soaked in glycerine. It was not until American researchers produced a catalyst called Hopcalite in 1920—an important breakthrough—that a fairly effective filter mask was made possible. For the first time some protection against carbon monoxide was available, as hopcalite converted it into less harmful carbon dioxide. The result became known as the Type N, or Burrill mask. It had a facepiece somewhat like a Second World War gas mask and a small canister connected to it by a flexible tube. The canister held layers of filtering materials including Hopcalite and activated charcoal.

The American Bureau of Mines approved the Type N mask in 1920, and it remained in widespread use in the Canadian fire service until supplanted by entirely self-contained types in the 1950s. Its great weakness was that it offered no source of oxygen if that was deficient in the atmosphere. Even with the Type N available, it was confined in most fire departments to occasional use and limited to perhaps a pair of masks on ladder and rescue trucks. In a way it was just as well, since this kind of mask could lull firefighters into thinking they were safer than was the case. Until the age of plastics most firefighters prided themselves on their ability to "eat smoke," considering a mask a hindrance and a sign of weakness. Cases of firefighter deaths due to carbon monoxide—even while wearing these masks—began to change their minds in the early 1960s.

In the meantime, efforts elsewhere to produce a practical closed system that supplied life-maintaining oxygen for the firefighter had produced results. The Siebe Gorman Company in England and Draegerwerke in Germany were making apparatus for mine rescue work around 1880. The basis was a small bag of air that was continually rebreathed by the mask wearer, but was scrubbed of moisture and carbon dioxide by chemicals in the bag, while oxygen was bled into the bag from small pressure cylinders. The equipment was used by firefighters and miners in Britain and Europe, often organized as Draeger teams, but its use was rare in North America, except for mine rescue.

This type of breathing apparatus has, even today, the advantage of long duration, four hours or more, and is still used for such needs, although long durations are considered a specialist task. A facepiece is usual, but a workhorse of the British fire services was for a long time the "Proto," with simply a mout hpiece for breathing and a clip to close the nostrils.

The implementation of improving technology for the tools and vehicles in the fire service was slowed by the Depression, when a damper was put on product development and sales. As the Depression wore off and apparatus manufacturers strove to rekindle customer interest in buying, the late 1930s would bring about substantial progress.

The most common version of the LaFrance Type 500 pumping engine seen in Canada was open-cab, like this one in Halifax, Nova Scotia. A modest number were sold before the war interfered with deliveries and the model was dropped. (BHC)

A New Generation

Striking changes in motor apparatus design in the 1930s brought more effective and safer tools to the firefighting scene in urban Canada. In 1912 and 1915, the two manufacturers who were to set the standard for fire apparatus in this country had found successful formulas upon which fire departments could convert from horse-drawn to gasoline-engined vehicles. By the end of the twenties, however, the little-changed basic designs had outlived their time and fallen behind automotive technology. The trusty T-head-powered LaFrance and Seagrave apparatus, their two-wheel brakes, exposed driver's seat, spring-hoist aerial ladders and gear pumps finally had to give way to more contemporary ideas. This happened in spite of the many conservative fire chiefs who were quite happy, or felt secure, holding on to their familiar equipment.

Late in the 1930s the new engines, pumps, aerial ladders and the vehicles on which they were mounted were a new breed, springing from a backlog of accumulating technology finally put to work. Unfortunately, the Depression, the Second World War, and the longevity of the older vehicles prevented a rapid proliferation of the new tools. It took another fifteen to twenty years for the fire service to come near to catching up with new technology.

V–12 Engines

The simple, rugged, straight six-cylinder T-head engine had been a faithful performer, but

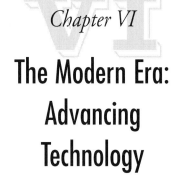

Chapter VI

The Modern Era: Advancing Technology

the basic designs could not be exploited for any more power. Further power with less bulk and weight was needed. Both LaFrance and Seagrave opted for twelve-cylinder vee engines, a type that had been used in high-powered automobiles like Cadillac, Packard and Pierce Arrow, as well as for aircraft and fast boats.

LaFrance developed two V–12 engines. The larger E model, introduced first, was their own design. It was rated initially for 244 bhp at 3200 rpm, had a 30-degree vee angle, a 4-inch bore and 5-inch stroke. The smaller engine, Type J, was derived from the well known Lycoming automotive engines, and produced from 190 to 215 bhp at 3200 rpm. One LaFrance catalogue lists a sixteen-cylinder engine, but no example can be found.

Both of these power plants were fitted with dual distributors, spark plugs and carburetors. Ignition was from both coil and magneto. The E engine was announced in 1929 and the first Canadian apparatus to have it was probably the quadruple combination, Master Series pumper-ladder truck delivered to Glace Bay, Nova Scotia, in 1933. Ottawa had a Master Series pumper with the V–12 engine driving a rotary gear pump.

About 1930 Seagrave bought the patterns, engines and stock for the V–12 engines that had been used in the now defunct Pierce Arrow cars. These became the basis for the smaller series of Seagrave twelve-cylinder engines in the area of 200 hp. Like LaFrance, Seagrave marketed a larger

In 1937 this Series 300 LaFrance for Vancouver was one of a few in Canada with a V-12 engine. However, it retained the rotary gear pump, mounted up front. Seen here is George Thomas, LaFrance Canadian General Manager until 1940. (LaFrance Fire Engine & Foamite Ltd)

In 1928 Montréal purchased two 100-foot wooden Magirus aerial ladders from Germany. European ladders were more advanced in their use of power-operated, self-levelling rear mounted aerials. Montréal favoured rear-mounts from then on. (John Daggett)

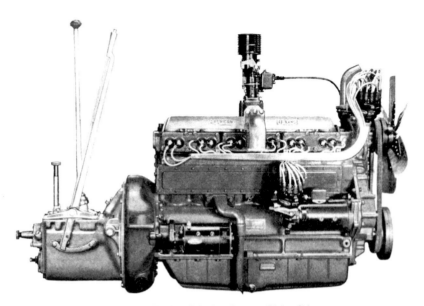

Fig. 29—Twelve-Cylinder Engine, Right Side

Fig. 30—Twelve-Cylinder Engine, Left Side

engine as well, in ratings up to 268 bhp. It appeared in Canada about the same time and also had dual ignition and carburetion. This particular engine was in use into the late 1950s. By then it had been boosted to 300 hp to meet competition from proprietary engines like Continental and Hall Scott. It was the last of the V–12s, and the last of the engines built by the fire apparatus builders.

Parallel-Series Pumps

Speed and horsepower were higher with both the V–12s and the newer proprietary engines favoured for fire apparatus. This performance, coupled with the highly flexible centrifugal pump that could work in either parallel or series modes, reopened the question of rotary gear versus centrifugal pumps for fire apparatus.

In the parallel-series pump the centrifugal impellers were mounted on a single shaft and the manipulation of a transfer valve directed half the water flow through each impeller or all of it through each one in succession. The engine-pump team can thus be made to deliver large volumes at lower pressures in parallel, or small volumes at high pressures in series, all at engine speeds reasonably near the maximum performance characteristics of the engine. This was the sort of flexibility the Ahrens-Fox piston pump had aimed at with its two banks of cylinders and the rotary gear with its two gear ratios.

Under these new conditions the rotary pump lost its strongest advocate, as LaFrance brought out their Centraflow parallel-series pump in 1933. This pump had one large, double-suction impeller for the first stage and a smaller single-suction impeller that operated as the second stage when in series.

The LaFrance Model J, V-12 gasoline engine started at 170 bhp and was derived from a Lycoming engine. Note the dual distributors and sparkplugs. The larger E Model engine was designed by LaFrance and put out 240 bhp. (BHC)

The battle was not over, however, for some fire chiefs. They particularly liked the rotary's prowess in drafting, or lifting, water from static sources. Rotary pumps were continued in production, notably by Bickle, into the Second World War. LaFrance built a few rotary gear pumpers with V–12 engines but, for their custom models, it would be chiefly the centrifugal from then on. Bickle continued to offer their rotary pump along with the Hale centrifugal on their own custom chassis as long as that type was produced. The first Hale centrifugal pump in Canada was used on a Bickle Underwriter model for Laval des Rapides, Québec, in 1935.

Seagrave further refined their compact bronze pump with a water-hydraulic transfer valve. The pump continued to be set down inside the chassis frame, with the suction inlets below the frame, a distinctive feature. Other manufacturers' pumps were on top of the frame and had manual transfer

Top: Like LaFrance, Seagrave had two V-12 engines, the smaller one based on a Pierce Arrow model. It, too, had dual ignition. The transverse cylinder at front top is the heat exchanger which uses water from the fire pump. (BHC)

Bottom: LaFrance introduced its Centraflow centrifugal, parallel-series pump in 1936. The most common configuration was this one in Series 500 and 600, with pump and suctions behind the cab, control panel and discharges in front. (BHC)

A Buda engine was used by LaFrance in an economy-model Series 400 pumper produced in 1932 and 1933. The modest price appealed to the city of Medicine Hat, Alberta which purchased this one. (LaFrance Fire Engine & Foamite Ltd)

The 1938 Bickle-Magirus aerial of Québec City, shown after the wood ladder was replaced with steel. It was handy in the old city's narrow streets. Ladder controls are on the ladder base, operated from the ground as there was no turntable. (BHC)

valves. While others followed the lead of Seagrave in using a small positive displacement vacuum pump to prime the main pump when drafting, LaFrance for a time employed the vacuum power of one bank of the engine cylinders for evacuating the pump. The Barton American front-mounted pumps installed on some light economy model pumpers also had an engine vacuum primer. In both cases a complicated device to prevent water from entering the engine was required. In their postwar models LaFrance abandoned this complicated and trouble-prone system in favour of an engine-exhaust-driven Venturi, or exhaust-ejector, primer. They also redesigned their pumps in the Tripleflow and Twinflow models, while producing a four-stage pump for high pressure fog.

Bickle Fire Engines continued their association with the Hale Pump Company, later adopting both the single-stage and parallel-series types. Beginning in 1935, however, as Bickle-Seagrave Limited, this company began using Seagrave pumps as well, while assembling complete Seagrave vehicles.

Front-Mount Pumps

Another type of centrifugal pump appeared in increasing numbers in the thirties. It was the single stage front-mounted style, with a gear or clutch connected to the front end of the truck engine. It had the advantages of simplicity, ease of installation, convenient location for approaching drafting sources, greater body space behind the cab for a large water tank and other equipment, and was able to operate while the truck was under way.

These features made the front-mount popular with village and rural fire departments. Commercial chassis engines could power them in capacities up to 500 gpm. After the war front-mount pumps with ratings as high as 840 l gpm became available, though not common. Such pumps were manufactured by Hale, Barton and Darley for export to Canada, many bought by small fire departments for local installation. A variation on this type of pump was the 500 gpm trailer pump, produced in large numbers during the Second World War by Thibault and Bickle for the armed forces and civil defence. Later these pumps were taken over by municipal fire departments and widely used for a variety of auxiliary pumping duties.

After the war, many pumpers with front-mount pumps were placed in service by small fire departments. The majority of them had the Barton American pump and were assembled by American Marsh Pumps (Canada) Limited in Stratford, Ontario, or by Saskatoon Fire Engine Company, first in Saskatoon, then in Calgary.

The Hydraulic Aerial Ladder

The spring-hoist manual aerial ladder had worked to everyone's satisfaction long after the introduction of self-propelled vehicles with their attendant possibilities for engine-powered ladders. The key factors in the demise of the spring-hoist ladder may well have been the promise of ladders longer than the previous maximum of 85 ft, with more than two extension sections. The unwieldy length of the two-section ladder was a liability in the thickening city traffic.

Except for a few electric motor or compressed air adaptations of the wooden aerials, it was not until 1935 that aerial ladders powered by the truck engine were in production by North American manufacturers. European builders had been using power take-off for many years before this. First in North America was Peter Pirsch Sons Company in Wisconsin. In 1931 after trying hydraulic raising cylinders and power take-off rotation and extension using a wooden ladder, they went into production with an all-metal ladder in 1935. This was a 100-ft, riveted aluminum alloy ladder in three sections, a new standard for this length. Pirsch stuck with this successful aluminum ladder although all others opted for welded steel for many years. Many would be the sales arguments for and against the

Built under the Bickle name, but using a Seagrave pump, this St. Lambert, Québec pumper was produced in 1935 under the newly established collaboration of these two builders at the Bickle Company's Woodstock, Ontario plant. (BHC)

two metals. Following the eventual demise of the Pirsch company, Sutphen Corporation carried on this system of ladder construction in a box-beam tower-ladder. Welded aluminum alloys eventually came into use in other companies' ladders.

LaFrance, then Seagrave, in a close race, brought out their welded steel, all-hydraulic ladders soon after, in 1935. Other builders followed and the hydraulic metal ladder in three or four sections took over the market, except in a few big American cities.

A bird's-eye view of the Seagrave V-12 Pumper of 1940 to 1950, assembled in Woodstock, Ontario. This 1940 unit undergoes an underwriters service test for the City of Montréal. (BHC)

New York and Chicago clung tenaciously to the spring-hoist wooden ladder even into the fifties. Some manufacturers were prepared to oblige them when large orders were at stake. By the late sixties, spring-hoist wooden aerial ladders had virtually disappeared from the Canadian scene.

Not long after the conversion of horse-drawn aerial ladder trucks with two-wheel, front drive tractors it was realized that the four-wheel tractor with a fifth wheel connection to a trailer aerial truck was more manoeuverable and, when jack-knifed, a more stable base for the ladder. From 1930 on, with a couple of exceptions, only this type was being built in Canada until four-section ladders became common.

The shorter 65- and 75-ft metal ladders, being in three sections, were built on four-wheel chassis since the truck could be a reasonable length, and stability less of a concern. The longer 85- and 100-ft ladders continued as always to be built on trailer trucks. By the beginning of the Second World War, however, LaFrance produced a four-section ladder on a four-wheel chassis of the cab over engine type. There was some head shaking over this, as many believed it unsafe without a jack-knifed tractor to improve stability when a ladder of such a length was raised.

This is not so hard to understand in view of the relative frailty of the ground jacks, or spuds, in use at the time. LaFrance equipped their truck with outrigger jacks that screwed manually against the ground. Seagrave had adopted hydraulic jacks on the running boards for their four-wheel trucks. On their 100-ft ladders they provided a lockout for the rear springs of the

After the Master series, in 1933, LaFrance modified the body and teamed their new V-12 engine to new parallel-series centrifugal pumps. In this Kitchener, Ontario 300 series pumper, the pump is entirely ahead of the cab, a short-lived design. Leading up to the Second World War LaFrance seemed to lose their sense of practical design. (BHC)

tractor and screw jacks on the trailer. Eventually, after the war, all manufacturers built 100-ft ladders on four wheels, although the tractor-tiller style would be preferred in some fire departments, especially in the United States, for many years.

A few, small, lightweight 55-ft aerials with electric raising mechanisms were placed in service in Canadian fire departments during the early postwar years. Most notable was a type designed by Peter Pirsch. Some of these were used by American Marsh Pumps,

The 1938 LaFrance 500 Series, V-12 powered pumpers had an all-enclosed, but inadequate equipment space.
The pump is under the cab, controls ahead, suction inlets behind. It proved too expensive to build and was dropped in 1942. Few reached the Canadian market. (BHC)

for example for Thetford Mines, and the Winnipeg Fire Department mounted them on several pumpers assembled in their own shops.

A light, economy model aerial ladder of 75 ft with a single hydraulic raising cylinder was introduced by Seagrave in the 1950s. It was designed for installation on commercial chassis, although custom chassis had been preferred by the majors heretofore. This model was soon discontinued, but since then, mounting regular aerial ladders on the heavier commercial chassis that had become available has been commonplace.

A 1937 Bickle-Seagrave, 65-foot aerial ladder with hydraulically operated steel ladder and ground jacks, but manual turntable rotation. It was followed by numerous 75- and 85-foot, all-hydraulic ladders in this series, quite popular across the country just before and after the war. (BHC)

The European Style Ladders

Fire departments in North America had already had a look at a possible alternative to the spring-hoist ladder in 1927. At that time, an attempt was made to market the German-built Magirus aerial ladder truck in Canada and the United States. The venture was not very successful, but possibly spurred the American builders to catch up in the technology race.

European manufacturers had developed engine-powered aerials very early in the automotive age and the Magirus reached a sophisticated state compared to the American product. Reportedly these ladders were developed for work on the construction and servicing of Zeppelins, which called for heights in the area of 160 ft. The Magirus ladder of the twenties was made of wood, in four sections with a steel truss rail on each beam. In the thirties an all steel ladder was adopted. All functions of elevating, training and extending were performed mechanically through separate clutches on a power take-off drive. In addition, a levelling device was provided to level the ladder when the truck was standing on a hill. There was also a strain gauge on the ladder to warn of overloading. Four screw jacks and a lockout for the rear axle springs were supplied for stability. The British Merryweather turntable ladders and other European ladders such as the Metz were similar. Before the Second World War, most of the world outside North America purchased aerial ladders from these companies.

The first 100-foot all-powered metal aerial ladder in Canada was this tractor-tiller rig supplied to Trois Rivières, Québec in 1937, by Bickle-Seagrave. The chassis with ladder was supplied by Seagrave Corporation in Columbus. (King-Seagrave Ltd)

The tillerman sat behind the ladder, not on top, on the LaFrance 100-foot tractor aerial. This one using the Series 500 tractor was supplied by LaFrance Fire Engine & Foamite Limited of Toronto for Westmount, Québec. (LaFrance Fire Engine & Foamite Ltd)

A rare enclosed-body style assembled by Bickle-Seagrave in 1939 for Swansea, Ontario.
The suction inlet and discharge outlet set below the frame, as well as the control panel, reveal a parallel-series Seagrave pump installation. (King-Seagrave Ltd)

The enclosed no-running-board 500 Series LaFrance of 1938 featuring the big Model E, V-12 engine, Centraflow pump had an awkward storage space for small equipment. It was replaced by the more practical 600 Series in 1942. (LaFrance Fire Engine & Foamite Ltd)

The turntable on which these ladders was mounted was located over the rear axle and the ladder in a retracted position extended forward over the front of the vehicle. This made for a very short wheelbase, and a compact vehicle suited to the narrow streets of European cities. On the other hand, the turntable and location of the raising mechanism ruled out the carrying of any number of hand-raised ground ladders. This did not bother the British and European firemen as they did not operate ladder companies as such, nor use the numbers of hand-raised ground ladders the North Americans did at that time. In recent years the latter have come to carry fewer ground ladders as well.

The lack of ground ladder accommodation, wariness of foreign products and the somewhat under-powered Magirus Deutz chassis resulted in failure of the Magirus attempt to make a serious dent in the North American market. They soon gave up, but a few fire departments had been impressed. It is possible, too, that American manufacturers had been stimulated to greater initiative in creating their own designs for power operated ladders. At any rate, several Magirus ladders were sold in the United States, while Calgary and Edmonton bought one each.

The Montréal Fire Department was particularly impressed. They had many problems manipulating two-section, wooden aerial ladders and the water tower through the narrow, old-world streets of the business district. They were also in the habit of dispatching at least two ladder trucks to all alarms. The department bought two Magirus trucks to serve these congested areas, pairing them with

A long-wheel-base LaFrance 600 Series quadruple combination pumper-ladder truck at Edmundston, New Brunswick. The hosebody formerly placed under the ladder racks has now been put on top for easier loading. (BHC)

city-service ladder trucks on all responses so there was no shortage of ground ladders on the scene. The two solid-tired Magirus, 100-footers went into service in 1929.

These two aerial ladders proved immensely successful in Montréal. A third, now of steel, was imported and installed in 1939 on one of their own chassis by Bickle. A year before, Bickle had done the same for Québec City, which also had narrow streets and hills. Both cities found that, not only could a heavy-calibre elevated stream be operated from the end of the lower ladder section, but another could be directed simultaneously from the top extension at considerable height. Profitable use of this capacity sealed the fate of Montréal's last water tower. All traditional water towers eventually succumbed to the superiority of the modern aerial ladder and elevating platform streams. Montréal's was probably the first.

During the Second World War the Montréal Fire Department worried about obtaining parts for the German ladders, but they performed without trouble. As soon as they were again available, Montréal bought a fourth Magirus on a Bickle-Seagrave chassis and, in the fifties, added several more. These were mounted on Mack B model chassis. The pre-war Magirus operating mechanisms were later re-used on new chassis with replacement steel ladders. In 1969, the Montréal Fire Department was operating with six Magirus, one Merryweather and two Thibault rear-mounted aerial ladders, setting a trend for the North American fire service.

In the 1950s, Magirus ladders were imported and sold in a number of cities, including Québec and Winnipeg. In addition a few British Merryweather and German Metz ladders were imported by Pierre Thibault Limited, for installation on their chassis. The first Merryweather ladders were mechanically operated like the

A more economical, and more traditional LaFrance design was the 600, wartime series, with pump and controls behind the cab. Few were sold in Canada. This one was bought by Niagara Falls. It was produced from 1942 to 1945, before the radical postwar 900 series was ready. (BHC)

Magirus, but elevated with a pair of worm gears instead of one. Later these gears were changed for hydraulic pistons. Hull, Montréal and Lévis had the former type, Westmount and St. Hyacinthe the latter. The two Westmount ladders and two Metz ladders in Montréal were reversed on their chassis with the turntables forward, a unique application permitting more ground ladders to be carried.

The suitability of the shorter wheel based, rear-end mounted turntable ladder in heavy traffic and the small space it occupied in front of a fire building were decided advantages for older cities. A trend toward designs of this type in which more adequate footage of ground ladders could be accommodated began to show itself in the sixties in both Canada and the United States. Thibault was a leader in this trend because of the demand in the province of Québec. They were now using their own 100-ft aerial ladders. LaFrance and Seagrave now offered such models in the United States. All other builders then followed suit as a free-wheeling era began in the design of fire service aerial devices.

As a result of favourable experience on the earlier Magirus aerials with the ladder levelling devices for hills, the Montréal Fire department demanded them on all subsequent aerial trucks. Bickle-Seagrave, as their principal supplier for some years, designed one for the Seagrave ladder with a manual hydraulic actuation. Like the Magirus, it tilted the ladder on its mounting. After the war,

A 1939 Thibault pumper for Drummondville, Québec is reminiscent of the LaFrance Series 500 in its wide body with suction hose carried inside the body. At first, Thibault used pumps by Darling Bros. of Montréal, among others. (Pierre Thibault Ltd)

LaFrance developed a system in which the entire turntable was tilted to horizontal by two hydraulic pistons. Generally in North America, there was little demand for these devices, though Montréal and Québec long considered them a necessity. San Francisco, understandably, was a customer as well.

Bickle and Seagrave

In 1930 the Seagrave Corporation of Columbus invaded Canada for the second time, setting up a final assembly plant in St. Catharines, Ontario. A number of units were turned out there, including the last of the F model pumpers, some Depression-era economy models, the Seagrave *Canadian* using Continental engines and the small *Suburban* models. Business did not develop favourably, however, and in 1935 an arrangement was concluded with Bickle Fire Engine Company to take over assembly of their apparatus under the name Bickle-Seagrave Limited. The last unit produced in the St. Catharines plant is said to have been the first V–12 unit in Canada, built for the City of St. Catharines.

The arrangement prospered, and Bickle spread Seagrave apparatus across the country to break out of the previous confinement of the latter's market. The Bickle organization now had a full range of aerial ladders and pumps on custom chassis, using V–12 engines and Seagrave pumps, as well as their own models. The collaboration was very successful.

By the late thirties, the Thibault factory in Pierreville, Québec was turning out a modest number of motor pumpers in this wide body style. As on this Ford pumper, it accommodated a centre aisle for men and equipment. (Pierre Thibault Ltd)

At this time, Seagrave designs were modified to provide a lower, more protected driver's seat and a windshield as standard equipment. By 1937, semi-cabs and a completely enclosed cab were available, including canopy cabs with an aisle through the body to sheltered seating for a crew of up to seven, a great luxury. In practice, when this option was taken, the aisle tended to fill with equipment, and the crew still rode the tailboard. Finally it was possible to get a good-sized crew inside, off the running boards and rear step, but they were in no great hurry to go.

LaFrance Enclosed Semi-Cab Models

LaFrance twelve-cylinder engines and centrifugal pumps were first installed in the open Master Series vehicles and it took several years for chassis and bodies to catch up with them. Apparatus with enclosed, semi-cab driving compartments without roofs became standard with LaFrance in their 500 Series of 1938. With the 600 Series of 1942, they enclosed everything with a vengeance. A streamlined body with no running boards and no side compartments made stowing small equipment difficult. A totally enclosed driving compart-

In 1938 American LaFrance introduced the first North American 100-foot aerial on four wheels with this pioneer cab-over-engine V-12 model. Second World War priorities prevented many municipal sales in Canada and the model was replaced. (BHC)

ment was available, but was not in demand. The Centraflow pump was mounted behind the cab in the usual way, but the operator's control panel and the discharge outlets were placed ahead of it next to the engine compartment. Production was limited by the war to only these models and few units were produced until the company's radically redesigned postwar apparatus appeared. Postwar safety conscious standards then required all firefighters to be accommodated within the vehicle, not clinging precariously to the rear and side steps.

Wartime Conditions

Canadian fire departments went into the Second World War equipped largely with the motor fire apparatus they had acquired to replace horses. These were the early models of the teens and twenties, frequently with two-wheel brakes, righthand steering and not even a windshield for protection against the weather. Most of the solid tires and some of the wooden spoked wheels had been replaced with pneumatic tires and steel wheels for better traction and a less jarring ride.

But the trusty T-head-engined custom vehicles of the major apparatus builders, obsolete in terms of the technology available, stood up well and were going strong into the fifties. Like steam locomotives they were built to last forever and only greatly improved designs hastened their replacement after the Depression and the Second World War. Most of the larger fire departments had just

A number of these International chassis pumpers with enclosed Bickle rotary pumps saw service at Royal Canadian Air Force bases during and after the Second World War. (King-Seagrave Ltd)

begun to try the new generation apparatus when the war intervened. As a result, there were a few hydraulic, steel aerial ladder trucks and a couple of centrifugal pumpers with semi-cabs here and there.

As large navy, army and air force bases blossomed across the country the small production lines of Canadian manufacturers were filled up, and stretched to provide protection for these vital facilities. The availability of chassis and components from American sources held up reasonably well until after the Japanese attack on Pearl Harbor in December 1941, when the United States intensified war production for its own use.

The fire protection load increased in some cities where large war production was established or population inflated by military activity. Halifax probably fared the worst in this respect.

Fortunately, the local fire department had made significant apparatus replacements just as war began, as a result of the disastrous Queen Hotel fire in which many lives were lost. The city benefited as well from the presence of the military fire services that were quickly expanded.

Municipal fire departments strove to keep their older, weaker vehicles running and prayed that they would not break down at the hands of inexperienced substitute operators. Considerable strain was caused by the war rush, congestion, inexperienced workers, old equipment and substitute firefighters. Gasoline was not as good as it had been and the new synthetic rubber tires were not too dependable.

The larger custom chassis apparatus grew scarce on the market and was subject to defence priorities that ranked much higher than

Top: A Seagrave *Suburban*, an economy model pumper with a small Seagrave pump, one of the few assembled at their St. Catharines, Ontario assembly plant. (BHC)

Bottom: The interior of the open cab LaFrance aerial truck of 1938, precursor of the post-Second World War designs, is shown in Etobicoke, Ontario. The hydraulic control pedestal and an elevating cylinder are at lower right. (BHC)

A number of these light, Ford front-mount pumpers were assembled in their own shops by the Canadian Army Service Corps for the protection of army bases during the Second World War. The bodies were of pressed fibreboard. (BHC)

municipal fire departments. Fire departments did obtain, in coastal cities especially, fire equipment of a sort in the form of civil defence trailer pumps and single-jacket hose that burst with dismaying frequency. The wartime models of regular apparatus that appeared were easily recognizable by their total lack of chrome trim.

Custom and commercial pumpers using both centrifugal and rotary pumps were turned out for military bases in much the same models as for structural protection in the city. Halifax and St. John's had sizeable naval fire departments, well equipped with LaFrance and Bickle-Seagrave custom apparatus. The army made use of a number of light pumpers built in its own shops—Ford trucks with front-mount pumps and bodies made of pressed fibreboard panels.

Large numbers of 420 Igpm trailer pumps on two wheels were built by the manufacturers using Ford and Chrysler automobile engines. A single-stage centrifugal pump was directly connected to the engine. This type of equipment had been pioneered long before in Canada, but was now being actively utilized by the British fire services during the Blitz. The idea was to produce a large quantity of simple, manoeuverable pumps that could be pulled by taxis or other small vehicles pressed into emergency service. Perhaps as many as 3000 were produced in Canada, over 1000 by Bickle-Seagrave. Some were very small, using 150 gpm rotary

Wartime fire apparatus production displayed little chrome plate or frills, like this Bickle-Seagrave triple combination pumper with Seagrave pump and chassis. Most such units were used at military bases. (King-Seagrave Ltd)

A considerable part of the Thibault pre-Second World War business was in Québec in apparatus for small town and village protection, particularly trailer pumps like this one for Repentigny. The company was using the trade name Richelieu at the time. (Pierre Thibault Ltd)

pumps and small Continental engines. They were noted for the number of lengths of wartime single-jacket 1½-inch hose they caused to burst due to chafing from pump vibration.

The trailer pumps were assigned to military camps and the civil defence auxiliary firefighting companies associated with the established municipal fire departments. Placed on barges, they substituted for fireboats at Vancouver and Halifax. After the war many of the larger units were taken over by the municipal departments, becoming valued auxiliaries for mopping up at major fires, pumping out basements, fighting rural and dump fires—things they had been doing already.

The trailer pumps, dubbed Village Queens after an earlier LaFrance model, were simple and spartan. Two-wheelers, they served well and some were still around in 1980. The single-stage centrifugal pump was direct-connected to the engine and the primer for drafting was of the Venturi exhaust ejector type. Each carried 400 ft of 2½-inch hose.

War's End

As the Second World War ended, municipal fire departments eagerly looked forward to new fire apparatus production, just as every other truck and automobile operator did. It took some time for the automotive industry to reconvert from military production to civilian. One expedient to cash in on the hunger for vehicles was to retool for the last prewar models without updating them with the new wartime inspired technology. The fire apparatus manufacturers did this, too. Surplus military vehicles became available but, surprisingly, few were converted to fire service. However, the leading manufacturers had been thinking about postwar models throughout the war. American LaFrance in particular was quick to come up with a dramatically new apparatus series. It caught the public's imagination sufficiently to make the cover of *Popular Science* magazine, something unusual in those times.

A Breathing Apparatus Safety Breakthrough

Wartime technology brought about a major improvement in firefighters' breathing apparatus. Descended from the Draeger was the postwar Chemox apparatus and other brands similar in principle, except that the scrubbing chemicals were located in a replaceable canister and included a chemical that released oxygen on contact with exhaled breath, instead of requiring a cylinder of oxygen. This particular rebreather apparatus was widely favoured after its introduction by the US navy in the Second World War. By the 1950s it was used in numerous Canadian fire departments and encouraged the increased use of masks, but, as with the Type N filter mask, they were few in number in any department. They were used for urgent and difficult jobs, not for general firefighting.

The most important breakthrough in breathing apparatus for all applications also came out of the Second World War. It was the automatic demand regulator, created for oxygen masks used in high-altitude aircraft. This device permitted the wearer's breathing process to control the supply of oxygen, or air, and made possible the modern compressed air breathing apparatus. It was first used for underwater diving (SCUBA) and now is almost universally in general use by structural firefighters around the world. Jacques Cousteau, the famous underwater researcher, played a key role in this development. With this apparatus the firefighter breathes fresh air from a high pressure cylinder carried on his back. "SCBA" as it is called in the fire service, came just in time to deal with the increasingly dangerous gases of combustion now prevalent in firefighting. Its use now is mandated by industrial safety standards.

The American LaFrance 700 Series of 1945 was a landmark design. This radical postwar model was the first of thousands of cab-ahead-of-engine fire trucks, built by all makers. It had five-man seating and a new pump. Westmount, Québec had this particular triple combination. (BHC)

The Rush to Catch Up

Municipal fire departments were impatient to acquire the first new fire apparatus off the assembly lines following the re-establishment of domestic production. Many needed to replace doddering vehicles or meet the postwar expansion that was soon underway. They were also looking forward to new technology stemming from intensive wartime development. Many fire departments were in a hurry, but had to be satisfied for a time with lighter, commercial chassis models, just as automobile buyers had to accept car models little changed from prewar.

LaFrance Sets the Postwar Trends

In their last models before the wartime freeze, LaFrance, as the industry leader, had introduced their big cab-over-engine aerial ladder truck on a 220-inch wheelbase. This permitted a four-section, 100-ft ladder on a four-wheel chassis for the first time. With the return to peacetime production, the company was ready to proceed with pioneering a radically new cab-ahead-of-engine design for both pumpers and ladder trucks. This strategy saved the company's life, as the big prewar models had been excessively expensive to build and the new ones were an inspired and popular design. In 1949 they were beginning to appear in Canadian fire departments, the Toronto Fire Department buying a dozen.

Chapter VII

Postwar to 2000: An Expanding Mission

Moving the engine back behind the driver's seat allowed greater visibility and provided convenient inboard seating for a crew of five with the introduction of the first, semi-enclosed, rear-facing seats on either side of the engine. This bold design was decried by competitors' salesmen as dangerous in the event of a collision, but by the late 1950s, all custom builders were following suit and, eventually, proprietary chassis of this type were produced. The first of these was made by International Harvester. It was usually equipped with a 285 hp, V–8 gasoline engine and was popular with smaller assemblers. Cab-over-engine commercial truck chassis became available about this time, emulating wartime military designs.

Regular commercial chassis cab-over-engine tilt-cab styles for fire apparatus grew popular as they came into general use for trucking. Various truck chassis specialists have since produced a variety of cab-ahead chassis specifically for the use of fire apparatus assemblers. Earlier ones included heavy truck builders like Scot, of Debert, Nova Scotia, and the American firms of Hendrickson, Spartan, Kenworth and Mack.

Automatic transmissions came into use on a small scale for fire apparatus in the fifties, although most fire departments adhered to manual gearshifts for a time because of the former's higher initial cost. Soon, however, lower upkeep of the automatics and a generation of new drivers with little previous manual shift experience forced a rapid change.

The introduction of the short-wheel-base cab-ahead chassis by LaFrance after the Second World War made the compact four-section 100-foot ladder popular. Previously ladders had always been in three sections and were tractorized for stability. (LaFrance Fire Engine & Foamite Ltd)

All fire apparatus benefited from the introduction of power and air brakes and power steering as well as greatly increased engine power and load ratings in available chassis. The range of suitable chassis and the greatly increased cost of the limited production custom types with their special engines resulted in a substantial decline in the demand for the latter by 1960. The long-popular idea that a fire truck chassis must be built expressly for the purpose by the fire apparatus assembler finally faded.

V–12 engines, outpaced in the horsepower race by mass production six- and eight-cylinder models, were succeeded in the late fifties by a range of proprietary engines, some with minor adaptations for fire service. Dual ignition, large displacement Continental engines of up to 350 hp were promoted, in the case of LaFrance in their 800 Series, and Waukesha engines in Bickle-Seagrave and Thibault chassis until diesel engines took over. The Hall-Scott gasoline engine was popular with some American manufacturers, but was seldom seen in Canada.

Following corporate changes of holding company owners on both sides of the border, in 1966 LaFrance Fire Engine and Foamite Limited of Toronto became independent of its parent in Elmira, but continued to use the American components in considerable part. Faced with sharing a highly competitive market with more manufacturers, disinterest by the owners and less demand for the custom chassis, the once dominant Canadian LaFrance firm faded and closed its assembly line in 1970. With an increasing trend towards the use of large production, proprietary pumps like Hale, Waterous and Darley, all of them American, the only large pumps made in Canada for fire service were now the Thibault line of single-stage and parallel-series models.

Post Second World War Manufacturers

The postwar period saw several new small and regional apparatus assemblers appearing on the scene in Canada. These were mainly users of commercial chassis and proprietary pumps who rode the

Carried away with their innovations, American LaFrance built this gasoline turbine-powered pumper and an aerial truck. They were not a success, being ahead of their time and thus without dynamic braking capability. (LaFrance Fire Engine Co)

boom of postwar catchup. They included American Marsh Pumps (Canada) Limited in Stratford, Ontario, which used Barton-American pumps of the single-stage front-mount type and their unique duplex-centrifugal midships type. The supplier, the American Pump Company, had a long history in pump development and manufacture. The latter pump had two different diameter impellers on separate shafts, capable of operating separately or together to cover a broad range of pressure conditions effectively. The American Marsh company supplied a considerable number of pumpers and quadruple combinations, including ten civil defence pumpers, but they ceased business in 1965, probably in the face of competitors with broader product lines.

The Barton-American pumps were also used by the Saskatoon Fire Engine Company, which became a significant player in the fire apparatus business in Saskatoon in 1959. Specializing in small town and rural pumpers with large water tanks and front-mount pumps, they later moved to Calgary, but closed down in 1979, not having grown beyond a western regional market. There was not enough room for both them and Superior Emergency, a newcomer, in Alberta.

A second western regional manufacturer commenced operations in the late 1950s in Abbotsford, British Columbia. Originally called Roney's of Abbotsford, the company was soon renamed Hub Fire Engines. They assembled pumpers with American made pumps, first with Waterous, then Darley. In addition to small town apparatus, Hub grew into the production of larger units, including pumpers for larger cities like Vancouver. They also built aerial ladder trucks using the first Grove ladder in Canada.

A number of military fire trucks, crash vehicles and a few municipal pumpers were supplied in Canada by the Four Wheel Drive Auto Company of Kitchener, Ontario, in the fifties. These

American Marsh Pumps (Canada) Ltd, of Stratford, Ontario, sold mainly to smaller communities, using front-mount pumps. This training pumper using the larger DMA duplex pump is one of ten 840 gpm units built for federal civil defence. (BHC)

were equipped with the FWD chassis and Waterous pumps, and the bodywork was performed in part by American Marsh Pumps and Pierre Thibault. Municipal units were supplied to Moncton, Saint John and Montréal. The company was active in the Canadian municipal fire apparatus field for only a short time during the fifties.

Mack Fire Trucks in Canada

In 1953, in Montréal, Mack Trucks Inc. established a fire apparatus division for the first time in Canada. An occasional Mack pumper had crossed the border from their long established American fire apparatus plant, Toronto and Nanaimo having bought earlier models. Mack had been building fire apparatus since 1910 in Allentown, Pennsylvania. The company, of course, used their own chassis which always had a strong public image for ruggedness, especially the long lived Bulldog AC model. Using mainly the conventional, engine-forward B Model chassis and later the five-man cab-ahead C Model, Mack assembled Canadian apparatus for seventeen years before suspending production. Only the Hale pump was mounted in Canada, although the American parent changed to Waterous. Mack chassis came into popular use by other assemblers, especially with new sought-after chassis produced in the eighties by the growing number of truck chassis specialists.

Large capacity pumpers in the custom class made up almost all of Mack's Canadian production. They were rated mainly at 1050 Igpm and used Hale parallel-series or single-stage pumps, popularizing the latter type to the benefit of all assemblers. Several smaller pumpers were sold, although only Mack chassis were employed, the engines being the Mack Thermodyne six-cylinder gasoline type of 225 to 276 hp. A couple of economy units had Chrysler industrial engines. Mack pioneered the use of diesel engines in fire apparatus in both the United States and Canada, promoting them hard before finally making a breakthrough. Their first sale in Canada was to Montréal in 1963.

Because Mack used only their own premium, heavy duty apparatus chassis, they specialized in large capacity pumpers for the big-city market. Among those purchasing more than one Canadian Mack pumper were Montréal with fifteen, and several each for Ottawa, Toronto, Hamilton, Winnipeg, Regina and Edmonton. Mack also claimed the first delivery of fire apparatus by air, a cargo plane taking a new pumper to Yellowknife, NWT. Mack Canada produced aerial ladder trucks with the German Magirus ladders for several cities including Montréal, Ottawa, Winnipeg and Québec. They also occasionally used the American Maxim ladder.

The Mack company's Canadian fire apparatus operations were under the direction of J. Gaston Tremblay, son of the one-time Montréal fire chief, Joseph Tremblay. The younger Tremblay, a huge and colourful individual widely known as "le gros Gaston," started out with his father's Fire Equipment Limited in Montréal in 1918, as salesman and painter. He then worked successively as salesman with W. E. Seagrave Limited, Tremblay Fire Engines Limited, the Bickle Fire Engine Company, Bickle-Seagrave Limited, and finally Mack Trucks—a unique record. Tremblay was, in fact, simultaneously the Mack Canadian fire truck assembly operation's manager, plant supervisor, salesman and delivery engineer. The line closed down when he retired.

King-Seagrave

After fifty years in the manufacture and supply of fire apparatus in Canada, the name Bickle disappeared from the scene in 1956. Apparently not anticipating a shrinking market share, Bickle-Seagrave ran into financial difficulties and a newly built plant in Woodstock closed its doors. It was revived briefly, then expired. Only a short time before the closure the company had completed the largest single order for fire department pumpers ever contracted in Canada. It was for forty small 420 gpm triple combination pumpers on Chevrolet chassis with five-man cabs. They were built for the federal civil defense organization in 1953 and distributed across the country in the care of municipal fire departments for use in training auxiliary firemen during the Cold War period. They were also available for assistance at major peacetime fires in their areas, but unfortunately were small and underpowered.

A new company, King-Seagrave Limited, was set up by Robert Bickle's nephew, Vernon Bickle King, by now a major manufacturer of trailers and truck bodies. King took over the franchise for the assembly of Seagrave apparatus in Canada. A full range of fire department apparatus using Seagrave aerial ladders, chassis and parts, along with Hale pumps, was re-established in Woodstock almost without interruption. This company also continued the production of commercial chassis fire trucks. Seagrave itself had by now become a division of FWD Corporation and had moved to Clintonville, Wisconsin.

King's connection with Seagrave lapsed, but the assembly of Snorkel elevating platforms and telescoping boom water towers on apparatus under the King name became an important part of King-Seagrave's production. Another reorganization in 1980 brought the operation under the control of the long-established Walters Company, longtime builders of four-wheel-drive crash fire trucks. Involvement in the municipal apparatus field declined after 1980 and the Canadian use of the Seagrave name disappeared.

The Thibaults, Growth and Division

Activity in the Second World War expanded the limited production of fire equipment on the part of Pierre Thibault and his nine sons, later incorporated as Pierre Thibault (Canada) Limited. Pierre was proud of his Canadian identity and apparently did not realize the word Canada in parenthesis would suggest his was an American branch plant. War production included substantial numbers of military and civil defense trailer pumps, hose fittings and firefighting

Bickle-Seagrave resumed production of Seagrave custom apparatus with gradual modifications of the pre-war designs. These included a rear accessed centre walkway and a variety of cab styles. This, with a two-man enclosed cab, is one of five for Montréal replacing Type F Seagraves in the fifties. (BHC)

vehicles on commercial chassis. Following the war, the company became an active contender for municipal fire apparatus sales, producing 420- and 625-Igpm pumpers in increasing numbers, primarily for the Québec market. For a time they were sold under the trade name Richelieu. After using Darling pumps, Thibault developed single-stage and parallel-series pumps very similar to the Hale. They were produced in the company's own foundry and machine shop facilities in Pierreville.

Mack Trucks, longtime builders of fire apparatus in the US, began assembly in Montréal in the fifties with their B Model, Thermodyne gasoline engine and Hale pump. This B Model in Montréal has the postwar Magirus 100-foot ladder. (BHC)

In 1950, Thibault, an entirely self-made entrepreneur, built his first custom chassis, powered by the Waukesha gasoline engine. The company subsequently standardized on this dual-ignition power plant. The first custom pumper was sold to the City of Valleyfield, Québec. For a time aerial ladders were bought from other builders, including the Peter Pirsch aluminum ladder as sold to St. Catharines and Trois Rivières, and Merryweather rear turntable ladders for Montréal, Hull, Lévis and St. Hyacinthe. Metz ladders were mounted on Thibault trucks for Montréal and Westmount. By 1960, Thibault were building their own steel, hydraulic aerial ladders, eventually in all standard lengths to 100 ft. Late in the decade, this company supplied other assemblers with aerial ladders for their apparatus, notably in the United States. Thibault became the only Canadian fire apparatus assembler to manufacture in-house complete vehicles including pumps and aerial ladders, but in this age, of course, not engines, which now required large-scale production.

Thibault fire apparatus spread across Canada in the 1950s, making this Francophone concern a national supplier in every sense. In the sixties, the export of Canadian fire engine technology and production to the United States was renewed for the first time since

Like all the major builders, Seagrave eventually went to the cab-ahead design as shown on this Simonds, New Brunswick pumper working with a rural tanker on an exercise. The company pushed its V-12 engine well over 300 bhp in the horsepower race before the diesel era left it behind. (BHC)

Waterous Engine Works moved south to produce steam fire engines in the 1880s. This time it was Pierre Thibault exporting pumpers and aerial ladder trucks. Even before this a modest export market in the Caribbean and South America had been established.

Corporate changes in the late 1960s, some years after Pierre Thibault's death, found the large Thibault family selling the company bearing their name. Then some of the older sons who had been prominent in the running of the old firm, set up in competition with the new owners from across the Richelieu River in St. François du Lac, under the name Pierreville Fire Trucks Limited. This new company grew rapidly, producing a full line of municipal fire apparatus using the Waterous line of pumps and building their own aerial ladders and telescoping boom devices. The firm grew to be the largest in the country by about 1980, with some export business to the United States and South America.

In the meantime, the original family plant, having undergone several changes in control, briefly came again under the management of a branch of the Thibault family. The result was direct competition between members of the same large clan, involving two generations with experience and skills in fire apparatus manufacture and sales.

Top: One of a fleet of Model C Mack 1050 gpm pumpers supplied to the Montréal Fire Department around 1960. They were typical of the early cab-ahead generation, seating five inboard. The gasoline powered unit is seen on duty at Expo 67. (BHC)

Bottom: Along with a smaller Ford, the first pumper with a Pierre Thibault-built chassis undergoes the underwriters' twelve-hour endurance pumping test at Pierreville in 1950. It was an endurance test for the engineers, too, at -20C. (Pierre Thibault Ltd)

For a time Pierre Thibault Limited had a significant export trade in South America, including eight pumpers and this aerial truck with pump on an International chassis for Bogota.(Pierre Thibault Ltd)

Both firms expired under more demanding competitive conditions in the eighties, but family members remained active in a number of fire apparatus and equipment firms, notably involving their background with aerial devices. A small new builder of apparatus, appropriately named Phoenix Fire Engines was among these efforts until it too foundered. Picking up the pieces in St. François du Lac was a company called Nova Quintech Corporation, with outside management and capital. In the era of free trade it grew thanks to its international connections and assembly sources. Going into the nineties, the name Thibault was again on the scene in Carl Thibault Fire Trucks Inc., and C.E. Thibault, assembling a variety of municipal fire apparatus.

Growth of the Regionals

The late 1970s and 80s saw a number of smaller fire apparatus assemblers appear on the Canadian scene from coast to coast. Seeking to carve out a share of the market, they catered to the perceived needs and loyalties of their own areas. Some grew to national stature as purchasers proved they were more interested in a good product for a good price. There was no lack of special fire truck chassis, pumps, aerial ladders and booms available to them. With the demise of King-Seagrave, Pierre Thibault and Pierreville Fire Trucks in the East, the production capacity for Canadian fire apparatus took a major shift to the West, as the regionals Superior, Anderson, Fort Garry and Hub turned their attention eastward to fill the gaps across the country. Later, free trade brought competition across the border from the US, cutting into this trade either directly or through partnerships and mergers.

A new Alberta regional manufacturer of ambulances and fire apparatus came on the scene in the seventies, expanding to take a major share of the apparatus market in Western Canada by the end of the decade. This was Superior Emergency Equipment Company

Earlier Thibault apparatus had this wide body with no running boards, but a centre section in the body available for ladders, a larger water tank, other equipment or riding space for volunteers. (Pierre Thibault Ltd)

of Red Deer. The company started with the American Marsh line of pumps—front-mount and midships—and a variety of commercial and special chassis, such as Hendrickson. By the nineties, in the free-trade era, Superior became a subsidiary of the major American manufacturer, Emergency-One Inc. of Ocala, Florida. The latter company had risen quickly to a dominant position in the industry with innovative chassis, with body and aerial ladder designs in aluminum. Superior uses these components as well as the various proprietary and mass production chassis, and the Hale and Waterous pumps.

Anderson Engineering of Langley, BC also grew into national stature, producing apparatus of all types on a variety of chassis. Anderson had an arrangement for the Simon-Duplex chassis, aerial ladders and towers from Simon-LTI in Pennsylvania. In the centre of the country, Fort Garry Fire Trucks of Winnipeg has grown like many others, from a modest assembler of tankers and small town front-mount pumpers to a major company. Now the company features the American Pierce and Freightliner chassis and Pierce aerial ladders, with the pumps of W. S. Darley of Chicago.

In the fifties the service ladder truck disappeared in favour of aerial trucks, quadruple combinations and three-section metal ladders on the pumpers. This Edmonton 1952, Bickle-Seagrave GMC with booster pump was one of the last service trucks built. (King-Seagrave Ltd)

The first apparatus manufacturer in the Maritime Provinces was started, like a number of others, by volunteer firemen who thought they could build a better fire truck. From a small farm machinery builder in Centreville, New Brunswick, Metalfab Limited has grown to building a range of pumpers and tankers mainly for a market in eastern Canada and Maine. Almonte Fire Trucks of Carleton Place, Ontario filled some of the gap that had been created in Ontario. This company started as a rebuilder of used apparatus and expanded into complete new apparatus assembly.

The Diesel Engine

British and European fire brigades—in fact most of the world—were early conscious of the merits of the diesel or compression-ignition engine, particularly its fuel economy. They also considered its lack of electrical ignition problems a significant reliability feature. In North America, while diesel power plants became highly developed in trucking and bus operations, their primary attribute of fuel economy was not important in low-mileage fire apparatus considerations. The higher cost of the diesel was, therefore, a drawback.

A diesel powered municipal fire department pumper was built in 1939 for the Columbus, Ohio, fire department by the Stutz Fire Engine Company. It provided good service for many years, but remained alone, as the fire services clung tenaciously to the familiar gasoline engine, in spite of vigorous attempts to sell them diesels, particularly by Mack Trucks.

A change of heart finally came in the sixties under a fresh campaign by Mack, keen on phasing out large gasoline engine production from its heavy truck lines. The Montréal Fire Department broke the ice in Canada in 1963 with the purchase of a Mack 1050 gpm pumper. Winnipeg and several other cities followed suit, while Montréal adopted a policy of using only diesels for large apparatus, based on excellent maintenance experience with their first units. In the beginning Mack supplied most of the diesel apparatus sold in Canada, but it was not long before all assemblers of large units were supplying diesel when asked. These included both two- and four-cycle types. Since then a large proportion has been Detroit Diesel, with Cummins, Caterpillar and others represented as well. In the sixties and seventies some larger fire departments engaged in extensive re-engining of their older gasoline powered trucks,

Top: Joining the crowd, Mack Trucks introduced their five-man cab-ahead C Model in Canada. This unit, Pump 25 in Montréal, was the first diesel municipal pumper in Canada, in 1960. It was a good sales promotion for the diesel engine with its flawless maintenance record. (BHC)

Bottom: Pierre Thibault Limited built their own custom chassis starting in 1950 using the Waukesha gasoline engine. This pumper for Valleyfield, Québec was the first one off the line. It used an 840 gpm parallel-series Thibault pump, said to be patterned after a popular Hale pump. (BHC)

Four Bickle-Seagrave triple combination pumpers undergo their acceptance tests at Montréal in 1953, the first enclosed cab major apparatus in the department. To keep the price competitive they had a Hale pump and Waukesha engine. (BHC)

Part of the order of forty civil defence training pumpers produced by Bickle-Seagrave in 1953 on Chevrolet chassis using 500 gpm Hale pumps. They were distributed about the country in the care of local fire departments. (King-Seagrave Ltd)

The Saskatoon Fire Engine Company enjoyed a market mainly in small town and rural pumper tankers in the west using Barton-American front-mount pumps. It migrated to Calgary, but folded in 1978 under increasing regional competition and a loss of market for these small pumps. (BHC)

The American Darley pump was used by the then regional manufacturer Hub Fire Engines in Abbotsford, British Columbia on this International pumper. It was rated at 625 gpm, the predominant size of the day. (Hub Fire Engines)

City-service ladder trucks carrying only hand raised ground ladders, tools and possibly a small booster water tank, disappeared from the assembly lines during the fifties. The "quint," "quad" and even triple combination pumpers with extra ladders handled their function. The almost universal phasing out at this time of the bulkier wooden ground ladders in favour of light alloy types was a contributing factor in these changes. With metal ladders, three-section extensions became feasible for mounting on pumpers. By the 1990s, better building and fire codes had reduced the need for firefighters to enter burning buildings from ladders, interior stairways now being safer.

For many years the usual minimum size of a fire department pumper had been the 500 US gpm or 420 Igpm rating, capable of producing two standard fire-streams. This became, about 1950, 500 Igpm, largely because more horsepower was available in the engines. In the late 1950s, the 625 gpm pump took over as the predominant size sold in Canada. Again, it was because the engines and chassis could handle it, the additional pump cost being slight. Also, because of chassis considerations, as well as the phasing in of preconnected $1^1/_2$-inch hoselines, booster water tanks grew steadily from 100 to 500 gal capacity.

Like other apparatus builders, Pierre Thibault sometimes used chassis specialist's products. This attractive unit was one of a number sold in parts of the United States, especially in the east central states. (Pierre Thibault Ltd)

Medium and larger sized cities operated for the most part the larger 840 and 1050 gpm capacity pumpers. This permitted more hand hoselines, higher pressures and greater capability for feeding large-calibre master streams. Numerous 1250 gal and larger pumpers are in service in some departments, but many hydrants cannot supply them during heavy fire demands. Among the largest pumpers delivered in Canada were four King-Seagrave units acquired by the Vancouver Fire Department in 1969 to compensate for the retirement of the fireboat *J.C. Carlisle* in the False Creek area. Larger still was the one-off 2000 gpm pumper of the Halifax department, built by Pierre Thibault in 1978.

Added to the basic firefighting vehicles in the modern fire-rescue organization there are a variety of specialized units to be found, including light and heavy rescue trucks, vans for hazardous materials, mobile command centres, and firefighter rehabilitation. The basic pumper has become a versatile emergency intervention vehicle. Increasing numbers are classified as rescue-pumpers for their role in emergency medical, automobile extrication and other, non-fire life safety activities.

The Fog-Spray Revolution

Like other fields, fire protection gained from technological advances that came out of the Second World War. Among the numerous improvements in vehicles, equipment and organizational patterns, one was undoubtedly the most dramatic in its effect on firefighting tactics. This was the development and rationalization of the spray or fog hose-stream for use as a general structural firefighting tool.

The smooth-bore nozzle and its solid stream of water had always, from the time of the fire syringe, aimed at achieving the longest reach and the greatest accuracy. The penetrating force of a solid jet of water was believed to be the most efficient way to extinguish a fire. Nevertheless, experienced firefighters all knew that, to cool down a blazing room, the nozzleman should aim first at the ceiling, causing the stream to break up and come down through the hot atmosphere in a coarse spray, soaking up heat. Fog was a major refinement on this idea.

Although some grasped this new weapon eagerly, it was an uphill struggle to persuade many "old dogs" in the fire service to learn the new tricks. During the fifties many old buildings on the outskirts of cities and towns were burned in demonstrations, training and experimentation in the use of fog techniques. One of the largest sessions of this sort was held in Montréal West, Québec, in 1956, when eight houses were burned over a period of a week for evaluation and demonstration purposes. Fog required higher pressures and the use of pumpers, whereas most fire departments had been accustomed to employing direct hydrant pressure streams for their initial attack, except for very large fires.

Variable spray nozzles like an over-sized garden hose had been tried from time to time since the 1880s, but without noteworthy results, due probably to their primitive designs. In the Second World War, a type of nozzle in which tiny impinging jets were broken up into fine droplets as they struck one another, was widely used for handling flammable liquid fires. These "fog" streams were used particularly aboard ships where oil fires were a special threat—hence the term marine nozzles. Firefighters soon found that a volume of fine spray directed into the superheated atmosphere of a burning compartment produced rapid cooling and smothering steam. Fog streams reached many times the efficiency of solid streams in their absorption of heat. Firefighting crews became more efficient, less water was needed and firefighters had a protective screen against the heat.

Over the period from approximately 1945 to 1955, fire departments generally adopted the fog techniques for structural firefighting, utilizing increasingly sophisticated nozzles. The stan-

dard quickly became an adjustable cone spray nozzle, capable of providing a discharge pattern ranging from a solid stream to a wide angle protective screen for the nozzlemen. Along with the fog nozzle, $1^1/_2$-inch (38 mm) diameter hose was widely adopted for interior firefighting in preference to the heavy $2^1/_2$-inch size. Previously the smaller size had been used chiefly for rural operations and for overhauling, ie, mopping up at the end of a fire. Most fire departments had carried little of it, if any.

So improved was the utilization of water that serious fires now could be extinguished with an amount of water that could be conveniently carried on board a triple combination pumper. The complication and delay of connecting to a hydrant could wait until after the initial attack had commenced. The 100 gal booster tank, into which the 30 and 40 gal chemical tanks had grown before the war, now was increased to 300 to 500 gals. Common practice on initial attack became the deployment of two lines of $1^1/_2$-inch hose, permitting a pumper

Top: In the sixties the Montréal Fire Department operated two heavy rescue companies equipped with the tools for the tasks of the day. The power tools available were run from the truck's big air compressor, rather than hydraulic pressure. (Montréal Fire Service)

Bottom: An early pumper by Fort Garry Industries of Winnipeg for Humboldt & District, Saskatchewan, follows the traditional form using a Dodge chassis. An ample rear step allows for riders on the back. (Fort Garry Industries)

Chassis specialist fire service models, like this Spartan Metrostar used by Fort Garry for Battleford, were a great help for smaller assemblers in competing with the major manufacturers' cab ahead apparatus. (Fort Garry Industries)

crew to deliver a two-angle punch to a threatening fire within seconds of their arrival on the scene.

This increased firepower came none too soon, for the shorter duty hours and rising wages of professional firefighters, as well as the increasing difficulty in raising volunteers, were reducing speedily available on-scene personnel resources. Even more than in the towns, the high yield per gallon of water was a great boon to burgeoning rural fire departments. Where previously great dependence had been placed on long relays of hose from wells and ponds, tank trucks on modern heavy-duty chassis and improved roads were able to ferry water to an attack pumper using its fog lines. This fast response with vehicles carrying hard-hitting self-contained strike power brought real fire protection to many rural and suburban areas of Canada by the 1960s. The capability was just in time to meet the rapid blurring of the lines between town and country in the latter part of the twentieth century.

Another line of development in fog firefighting was the ultra-high-pressure stream. Delivering only about 20 to 30 gpm but at pressures of 600 to 800 psi, small high pressure hoselines and special pumps were required. At first the pumps were small three-cylinder piston pumps derived from agricultural spray systems. The leading producers were Food Machinery Corporation (FMC) with its John Bean equipment and the Hardie fog gun. Early in the 1950s FMC moved into the fire apparatus business in the United States, when high pressure fog was in vogue, but they did not stay in the business long as enthusiasm soon faded.

The traditional manufacturers of fire pumps responded by offering a small third-stage addition to their large pumps, capable of boosting pressure on small flows to about 600 psi. Many Canadian fire departments at the time obtained pumpers with these modified pumps. The high pressure fog stream was a finely atomized mist of high heat-absorption efficiency, but because of the cost, limited gallonage and air entrainment in the stream this form of application declined rapidly in favour by the end of the decade. Like many ideas, it was good in theory, but not so good in practice because of the range of conditions experienced in fire service.

Improving Upon Water

Water has been the universal fire extinguishing medium—plentiful, cheap and relatively easy to deliver on a fire. It both cools and smothers, leaving the combustible material wet and slow to re-ignite. Water has the disadvantage, however, of being very damaging to many surfaces. With some fuels it may make the situation worse, such as causing flammable liquids to boil over. The fog nozzle has helped reduce both these problems, but a variety of additives have been developed to further improve water's extinguishing efficiency.

The old licorice based chemical foam for oil fires was replaced as a result of the wartime perfection of a family of protein foams in which the bubbles were produced mechanically instead of chemically. This originated in the pressing demands of shipboard firefighting. These flammable liquid foams are designated Class B. In the sixties, high expansion air-detergent foams with expansion rates of up to 1000 times were produced by blowing a large fan against a screen over which a detergent fluid flowed. The resultant high volumes of foam were capable of filling inaccessible areas such as basements and ships' holds, cutting off the air supply to the fire. It was very effective in such special cases. Many fire departments acquired the equipment, but few made much use of it. High expansion foam had its greatest acceptance mainly in marine and fixed industrial applications.

A detergent additive that gave water greater penetration power similarly had a brief vogue and faded from sight. It was called wet water and was particularly effective on porous materials like baled textiles and hay. Surfactant solutions and detergent or Class A foams have more recently been added to the arsenal to improve water extinguishing efficiency even further.

Despite its effectiveness and acceptance in fixed installations, ultra-high-expansion foam failed to become a regular part of fire department operations. Wet water went the way of high pressure fog. The more recent foams, however, have been adopted and installed on numerous pumpers, and are found particularly useful in the increasing number of highway and rural fires. A new foam featuring the penetrating characteristics of wet water was the most exciting development in fighting Class A fires in the eighties and nineties. The new foam promised greater effectiveness in the use of water in structural and wildland firefighting. Even so, urban fire services did not rush to adopt it, proceeding with their traditional caution until convinced by successes in the field of forest firefighting. However, some fire departments are equipping their new pumpers with both Class A and Class B foams.

Standardized Apparatus Specifications

Much of Canadian motor fire apparatus design had long been based on the engineering of components by American affiliates and suppliers. The resulting vehicles thus generally followed the same standards of performance. After the days of hand engines and steamers there had been no influence from Britain or Europe, the general philosophy of fire protection there being different. One way in which Canadian performance exhibited a difference arose after the Second World War with a trend toward expressing pump ratings

Pierre Thibault-designed and fabricated aerial ladders were very competitive and sold widely. Nepean, Ontario, purchased this quintuple combination with a conventional North American style mounting on the popular Ford chassis. (Pierre Thibault Ltd)

in Imperial gallons instead of the smaller US gallons. Considerable confusion resulted, largely because of rather loose transpositions from the original designed ratings in US gallons. Salesmen seized advantage of this confusion to arbitrarily increase ratings.

Since the early endurance tests to prove the reliability of automobile apparatus for pumping water, American pumping engines had been processed through the free testing programs of the NFBU and local insurance rating bureaus. General specifications published by the NFPA were widely recognized.

In 1952, Standard B89.3 of the Canadian Standards Association (CSA) was completed by a committee of interests involved in the production and use of municipal fire apparatus. It laid down basic performance requirements and standardized pump ratings in Imperial gallons of 420, 500, 625, 840, 1050 and 1250 gpm. The long-standing pressure rating of pumps at 120 psi was relegated to what was called Class B, while the recently appeared ratings at 150 psi were called Class A. Within a few years Class B pumpers disappeared from the market. More recently, the pump ratings have been converted to SI (metric) units. The standard fire stream of 250 US gpm (208 Igpm), of which pump ratings had been multiples, became 1000 litres per minute (L/min). Thus an 840 Igpm pump became 4000 L/min and 1000 kilopascals replaced 150 psi net pressure.

On the basis of this standard, the DBIU and their successor the CUA offered a testing program at no cost to determine compliance with pump, road performance and design requirements. All municipal pumping engines were passed through this service with considerable benefit to the standard of performance. In 1968, the work was taken over on a fee basis by Underwriters Laboratories of Canada, including the ongoing standards development. In the early days of this testing work, the watchdog activity of the fire insurance underwriters was more significant than in recent times. The policing had paid off and, as well, the general run of apparatus chassis and engines grew bigger and less likely to prove insufficient, as had often been the case previously. However, the hopes of some that a standard performance specification would lead to lower cost, assembly line production of standardized fire apparatus was not realized. In spite of attempts by some manufacturers to market "off the shelf" pumpers, fire chiefs continued to demand a variety of options and a somewhat tailor-made vehicle.

The New Water Towers

By the end of the Second World War, the four traditional water towers in Canada had fallen by the wayside, their work being taken over reasonably well by elevated streams from metal aerial ladders. Some large American cities, notably New York and Chicago, continued using water towers after this, also clinging to wooden aerial ladders and their weaker ladder streams.

In the early 1950s, at a major fire in New Westminster, Bristish Columbia fire department hoselines were attached to a new hydraulic, articulated boom device on a city utility truck in order to secure elevated streams. The boom was of tubular steel in two sections with a hinged elbow joint. A man standing in a basket at the end of the boom could use the high degree of mobility in the boom to put himself in a variety of elevated positions. The machine had been developed by the Trump Company in Oliver, BC and was called a Giraffe. Becoming popular with public utilities for work on power lines and trimming trees, it had been designed originally for fruit picking and is still sometimes referred to by some firefighters as a cherrypicker.

After the New Westminster fire, the Trump Company saw the possible application the cherrypicker might have in firefighting on a regular basis. They tried to interest the fire service, but not for several years did any fire service take action in this direction. Then the Chicago Fire Department borrowed one of the units, built by an American licensee, the Pittman Company, from a municipal utility. The department proceeded to adapt it with a line of fireboat hose to carry a large capacity elevated stream. The old traditional Chicago water towers were becoming decrepit by now. Soon christened "the Snorkel", after the German U-boat breathing device, it proved exceedingly useful for gaining mobility in master streams, for certain types of rescue work and for getting over the tops of roofs and power lines by virtue of its elbow joint. The idea of using this progenitor of a large array of aerial devices for firefighting is generally believed to have occurred first in Chicago, but the evidence is to the contrary. The Chicago Fire Department did develop and publicize its wide use, however.

In most cases, Canadian fire departments using elevating platforms (the adopted generic term) employed them as substitutes for one or two aerial ladders. The new vehicles supplemented the traditional aerials, functioning in the form of ladder companies or for combined pumper ladder service. The first of these devices to go into fire department service in Canada was a 65-ft model purchased by Fredericton, New Brunswick.

Canada's first "Snorkel" or elevating platform was placed in service by the Fredericton, New Brunswick, Fire Department. Here it is supplied by a 900 Series LaFrance pumper at draft. (BHC)

Elevating platforms were soon produced on either articulating or telescoping solid-box booms, trussed booms and, in competition, on the end of traditional aerial ladders. The obvious initial advantages were the basket that served as a convenient work platform or as a rescue vehicle, the presence of operating controls both in the basket and at ground level, and a built-in waterway to one or two master stream nozzles. It would take another thirty years for aerial ladder manufacturers to perfect the built-in waterway for all aerial ladders in order to produce fast heavy-stream deployment at heights.

Most elevating platforms had been installed on ladder trucks or quints until the eighties, when the smaller platforms became popular on triple combination pumpers. Platform working heights vary from 55 to 90 ft, with a few of much greater size, to 150 ft or more. The earlier builders were Trump, their American licensee Pittman and their successor the Snorkel Company, as well as American LaFrance, Mobile Towers, Pierre Thibault and King-Seagrave.

More recently, most aerial ladder builders have supplied ladder models with platforms or the boom type devices in addition to the

White has come into favour again, as part of the apparatus colour scheme. North Cowichan, British Columbia went all the way with this pumper on a Ford by Superior with a cross-mount pump panel. (Superior Emergency Vehicles)

basic ladders. The American Grove aerial ladder, used by numerous assemblers, was taken over by Ladder Towers Inc (LTI) which has produced a family of aerial devices.

Rapidly expanding in the eighties, Emergency-One Fire Trucks of Florida also brought out a family of aerial devices, these in aluminum construction. Many of these American aerial devices have been mounted by Canadian assemblers. With the coming of the box-boom type aerial devices, much improved hydraulics and outrigger stabilizing jacks were used for all booms and ladders. Along with the changes in apparatus design centred around the aerial devices there has been a significant reduction in the number of manually raised ground ladders demanded by the fire service. This has allowed for more compartment space for the proliferation of small tools, the rear mounting of aerial device turntables and greater use of the quintuple combination configuration.

The Last Quarter of the Century

The 1970s saw the continuing evolution of firefighting vehicles in response to the ambitious sales goals of manufacturers and the fire chiefs' perceptions of their needs. The hydraulically raised box section booms with integral pipelines for elevated streams created an interest in a modern version of the traditional water tower. The need to mechanize a costly, labour-intensive operation was a significant factor.

A departure from the articulated boom was a telescoping type, first with two sections, later with three. It was produced by Snorkel Fire Equipment Limited, in the United States and was called the Telesqurt. The trade name soon became generic. Easily mounted on a pedestal at the rear of even a triple combination pumper, it met with wide acceptance in both countries and, eventually, had imitators at home and all over the world. King-Seagrave acquired Canadian rights to the Snorkel products in 1969 and Pierreville Fire Trucks produced early models. By the eighties, combination articulated and telescoping boom platforms were produced to gain greater heights. Those of Calavar in California and Bronto in Finland could reach heights of 150 ft or more. Major Canadian cities including Vancouver, Calgary, Toronto, Mississauga, and Montréal have operated these taller units.

In reply to the challenge of the elevating platform and other boom devices, aerial ladders were strengthened, and sprouted their own platform baskets with operating controls and built-in waterways. Another aspect of these changes in aerial devices was greater stability with stronger frames and wider stance hydraulic stabilizing jacks. These are strong enough to lift the entire vehicle off the ground.

Changes in the basic workhorse, the triple combination pumping engine, show how some fire departments have kept up with faster moving technology through innovation and experimentation. Less technical was the complete abandonment of the open cab as a desirable feature for fire vehicles. Other innovations included the steady increase in available gross vehicle weights, the transverse boxes for preconnected, fast attack hoselines, greater subdivision of the main hose body for a variety of hose sizes and the elimination of hard suction drafting hose when not needed, to satisfy the pressing demand for more compartment space.

Chassis built by the apparatus assemblers themselves became relatively rare in the seventies. Taking their place were popular production models such as large tiltcab Fords with diesel engines and a canopy added on the cab to accommodate the full crew. In the eighties, a wide choice of American specialty chassis intended for fire service was produced by Spartan, Pemfab, Freightliner, Kenworth, International, Duplex, Volvo, and Mack. For a time a popular chassis was built for fire service by the short-lived Scot Trucks in Debert, Nova Scotia, whose main purpose had been to build trucks for the numerous Irving industries.

To go with this variety of chassis were a somewhat smaller number of diesel engines and an even smaller number of large capacity pumps. Popular engines were Detroit Diesel, Cummins, Caterpillar, Volvo and Mack. In the eighties the major pumps were all American made, limited largely to the models built by the long-enduring companies of Waterous, Hale, American and Darley. The single stage pump came to dominate the parallel-series type, with some signs of a challenge on the part of power-takeoffs to the traditional midships mounting with driveshaft gear box. The rear mounted pump in the European style also appeared with the advent of very large enclosed bodies, but the once popular front-mount pump has all but disappeared.

Some fire departments began to prefer a new style of transverse pump control panel that ran across the chassis behind the cab. Safety for the pump operator and all-round visibility were the desired benefits. With the later advent of the very large standup cab, this operator's position was also incorporated. The fully enclosed

Top: This rescue and command vehicle with a walk-in body on a GMC T8500 chassis by Superior Emergency Vehicles, was built for Portage la Prairie, Manitoba. (Superior Emergency)

Center: Superior Emergency supplied Regina with enclosed pump-rescues on Emergency-One Cyclone chassis, carrying 1250 gpm Hale pumps and A and B foams. The height of modern pumpers has spawned the hydraulic rack for ground ladders as shown. (Superior Emergency Vehicles).

Bottom: In this 2000 Pierce heavy rescue truck of "walk around" type delivered to Stoney Creek, Ontario, equipment is reached from outside through rollup shutters rather than from an aisle inside the body. (Hamilton Fire Dept)

Top: Canadian military bases like CFB Esquimault joined small city fire departments in the late century with the use of quintuple combination pumper-aerials or telescoping boom towers for greater versatility. (Superior Emergency Vehicles)

Bottom: The GMC Suburban has made a position for itself in many fire departments by its versatility as a command, light rescue or other auxiliary emergency response vehicle. (Hamilton Fire Dept)

six-man cab logically appealed to the cold city of Edmonton, among the first. Generally, the fully enclosed personnel space, long common in Europe, did not seem to interest the Canadian fire department until about 1990. Air conditioning was then not far behind. A large-scale change came in the late eighties with the intensification of interest in safety for firefighters enroute to a blaze. The large standup full crew cabs even permitted some pumpers to function as ambulances.

The great size to which triple combination pumping engines were growing in the sixties and seventies inevitably led to the appearance of a small unit that would compensate for some of the drawbacks of large size. An evolution from the small grass-and-brush fire truck, the light attack vehicle, trade-named Minipumper, gained considerable appeal for its high power to weight ratio. This pumper sat on a chassis of around 10,000 lbs GVW rating, and had a presumed ability to get through traffic quickly. Its 200 to 300 gal water tank and light-weight, two-member attack team could cope with, or hold, the majority of calls. But it had a poor cost-to-firepower ratio, and there was the constant threat of its being caught short in firefighting capability. The concept was remarkably like that of the chemical cart in the horse-drawn era. Familiar too were the suggestions that it was a panacea. It had an on-and-off popularity, serving a useful role in some fire departments in some situations. Québec City was pleased with the performance of a number of them over some years. Its often ambivalent reception has been reflected in the inability of the fire service to settle on a name for it—Rapid Attack, Initial Attack, Light Attack and the trade name Minipumper all being applied.

Into the Nineties: Towards 2000

The 1980s and early 1990s were destined to bring both continuing technological innovation in firefighting equipment, and difficult financial problems for municipalities trying to provide fire protection for their citizens. A need to economize and equip to meet expanding emergency service challenges occupied the minds of fire chiefs and administrators when considering new apparatus and equipment. They were to be involved as well in substantial programs to rebuild older apparatus and in elaborate testing to ensure that ageing aerial ladders remained safe and reliable. Several companies established viable businesses rehabilitating and selling second-hand apparatus—Customtec, Dependable and CET, for example.

Top Left: The light attack, fast attack or "Minipumper" has seen favour off and on, especially in small and rural fire departments. A 1983 GMC 4x4 with 250 gpm pump can supplement other apparatus in Stoney Creek, Ontario with larger crews. (Hamilton Fire Dept)

Top Right: Increasingly popular in city fire departments is the large cab with standby section where crew have shelter for adjusting masks, first aid and pump control. An Emergency-One chassis with body by Superior. (Superior Emergency)

Bottom Right: Though not so common as before, the front-mount pump still has a small market, in larger sizes. Lougheed, Alberta has this recent Superior-GMC8500, 840 gpm pumper tanker. (Superior Emergency Vehicles)

Free trade across the American border has led to an invasion of fire apparatus and its manufacturers into Canada. The fast moving times brought many new manufacturers' names into Canadian fire stations and spawned shared construction and components. A few of the American names were Emergency-One, Grumman, Salisbury, Ferrara, Pierce, Smeal, and Sutphen. Even the venerated name of American LaFrance was revived, backed by the Freightliner Corporation. LaFrance, a re-born manufacturer, was using newly designed LaFrance chassis, pumps with aerial devices by LTI Ladders and others. The LaFrance chassis reviving the old names Metropolitan and Eagle, and the Freightliner chassis are also frequently being used by a variety of other final assemblers. The Seagrave name has reappeared in Canada as well, Almonte Fire Truck Company in Carleton Place, Ontario, undertaking to install bodies on the FWD Seagrave chassis. In a shrinking world international differences in firefighting vehicle design have also receded, major manufacturers of vehicles, aerial devices and pumps now selling world-wide. It is not unusual to see an Australian fire truck built in the British style on a Japanese chassis with an American pump!

Fire departments continue to go their respective ways, some with yellow or lime-yellow trucks, most retaining or returning to the traditional red with reflective striping, as it suits them. Under the paint, steel has changed to aluminum bodies and fibreglas water tanks. The changing role of the municipal fire service is indicated

Top Left: A compact triple combination pumper with extended cab by Simon Duplex for Stoney Creek, Ontario, a 1992 model rated at 1050 gpm. (Hamilton Fire Dept)

Bottom Left: This 1998 Freightliner tanker for rural areas of Stoney Creek has a 280 gpm pump with a shuttered control panel. It carries 2500 gallons of water in a body by C-Max Transportation of St. Jacob's, Ontario. (Hamilton Fire Dept)

Top Right: A 1980 Mack-King triple combination with added crew canopy. Safety bars across the aisle help keep firefighters from falling out. This King pumper is rated at 1050 gpm and has a 350 gallon water tank. (Hamilton Fire Dept)

Bottom Right: The Thibault-built Canadian 30-metre ladder was widely used in the sixties and seventies, and some were exported. This Dundas, Ontario unit was equipped with a Thibault pump. (Hamilton Fire Dept)

by the increase in foam installations and the new emphasis on non-fire emergency service.

This multi-faceted role calls for widely divergent equipment—vehicular accident extrication tools, emergency medical capabilities (including defibrillators), and hazardous materials spill kits. Large capacity equipment compartments with rolling shutter doors have recently become popular. Increasing instances of combined firefighting and emergency medical functions in one vehicle are symptomatic of the trends. All this, unfortunately, results in an increase in size of the basic firefighting vehicle at a time when greater manoeuverability in heavy traffic is needed.

Counter to all the increased specialization in vehicles during the preceding decades was the growing trend of the nineties to use quintuple combination pumper-aerial-ladder vehicles in place of the traditional triple combination pumper. The rescue truck was also combined with the pumper in many cases, the latter often being designated rescue-pumpers. The intention was to have widely diversified capability in the individual fire company, avoiding the previous situation where a ladder or rescue company found itself alone at a fire without the ability to attack it, or pumper crews waited for an aerial ladder or rescue unit. Versatility has become the motto in the face of more stringent

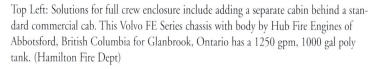

Top Left: Solutions for full crew enclosure include adding a separate cabin behind a standard commercial cab. This Volvo FE Series chassis with body by Hub Fire Engines of Abbotsford, British Columbia for Glanbrook, Ontario has a 1250 gpm, 1000 gal poly tank. (Hamilton Fire Dept)

Center Left: A recent Ancaster Fire Department acquisition was their Pump 21, a 1999 full crew cab Spartan model rated at 1050 gpm. (Hamilton Fire Dept)

Bottom Left: The telescoping box boom with light ladder attached gained favour in the eighties for its built-in elevated master stream capability. Ancaster, Ontario's Tower 21 had this 75-footer on a 1972 International Harvester chassis with 1050 gpm pump. (Hamilton Fire Dept)

Top Right: Stoney Creek, Ontario Pump 14 is a year 2000, Pierce 1050 gpm unit with a fully enclosed crew cab, cross-mount pump control panel and the recently popular rollup shutters. (Hamilton Fire Dept)

Center Right:: This C900, 840 gpm pumper from Dundas, Ontario was fairly typical of the popular diesel Fords of the seventies. The crew extension tilts with the original cab for engine servicing. Hard suction hose for drafting was still being carried. (Hamilton Fire Dept)

Bottom Right: An example of a more traditional design, a 1980 Mack-King triple combination with open back cab, hard suction hose and limited compartmentation. (Hamilton Fire Dept)

The tallest aerial devices in Canada have been articulated telescoping booms, first built by Calavar of California and lately by Bronto of Finland. This Calgary HLA Bronto extends 50 metres, is mounted on an E-One Hurricane chassis with 470 hp engine. (Superior Emergency Vehicles)

budget limitations coupled with widening service expectations by the public.

A proliferation of options allows the fire department to tailor its firefighting vehicles to its particular style of operation. There is, nevertheless, a general standardization of the basic vehicles, although not enough to promote low costs. But fire apparatus tailored to a local need is cheap compared to the cost of career crews to staff it around the clock. As well apparatus that is effective, while also having features fire crews can be proud of, encourages the volunteers as always, a distinct cost benefit. Competent and dedicated firefighters are the key to effective fire departments, and it is good, faithful equipment that keeps them that way. Canadian municipalities are quite well served by the available fire apparatus, thanks to the dedication of thinking, better-qualified fire chiefs, municipal officials, manufacturer's designers, the automotive industry, committees of standards writers and testing agency staff.

Canadian and American standards for firefighting vehicles and their operational methods have long been very similar, but not close enough to be interchangeable. The new era of free trade has allowed a free flow of firefighting vehicles across the border. The number of brand names seen in the Canadian fire service has proliferated with many American companies making sales or buying into builders in the Canadian market. A few Canadian fire trucks go south as well.

Appendix

This appendix is comprised of extracts from contemporary documents which provide an insight into the resources of firefighting apparatus available to fire departments. It illustrates the nature of the tools available to the firefighting forces over the past century.

Saint John Volunteer Fire Brigade, 1857

Engine Company	Engine House	Apparatus
1. Wellington	Queen St. betw Germain and Charlotte Sts.	1842 Phoenix Foundry engine, two-wheel hose cart
2. Union	Sydney St. opp. King Square	1856 Fleming and Humbert engine, two-wheel hosecart
3. Cora Linn	Union Street	1853 Hunneman fore & aft engine, two-wheel hose cart
4. Emerald	Market St. near Germain St.	1856 Smith piano engine, two-wheel hose cart
5. St. George "Silk Hats"	Germain St. near Kirk	1856 Smith piano engine, Smith four-wheel hose cart
Hook and Ladder	Great George St.(King) at Carmarthen St.	Hook and ladder cart
6. Faugh a Ballagh	Princess St.	1852 Smith piano engine, four-wheel hose cart
7. Western Star	King St. West	1852 Smith piano engine, two-wheel hose cart
8 Prince of Wales	St. John St. West	1853 Smith piano engine, four-wheel hose cart

Manpower: Each company comprised an assistant engineer, foreman, assistant foreman and sixty firemen, all under the direction of the chief engineer. All were volunteers.
(Compiled from data in the Colwell Collection of papers and representing the peak of the all-volunteer service in Saint John.)

Toronto Fire Department, 1866

Station	Apparatus	Fulltimers
1. Court Street	Hose cart; Hook and Ladder; Silsby Steamer*	1 Driver; 1Driver; 1 Driver & Engineer
2. Bay St. at Temperance St.	Hose cart; Silsby Steamer	1 Driver; 1 Driver & Engineer

* At some point both steamers may have been at Station 2.
Reserves: 1 Silsby steamer, 1 hose cart and a fuel wagon.
Personnel: Chief Engineer, First and Assistant Steamer Engineers, and on call or part-paid force of a bugler, 17 branchmen and 12 laddermen.
Water Supply: 85 hydrants, some with very poor pressure, and 28 street tanks for steamer suction.

Hose: 2400 feet of rubber type.
Alarm System: Ringing of tower bell at nearest fire station.
Fire Record for Year: 55 fires, 25 false alarms, loss of $47,000.
(From the Fire Department By-law of 1862 and the accounts of J.R. Robertson)

Montréal Fire Department, 1869

Station	Horses	Men	Hose (ft)	Apparatus*
1. Craig St. at Chenneville St.	2	4	489	Double Reel; Ladder Truck
2. Court House Square	1	3	439	Double Reel; Sleigh Reel
3. Wellington St. at Dalhousie	2	3	483	Double Reel; Ladder Truck
4. Chaboillez Square	1	3	479	Double Reel
5. St. Catherines near Bleury	1	4	485	Perry Engines 1st and 2nd Class; Double Reel
6. German St.	1	4	493	Hand Engine 2nd Class; Double Reel
7. Dalhousie Square	1	3	479	Double Reel
8. Craig St. at Visitation St.	2	3	490	Ladder Truck; Double Reel
9. St. Gabriel Market	1	2	487	Hand Engine 2nd Class; Double Reel

* For every vehicle except the hand engines there was a sleigh reel or ladder sleighs for winter use.

Manpower: The "Fire Police" of Montreal was the first fully career firefighting force in Canada, the last volunteers having been retired two years before. At this stage the department operated with hydrant streams only, except where hand engines were sometimes used in the higher elevations.

In 1904 the Montreal Fire Department had grown to a population of 280,000 in a metropolitan area of 370,000, covered by 20 fire stations housing 238 firefighters on a continuous duty system.

Apparatus, 1904

- 11 steam fire engines rated up to 1300 gpm, hauled by 2 to 4 horses.
- 2 2-horse chemical engines of 100 gallons capacity.
- 1 75-foot Champion water tower drawn by 4 horses.
- 4 Aerial ladder trucks: 1 85-foot Hayes, 1 75-foot Dorval, 1 95-foot Colleret and 1 85-foot Chicago Babcock, each drawn by 4 horses.
- 11 service ladder trucks with hand ladders up to 65 feet long.
- 11 2-horse hose wagons.
- 10 2-horse hose reels.
- 15 1-horse reels, with 22 winter sleighs.

(These excerpts are from the annual report of Chief Bertram.)

Halifax Fire Department, 1910

Manpower: The permanent (Career) force consisted of the Fire Chief, Chief Mechanical Engineer, 3 chemical operators, 3 assistant chemical operators, 2 blacksmiths and 22 drivers. The Call (part-paid) force included 2 assistant chiefs, 5 engineers and 78 hosemen. There were 10 fire stations.

Apparatus, 1910

- 8 steam fire engines of 300 to 800 gpm
- 2 chemical engines of 120 gallons
- 1 combination chemical service ladder truck
- 9 hose wagons
- 1 turret wagon
- 1 buggy and sleigh for chief
- 1 Horton 85-foot aerial ladder truck
- 2 service ladder trucks
- 2 ladder sleighs
- 8 hose sleighs
- 3 working sleighs
- 1 racing reel

Total hose 11,850 feet of $2\frac{1}{2}$-inch, 3500 feet cotton jacketed, the balance plain rubber.

- 34 horses each with blanket,
- 3 sets of 3-horse snap harness, 8 sets double snap harness and 7 sets single snap harness.

(Excerpted from the Annual Report of Fire Chief P.J. Broderick)

Regina Fire Department, 1910

Manpower: The fire brigade consisted of 35 men including the chief, and 5 fully paid firemen, 2 steamer engineers part-paid and 27 volunteers, 10 of whom slept at the firehall. The last was located on Hamilton Street between 11th and 12th Streets. (Only five years later, the fast-growing city would have 4 fire stations, 36 career firefighters and several pieces of motor apparatus.)

Apparatus, 1910

- 2 hose wagons, 100-foot hose on wagons
- 1 hose sleigh, 500-foot hose on sleigh

Total hose 5200 feet of $2\frac{1}{2}$-inch

- 1 Seagrave service ladder truck with 8 ladders to 60 feet
- 1 Ronald steam fire engine of 350 gpm
- 1 hand drawn Lindgren chemical engine of 70 gallons

1 chief's buggy
4 horses.

Vancouver Fire Department, 1913

Manpower: This rapidly expanding fire department had 165 fulltime members and 14 fire stations in a period when there was a mixture of automobile and horse drawn apparatus. Nine of the stations had at least 1 automobile hose wagon.

Apparatus, 1913

6 steam fire engines, mainly Waterous horse drawn.
1 Amoskeag self-propelled steam fire engine.
(1 automobile pumper on a Commer chassis on order).
7 chemical engines: 5 double 60-gallon Seagrave autos, and 2 horse drawn.
15 hose wagons, including 1 LaFrance motor and 1 horse drawn chemical combination, 6 Seagrave and 2 LaFrance automobile types and 5 horse drawn, all plain wagons.
1 85-foot Webb-electric aerial ladder truck.
1 75-foot Seagrave motor aerial truck.
1 60-foot Hayes-Waterous horse-drawn aerial truck.
1 Seagrave horsedrawn service ladder truck.

St. John's Newfoundland, 1943

During the Second World War St. John's was an important seaport, overcrowded with many flammable wooden structures. The fire department was a division of the Newfoundland Constabulary. Members were on continuous duty, with one day off in eight. There were 7 horses, and winter sleighs for horse drawn apparatus.

Fire Stations	Men	Apparatus
Central Bonaventure Ave, Fort Townsend	26 men	Merryweather 850 gpm motor pumper, 1935; Bickle 833 gpm pumper, 1938; LaFrance hose and chemical wagon, 1920; LaFrance 65-foot aerial truck, 1923; LaFrance horsedrawn service ladder truck; 3 light motor hose trucks; 1 civil defence hose truck; 2 civil defence trailer pumps, 420 gpm.
West End New Gower St. at Bambrick St.	14 men	LaFrance 625 gpm pumper, 1923; Horsedrawn hose wagon; 1 civil defence hose truck; 1 civil defence trailer pump, 420 gpm.
East End	14 men	LaFrance hose and chemical wagon, 1920; Horse drawn hose wagon; 1 civil defence hose truck; 2 civil defence trailer pumps, 420 gpm.

Bibliographical Notes

In recent years a number of histories of municipal fire departments and short papers on individual manufacturers have been published which help to illustrate the major steps in the evolution of firefighting technology. The history of fires, firefighting and fire departments in Canada was explored by the author in *The Story of Firefighting in Canada*, published in 1986.

Even so, no comprehensive story of the development of firefighting apparatus in Canada has been available, until now. A significant technological element in the development and preservation of the community's physical assets was thus left undocumented.

There are a number of books on the history of fire apparatus in the United States, but none of a definitive nature. The more complete works are confined to particular eras. Some dealing with the hand engine period are good. Many books on the fire service have been strong on pictures and weak on text, and focus on the time of motor apparatus.

Early research for the material in this volume originated in an attempt to rectify the scarcity of published works with respect to Canada at a time when data seemed to be fast disappearing. Twenty years ago some of the documentation was prepared by the author for the National Museum of Science and Technology, Ottawa, and it is used here with the kind permission of the museum. The material comes from a great variety of sources. They include magazine articles written over many years by well known authorities in special areas, manufacturers' catalogues and manuals in archives and private collections, and the periodic reports of the fire insurance underwriters. As well, there are interviews with students of the field and old-timers who were there first-hand.

The author's own intimate involvement with Canada's fire service over many years has resulted in an accumulation of information from uncounted sources on this subject. This background has been of great help in plugging, with care, the copious holes found in formal records.

Chapter 1

A good account of the earliest hand pumping engines is found in Ewbank's *Hydraulics and Mechanics*, a work written in the mid nineteenth century illustrating the steps of the German, Dutch, French and English inventors who improved on the legacy of Egypt and Rome. Ewbank provides good detail on the engines of Hautsch, Van der Heide and Newsham.

Cannon et al, in *Heritage of Flame*, reproduce original documents and drawings that cover the Newsham engine and provide excellent detail on the American hand engines.

The consolidations of the early English makers under the Merryweather name are documented by the Science Museum, London.

Roy's *La Ville de Québec sous la Régime Française*, Vol.II, quotes the *Gazette de Québec* on the proposal and permission for Québec merchants to buy the fire engine that never arrived—but would have been the first in Canada by far.

Alfred Perry's description of the Montréal Fire Department in the early part of the nineteenth century, and scattered references elsewhere, give us a fairly accurate picture of the hand fire engine roster of Canada's major city of the time.

Some information on the first engines in Halifax is available in *Halifax Fire Companies*, Public Archives of Nova Scotia (PANS); in Québec in Mainguy's history of the Quebec Fire Department; and for a number of eastern cities, from the reports to the Phoenix Assurance Company by Jones in 1807 and Broomfield in 1845.

The accounts of Alfred Perry's exploits in London are taken from more detailed stories in the author's biography of Perry which relied on Perry's own writings, and contemporary newspaper and magazine reports.

The records of the fire engines in use in Saint John and adjoining Portland, NB were compiled by the late Deputy Chief A. Montrose Colwell of Saint John, mainly from the papers and personal accounts of E.P. Leonard, whose life bridged the hand, steam and gasoline fire engine eras, and who was a steamer engineer in both departments.

Retired Fire Chief Harold Doherty of Fredericton, NB, was one of the rare fire chiefs who worked on the history of his department, contributing substantially to the Public Archives of New Brunswick (PANB) files.

The origins of fire hose in Europe are traced by Ewbank and the history of the Merryweather Company reveals a connection through English manufacture to the American improvements with rivetted seams. An internal history compiled for the St. Catharines Fire Department outlines the recurrent problems of a volunteer fire department with leather fire hose.

The services of the water carters in fire protection is told in some detail by Perry and Sandham in the case of Montréal and in Toronto by Robertson, Volume II, Chapter 196, and Firth. They were essentially similar in a number of cities. Robertson supplies good detail on the hand engines of Toronto and their crews, and he may have worked the brakes himself as a member of a boys' company.

The purchase of the first fire engine in the West, the Merryweather bought by the Hudson's Bay Company, is documented in the archives of the company at the Public Archives of Manitoba (PAMan).

Laing's and Lamb's paper "The Fire Companies of Old Victoria" describes the first fire engines in Victoria, BC, and the occasion of their arrival.

Chapter II

The first essays on producing a steam powered fire engine in England and the United States, together with the difficulties in having them accepted, are recorded in a number of treatments including William King's "The American Steam Fire Engine," Fire Engines and Fire Fighting," by David Burgess Wise, and Holtzman's "The Romance of Firefighting." Ewbank also mentions this promising new invention.

Statistics on the numbers and types of steam fire engines manufactured and in service are based on Grove Smith's "Fire Waste in Canada," the early reports of the Canadian Fire Underwriters Association and its regional counterparts, as well as lists culled from old records and catalogues. These materials have been passed around by generous enthusiasts, notably the late Paul Cleveland of the Nova Scotia Firefighters' Museum, Yarmouth.

Data on the design of the various makes of engine are from the makers' original catalogues and reproductions therefrom, together with manufacturers' operating manuals and old textbooks such as Roper's *Handbook of the Modern Steam Fire Engine*. The Nova Scotia Firefighters' Museum has many of these.

Old fire department training manuals and regulations as well as contemporary treatises such as Roper's help piece together the methods of fire departments in firing and running their engines.

Chapter III

With no previous consolidation of material, information on conditions and equipment during the period when horses provided the locomotion for fire departments, has been pieced together from a great variety of sources, both Canadian and American. Details of the design, development and use of the different kinds of horse-drawn fire apparatus—including chemical engines, aerial ladders and water towers—is found in manufacturers' publications and the work of reputable researchers like Clarence Meek of the Fire Department of New York Museum (FDNY) and Harold Walker, both of whom wrote for *Fire Engineering* magazine in the 1950s.

The writings of Alfred Perry and William McRobie, who were intimately connected with the Montréal Fire Department, enlarge upon the dry statistics taken from the beginning of the horse-drawn fire departments, particularly McRobie's affectionate stories of his horse.

Surviving old reports on municipal fire protection by the Canadian Fire Underwriters Association and related regional associations have fine detail on firefighting equipment and supply a clear insight into the operating methods and tactical considerations of individual fire departments. These reports cover the years 1904 to 1943 and have been made available through the kindness of the Insurers Advisory Organization, heir to all these associations.

To go farther back than the underwriters' reports we have the annual reports of individual fire departments, notably Montréal's, that include substantial detail and inventories dating from the 1860s. The nature of fire service tactics using horses are fairly well shown in old copies of department operational regulations, the underwriters' reports and the writings of those who lived in the horse-drawn era, such as Clarence Meek and Robert Holtzman.

Chapters IV and V

As in the case of horse-drawn apparatus, data on the motorization of fire departments has come from a great variety of sources, including manufacturers' manuals and catalogues, fire underwriters' reports, magazine articles and books. The author received notable help when dealing with early motor apparatus from recognized authorities such as Eric Sprenger of Montréal and Paul Cleveland of Yarmouth, together with George Fox, longtime president of LaFrance in Toronto, and Gaston Tremblay of Seagrave, Bickle and Mack. Fox and Tremblay were both active in the manufacture and sale of Canadian fire trucks for over forty years. Veteran fire department mechanics from Tommy Venelle of Vancouver to Fred Travis of Saint John knew a lot about the apparatus of this period, as did Billy Latter, legendary LaFrance delivery engineer and Hubert Walker, longtime chief engineer of American LaFrance.

Fire Engineering magazine has carried many useful articles over the years dealing with aspects of motor fire apparatus. Of special value have been articles in *Enjine! Enjine!*, the magazine of the Society for the Preservation and Appreciation of Motor Fire Apparatus in America.

A number of early fire trucks are still preserved in fire departments and museums, many of them in running order. The author is old enough to have operated or tested a number of them when they were long in the tooth, but still in service around the country.

The development of breathing apparatus has been well described by George L. Morse in *Firemen* magazine, in the October, 1959 issue, and by Edwin J. Kloos in *Fire Engineering* of July, 1963.

Chapters VI and VII

The author, in a career that has involved the testing, evaluation and writing of standards for fire apparatus from the V–12 era to the present, has been closely concerned with the evolution and use of modern firefighting apparatus. He has associated with the principals in the manufacturing companies and with fire chiefs. For this reason, the content of these chapters comes in large part from his own experience and current literature. These sources are augmented by the assistance of a number of fire apparatus history buffs and some professionals in the field whose memories are even longer than the author's.

Bibliography

Baird, Donal M.. *The Story of Firefighting in Canada.* Toronto: Boston Mills Press, 1986.

Broomfield, John J. Reports and Letters to Phoenix Assurance Office in 1846. In files of Phoenix Assurance Company, Toronto.

Burgess-Wise, David. *Fire Engines and Firefighting.* London: Octopus Books Ltd., 1977.

Canadian Fire Underwriters Association, Numerous reports on individual cities and towns in Canada by this and affiliated regional associations prior to World War II. Insurers Advisory Organization, Inc., Toronto, is successor to all these associations.

Cannon, D.J., Editor. *Heritage of Flame.* Garden City, New York: Doubleday and Company Inc., 1977.

Colwell, A. Montrose. Collection of papers including scrapbooks of E.L. Leonard. Archives of New Brunswick Museum, Saint John, NB.

Doherty, Harold F. Collection of papers, Public Archives of New Brunswick, Fredericton.

Dunshee, Kenneth H. *Engine! Engine!* New York: The Home Insurance Company, 1939.

Ewbank, Thomas. *Hydraulics and Mechanics.* New York: Bangs and Platt & Company, 1850. A later edition is called *Hydraulics and Other Machines.* New York: Scribner, Armstrong and Company, 1876.

Firth, Edith. *The Town of York, 1739 - 1815.* Vol II. Toronto: The Champlain Society, 1962.

Holden, John. *The Canadian LaFrance Story.* Toronto: Ontario Fire Buffs Association, undated.

Holtzman, Robert. *The Romance of Firefighting.* New York: Bonanza Books, 1956.

Jones, Jenkin. Reports to the Phoenix Fire Office in 1808. In the files of Phoenix Assurance Company, Toronto.

King, William. *The American Steam Fire Engine.* Chicago: Owen Davies, 1960.

Laing, F.W. and W. Kaye Lamb. "The Fire Companies of Old Victoria." *British Columbia Historical Quarterly.* Vol. 10, No. 1. Victoria, B.C.

Mainguy, Cyrille. "Le Service de Protection Contre l'Incendie de la Ville de Québec." Quebéc Fire Prevention Department, unpublished, 1976.

McCall, W.M.P. *The Bickle Story.* Toronto: Ontario Fire Buffs Association, 1973.

McRobie, William O. *Fighting the Flames.* Montreal: Witness Printing House, 1881.

Montreal City Archives. *Dossiers on the Montreal Fire Service* and *Annual Reports of the Montreal Fire Department.* Montreal City Hall.

Perry, Alfred. Numerous newspaper articles from the 1880s and 1890s and part of an unpublished autobiography. In possession of A. Leslie Perry, MRAIC, Westmount, QC, and the files of the late *Montreal Star.*

Robertson, John Ross. *Landmarks of Toronto.* Vol. II. Toronto: Republished from the *Toronto Telegram* by J.R. Robertson, 1895.

Roper, Stephen. *Handbook of the Modern Steam Fire Engine.* Philadelphia: E. Claxton and Company, 1883.

Roy, Pierre George. *La Ville de Québec sous la Regime Francaise.* Vol. 2. Québec: Queen's Printer, 1930.

Sandham, Alfred. *Ville Marie, or Sketches of Montréal Past and Present.* Montréal: George Bishop and Company, 1870.

Smith, J. Grove. *Fire Waste in Canada.* Ottawa: The Commission on Conservation, 1918.

Index

Aerial ladder 85
Aerial ladder trucks 159
Ahrens-Fox Company 121
Ahrens-Fox piston pumpers 152
Ahrens-Fox pump 123
Air chamber 11, 15
Air-cooled engines 111
Almonte Fire Trucks 210
American LaFrance Fire Engine
  Company. (See also LaFrance) 56, 81,
  88, 114, 228
American Marsh Pumps (Canada)
  Limited 178, 201
American Pump Company 201
Amoskeag Manufacturing Company 44
Anderson Engineering 209
Apparatus Types 213
Automatic transmissions 199
Automobile tractors 103

Babcock aerial ladder 88
Babcock Manufacturing Company 81
Bangor ladder 85
Barton-American pumps 178, 200
Bedposter 15
Bickle Fire Engines Limited 117, 141
  Bickle and Ahrens-Fox 152
  Bickle and Seagrave 189
  Bickle and Webb 117
  Bickle chassis 154
  Bickle King, Vernon 154, 204
  Bickle Northern rotary pumps 129
  Bickle, Robert S. 83, 85, 94, 117,
    204
  Bickle rotary pump 154
  Bickle-Seagrave Limited
    (See also Seagrave) 189, 203
Booster water tank 161, 217
Brakes 15, 30
Breathing apparatus 168, 197

Bronto 224
Brussels Steam Fire Engine Works 51
Buckboard 109
Bucket brigade 29
Burrill and Johnson 57
Button and Company, Watertown, NY
  24
Button engine 57

Cab-ahead-of-engine 199
Cab over engine 180, 199
Cable and Windlass 87
Calavar 224
Canada's first steam fire engines 45
Canadian Fire Engine Company 51, 85
Canadian Standards Association, CSA
  221
Canadian Underwriters' Association,
  CUA 222
Canopy cabs 190
Carl Thibault Fire Trucks (See also
  Thibault) 208
Carlisle, John C. 109
Carters 29
Champion 81
Champion water tower 93
Chemical Engines 78
Cherrypicker 222
City-service ladder trucks 215
City-service truck 85
Civil defence 204
Clapp and Jones engines 47
Class A foams 220
Class B pumpers 221
Cole Brothers 57
Cole engine 51, 57
Colleret ladder 87
Combination wagons 81, 84
Commercial automobiles 105
Commercial chassis fire apparatus 106

Condensing case 15
Continental engines 200
Conversion from horses 133
Couple-Gear Freight Wheel Company
  107
Crane-neck frame 45
Custom fire apparatus 106, 137
Custom chassis 108

Darley pumps 178
Darling pumps 205
Dederick ladder 90
Diesel engine 210, 225
Duplex-centrifugal pump 201

Early chassis 130
Electric Trucks 107
Elevating platforms 223
Emergency medical functions 229
Emergency-One Fire Trucks 224
Emergency-One, Inc. 209
Engine company 76
English engines 47
European style ladders 183
Exhaust-ejector, primer 178, 197

Fire company 15, 30
Fire engine 13
Fire Equipment Limited 87, 94, 129
Fire Hose (See also Leather hose) 27, 167
Fire insurance companies 12, 15-17
Firing and running 61
First engines in Canada 15
First steam fire engine 39
Flying squadron 132-3
Foamite 84
Fog-spray 217
Force pump 11
Fore and aft pump 51
Fore and aft style 18-20

Four-cylinder engines 157-9
Four Wheel Drive Auto Company 201
Four wheel tractor 180
Fox George 117
Free trade 227
Freightliner 209
Front-mount pumps 178
Front wheel drive conversion 118
F.S. Seagrave Company (See also
  Seagrave) 89
Fuel wagons 94

Gasoline-electric drive 107
Gleason and Bailey 85
Gooseneck 13
Gorman three-stage pump 126
Gotfredson truck 142
Gramm chassis 107
Grove aerial ladder 201, 224

Hale centrifugal pump 175, 204
Hale Motors Company 127
Hale Northern rotary pump 127-9
Hand fire engines 15, 17, 30
Hand tub roster 33-4
Harness 96
Harp engine 45
Hayes and Babcock ladder 87
High expansion air-detergent foams 220
High pressure fog 219
Holloway Company 81
Holly rotary engine and pump 41
Hook and ladder 33
Horses 75, 96
Hose jumper 28
Hose reels 28, 71
Hose wagons 71
Hub Fire Engines 201
Hunneman Company 20
Hydraulic aerial ladder 178

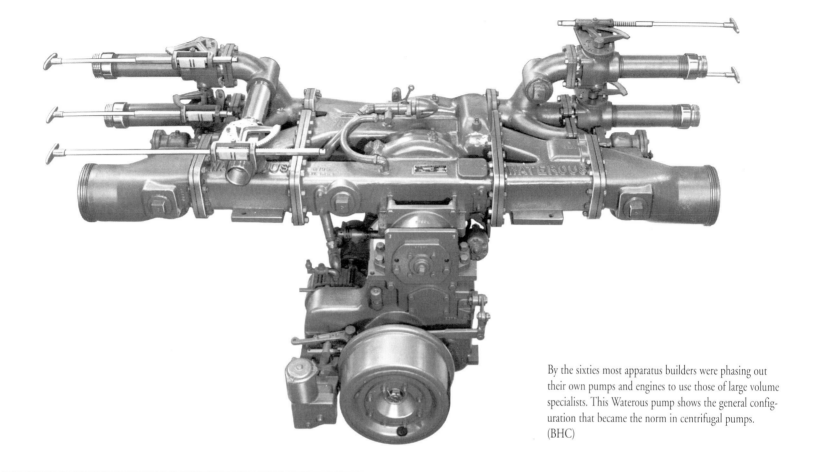

By the sixties most apparatus builders were phasing out their own pumps and engines to use those of large volume specialists. This Waterous pump shows the general configuration that became the norm in centrifugal pumps. (BHC)

particularly the old V–12 driven pumpers. The diesels came along at the right time, when engine manufacturers were reducing their lines of large gasoline engines.

Apparatus Types

Following the Second World War the availability of heavier chassis encouraged the use of the quadruple combination, combining the functions of the triple combination pumper and the service ladder truck. During the fifties, the quintuple combination aerial ladder truck and pumper became a familiar sight on the manufacturers' assembly lines. Although technically workable with the four-wheel aerial chassis, these heavier vehicles suffered the weakness of tactical inflexibility. With too many functions expected of one vehicle, the aerial ladder and pumper combination was never staffed sufficiently for full utilization. Not until the late eighties did builders provide chassis and designs that would promote large scale adoption of pumpers with aerial and water tower capability. Heavier "firepower" in the delivery of water on serious fires was the result.

Hyslop and Ronald 51

International Harvester 199

J.D. Ronald Fire Engine Company
(*See also* Ronald) 49, 51, 85

King-Seagrave Limited 203

Ladder levelling devices 188
Ladder trucks 85, 87
LaFrance Fire Engine Company of
  Canada 117
    LaFrance Fire Engine and Foamite
      Limited 85, 200
    LaFrance enclosed semi-cab models
      190
    LaFrance motor apparatus pump
      125
    LaFrance rotary gear pump 156
    LaFrance T-head engine 155
Largest pumpers 215-17
Last horses 99
Leather hose 27-8, 167
Lemoine engine 25
LePage engine 25
Light attack pumper 227
Lime-yellow trucks 228
LTI company 224

Mack Fire Trucks 203
Magirus aerial ladder 183
Maintenance 163
Major pumps 226
Manistee four-stage pump 126
Manufacturers 94
Marks, William 27
Master Series 157
Merryweather and Sons 15, 34, 47
Merryweather turntable ladders 183,
 205
Metalfab Limited 210
Metropolitan Series 157
Metz ladders 205
Minipumper 226

Mongrel pump 45
Motor pumper standards 163
Muster competitions 37

National Board of Fire Underwriters,
  NBFU 221
National Fire Protection Association,
  NFPA 221
Newsham's engine 15
Newsham, Richard 13
Nova Quintech Corporation 208

Osborne-Killey Company 57

Pacific Coast 35
Parallel-series pumps 174
Perry brothers 20
Perry engine 20-3
Peter Pirsch aluminum ladder 178, 205
Peter Pirsch Sons 178
Piano engine 24-5
Pierre Thibault (Canada) Limited (*See
  also* Thibault) 204
Pierreville Fire Trucks Limited 208, 224
Piston pump 152
Pittman Company 222
Pope-Hartford 110, 111
Post Second World War manufacturers
  200
Postwar trends 199
Pre-connected lines 167
Protein foams 220
Pumping test 121

Quadruple combination 213
Quintuple combination 213
Quintuple combination pumper-aerial
  229

Rated capacities of pumps 163
Rear mounted aerial ladders 187
Rear mounted pump 226
Reels and carts 33
Rescue-pumper 217
Richelieu 205

Ronald engines 51
Ronald, Hyslop and 51
Roster of horse power 99
Rotary gear pump 120-1, 174-5

Saskatoon Fire Engine Company 178,
  200
Salvage wagons 94
Seagrave, F.S Company 89
    Seagrave 85
    Seagrave aerial ladders 204
    Seagrave Centrifugal 125
    Seagrave, Frederick 89
    Seagrave hose wagon 109
    Seagrave Model F 143
    Seagrave pump 145
    Seagrave Standard engines 145
    Seagrave tower 93
    Seagrave tractors 111
    Seagrave, W.E. 93
Self-propelled Amoskeag engine 103
Self-propellers 57, 103
Shand Mason 47
S.I. units 222
Silsby Manufacturing Company 41
Single-stage pump 226
Size and gallonage classes 66
Skinner ladder 87
Sleighs 75
Smith, James 24
Snorkel elevating platforms 222, 204
Snorkel Fire Equipment Limited 224
Soda-acid chemical engines 81
Soda-acid extinguisher 81
Soda-acid solution chemical tank 159-61
Solid rubber tire 119, 130
Specialty chassis 226
Spring-assist aerial ladder 89
Spring-hoist aerial ladder 90
Squirrel-tail 25
Squirt 11
Standard fire stream 222
Standardized apparatus specifications
  220
Steam automobiles 103

Suction hose 28
Superior Emergency Equipment
  Company 208

T-head configuration 145
Tactical operations 58
Tactics with motorization 131
Telesqurt 224
Thibault, Charles 94, 129
Thibault, Pierre 129, 204
Tractor-tiller 181
Tractor units 67-8
Tractorization 117
Trailer pumps 104, 129, 161, 178, 194
Transverse pump control panel 226
Tremblay Fire Engine Company 129,
  161
Tremblay, Gaston 203
Tremblay, Joseph 94, 105, 129
Triple combination pumper 133, 226,
  229
Trump Company 222
Two-piece company 133
Type 12 156

Underwriters Laboratories of Canada
  222
U-tank engine 45

V–12 Engines 171, 200
Vacuum primer 178
van der Heide, John and Nicholas 13
Village Queene 197
Volunteer fire companies 12

Water towers 93, 222
Waterous Engine Works Company 55,
  129
    Waterous boilers 55
    Waterous Charles H. 52
Wartime conditions 191
Waukesha engine 154, 200
Webb Company 107
Wet water 220